FOREIGN POLICY OF THE UNITED STATES

U.S. LED SANCTIONS ON IRAN

Foreign Policy of the United States

Additional books in this series can be found on Nova's website under the Series tab.

Additional E-books in this series can be found on Nova's website under the E-book tab.

Politics and Economics of the Middle East

Additional books in this series can be found on Nova's website under the Series tab.

Additional E-books in this series can be found on Nova's website under the E-book tab.

FOREIGN POLICY OF THE UNITED STATES

U.S. LED SANCTIONS ON IRAN

ROBERT K. FIGG
AND
DANIELLE A. WILSON
EDITORS

Nova Science Publishers, Inc.
New York

For permission to use material from this book please contact us:
Telephone 631-231-7269; Fax 631-231-8175
Web Site: http://www.novapublishers.com

Library of Congress Cataloging-in-Publication Data

Library of Congress Cataloging-in-Publication Data

U.S. led sanctions on Iran / editors, Robert K. Figg and Danielle A. Wilson.
p. cm.
Includes index.
"CRS report for Congress prepared for members and committees of Congress."
ISBN 978-1-62100-414-1 (hardcover)
1. Economic sanctions, American--Iran. 2. Economic sanctions--Iran. I. Figg, Robert K. II. Wilson, Danielle A. III. United States. Government Accountability Office. IV. Title: United States led sanctions on Iran.
HF1413.5.U16 2011
327.1'17--dc23

2011033674

Published by Nova Science Publishers, Inc. † New York

CONTENTS

PREFACE

This book provides an overview of U.S. led sanctions being imposed on Iran. There is broad international support for imposing progressively strict economic sanctions on Iran to try to compel it to verifiably confine its nuclear program to purely peaceful uses. However, there is not a consensus on how effective the sanctions are on core Western goals. In January 2011, Secretary of State Clinton claimed that sanctions have accomplished a core objective of slowing Iran's nuclear program. But, nuclear talks in December 2010 and in January 2011 made virtually no progress, suggesting that Iran's leaders do not feel sufficiently pressured by sanctions to offer major concessions to obtain a nuclear deal. Because so many major economic powers have imposed sanctions on Iran, the sanctions are, by all accounts, harming key sectors of Iran's economy by reinforcing the effects of Iran's economic mismanagement.

Chapter 1- There is broad international support for imposing progressively strict economic sanctions on Iran to try to compel it to verifiably confine its nuclear program to purely peaceful uses. However, there is not a consensus on how effective the sanctions are on core Western goals. In January 2011, Secretary of State Clinton claimed that sanctions have accomplished a core objective of slowing Iran's nuclear program. But, nuclear talks in December 2010 and in January 2011 made virtually no progress, suggesting that Iran's leaders do not feel sufficiently pressured by sanctions to offer major concessions to obtain a nuclear deal.

Chapter 2- Iran is obtaining U.S. military and dual-use goods (civilian goods with potential military applications) that are illegally transshipped through intermediaries in third-party nations, most notably the United Arab Emirates, Malaysia, and Singapore. U.S. agencies have conducted investigations to uncover Iranian procurement networks and prosecuted at least 30 firms and individuals between 2007 and 2009. The Comprehensive Iran Sanctions, Accountability, and Divestment Act of 2010 requires the President to designate a country as a Destination of Diversion Concern if certain criteria are met. Moreover, the President shall impose a licensing requirement upon certain U.S. exports to the designated country unless the President makes a number of determinations, including determining that it is appropriate to provide technical assistance to strengthen the country's export control systems.

Chapter 3- Based on our review of open source information, we identified 41 firms that had commercial activity in the Iranian energy sector between 2005 and 2009. Of these firms, seven had contracts with the U.S. government. From fiscal years 2005 through 2009, the U.S. government obligated almost $880 million in contracts to these seven firms. U.S. agencies obligated almost 90 percent of these funds for purchases of fuel and petroleum products overseas. Thirteen of the 41 firms listed in our March 2010 report responded to our inquiries regarding their commercial activities in Iran, including two of the seven firms with U.S. government contracts. Since the report was released, four more firms responded, including one firm that noted it had not made a decision about finalizing its commercial activities in Iran.

Chapter 4 On March 23, 2010, we issued a report entitled *Firms Reported in Open Sources as Having Commercial Activity in Iran's Oil, Gas, and Petrochemical Sectors*. Based on open sources, we identified 41 foreign firms as having commercial activity in these vital sectors of Iran's economy from 2005 to 2009. As you requested, this report identifies which of the 41 firms in our March 2010 report had contracts with the United States government from fiscal years 2005 to 2009.

Our March 2010 report and this report are intended to support congressional consideration of U.S. sanctions against Iran, including proposed legislation to expand the Iran Sanctions Act (ISA). We did not use ISA criteria or monetary thresholds when identifying firms and did not attempt to determine whether firms meet the legal criteria for an investment specified in ISA. Under the existing Iran Sanctions Act, persons, including firms, that invest more than $20 million in Iran's energy sector in any 12-month period may be banned from U.S. government procurement. In 1998, the United States made its first and only determination that a firm's investments constituted activity covered by the Iran Sanctions Act. The sanctions were waived because the Secretary of State determined it was in the national interest to do so. The U.S. Senate and House of Representatives have passed separate bills to expand U.S. sanctions against Iran and are now working to resolve differences.

Chapter 5- Iran's oil and gas industry is vital to its economy and government. Oil export revenues have accounted for more than 24 percent of Iran's gross domestic product and between 50 and 76 percent of the Iranian government's revenues in recent years. Iran has the world's third largest oil reserves and second largest gas reserves, according to the Congressional Research Service (CRS), and is the world's fourth largest producer of crude oil, according to the Central Intelligence Agency (CIA) World Factbook. However, Iran has not reached peak crude oil production levels since 1978, does not produce sufficient natural gas for domestic use, and lacks the refining capacity to meet domestic demand for gasoline, according to the Department of Energy (DOE) and IHS Global Insight. IHS Global Insight reports that Iran's priorities for the next five years are to (1) raise oil production and exports as much as possible, (2) increase natural gas production for domestic use, and (3) expand refining capacity if financially and technically possible. CRS reported that the Deputy Minister of the National Iranian Oil Company said in November 2008 that Iran would need about $145 billion in new investment over the next 10 years to build a thriving energy sector. Accordingly, Iran is seeking the participation of foreign firms in providing financing and technical assistance in numerous oil, gas, and petrochemical projects, according to DOE. Although Iran prohibits non-Iranian firms from obtaining an ownership interest by investing in oil and gas fields, Iran allows them to enter into "buy-back" arrangements in which the foreign firms may receive entitlements to oil or gas for a limited time in exchange for the funds they expend on the project, according to DOE.

Chapter 6- In 1995, the United States banned exports to Iran of most U.S. goods without a Treasury Department license. In 2008, the U.S. media, citing U.S. government statistics, reported that U.S. firms were exporting numerous goods to Iran. The statistics are maintained by the Census Bureau and are based on data filed by exporters or their agents. The United States has also generally banned unlicensed transshipments of U.S. goods to Iran via other nations. In this report, GAO assesses the extent to which (1) U.S. trade statistics accurately depict exports to Iran, (2) Treasury licenses exports to Iran in accordance with the trade restrictions and provides licensing data to enforcement agencies and Congress, and (3) Iran obtains U.S. military and dual-use goods through transshipment. GAO analyzed Census export data, a randomly selected sample of Treasury export licenses, Treasury licensing information systems, and U.S. government transshipment data. It also interviewed relevant U.S. government officials.

In: U.S. Led Sanctions on Iran
Editors: Robert K. Figg and Danielle A. Wilson
ISBN: 978-1-62100-414-1

Chapter 1

IRAN SANCTIONS*

Kenneth Katzman

SUMMARY

There is broad international support for imposing progressively strict economic sanctions on Iran to try to compel it to verifiably confine its nuclear program to purely peaceful uses. However, there is not a consensus on how effective the sanctions are on core Western goals. In January 2011, Secretary of State Clinton claimed that sanctions have accomplished a core objective of slowing Iran's nuclear program. But, nuclear talks in December 2010 and in January 2011 made virtually no progress, suggesting that Iran's leaders do not feel sufficiently pressured by sanctions to offer major concessions to obtain a nuclear deal.

Because so many major economic powers have imposed sanctions on Iran, the sanctions are, by all accounts, harming key sectors of Iran's economy by reinforcing the effects of Iran's economic mismanagement. Among other indicators, there have been a stream of announcements by major international firms since early 2010 that they are exiting the Iranian market. Iran's oil production has fallen slightly to about 3.9 million barrels per day, from over 4.1 million barrels per day several years ago, although Iran now has small natural gas exports that it did not have before Iran opened its fields to foreign investment in 1996. In addition, Iran's overall ability to limit the effects of sanctions has been aided by relatively high oil prices in mid-2011.

The United States and its allies appear to agree that sanctions should continue to target Iran's energy sector and should try to isolate Iran from the international financial system. The energy sector provides about 80% of government revenues. Iran's large trading community depends on financing to buy goods from the West and sell them inside Iran. Using the authorities of U.N. Security Council Resolution 1929, adopted June 9, 2010, measures adopted since mid-2010 by the United Nations Security Council, the European Union, and several other countries target those sectors. These national measures complement the numerous U.S. laws and regulations that have long sought to try to pressure Iran, particularly the Iran Sanctions Act (ISA)—a 1996 U.S. law that mandated U.S. penalties against foreign companies that invest in Iran's energy sector. In

* This is an edited, reformatted and augmented version of a Congressional Research Service 7-5700 publication RS20871, dated June 22, 2011.

the 111th Congress, the Comprehensive Iran Sanctions, Accountability, and Divestment Act of 2010 (CISADA, P.L. 111-195) expanded ISA to sanction Iran's ability to obtain or make gasoline, for which Iran depends heavily on imports. Sales to Iran of gasoline have fallen dramatically since.

CISADA also contained a broad range of other measures further restricting the already limited amount of U.S. trade with Iran. It also contained provisions to promote the cause of the domestic opposition in Iran by sanctioning Iranian officials who are human rights abusers and facilitating the democracy movement's access to information technology—a trend that is increasingly taking hold in the Obama Administration and in partner countries. The increasing emphasis on human rights-related laws and sanctions reflect a growing belief that there are few new economic sanctions that can be successfully agreed on or imposed. In the 112th Congress, legislation has been introduced to enhance both the economic sanctions and human rights-related provisions of CISADA and other laws.

OVERVIEW

The Obama Administration's policy approach toward Iran has contrasted with the Bush Administration's by attempting to couple the imposition of sanctions to a consistent, direct U.S. effort to negotiate with Iran on the nuclear issue. That approach was not initially altered because of the Iranian dispute over its June 12, 2009, elections. However, with negotiations yielding no firm Iranian agreement to compromise, since early 2010 the Administration and Congress have focused on achieving adoption of and implementing additional U.S., U.N., and allied country sanctions whose cumulative effect, it is believed, could compel Iran to accept a nuclear bargain.

U.N. sanctions on Iran (the latest of which are imposed by Resolution 1929, adopted June 9, 2010) are a relatively recent (post-2006) development. U.S. sanctions, on the other hand, have been a major feature of U.S. Iran policy since Iran's 1979 Islamic revolution. Many of the U.S. sanctions overlap each other as well as the several U.N. sanctions now in place. Some U.S. sanctions, particularly the 1996 Iran Sanctions Act (ISA), caused differences of opinion between the United States and its European allies because it mandates U.S. imposition of sanctions on foreign firms. Successive Administrations have sought to ensure that U.S. sanctions do not hamper cooperation with key international partners whose support is needed to adopt stricter international sanctions.

SANCTIONS TARGETING IRAN'S ENERGY SECTOR: THE IRAN SANCTIONS ACT (ISA) AND CISADA AMENDMENTS

The Iran Sanctions Act (ISA) is one among many U.S. sanctions in place against Iran. Since its first enactment, it has attracted substantial attention because it is an "extra-territorial sanction"— it authorizes U.S. penalties against foreign firms, many of which are incorporated in countries that are U.S. allies. (U.S. firms are barred by executive orders, discussed below, from dealing with Iran.) When it was first enacted in 1996, Congress and the Clinton Administration saw ISA as a potential mechanism to compel U.S. allies to join the United States in enacting trade sanctions against Iran. American firms are separately restricted from trading with or investing in Iran under separate U.S. executive measures, as discussed below. As noted, a law enacted in the 111th Congress (CISADA, P.L. 111-195) amended ISA to try to curtail additional types of activity, such as selling gasoline and gasoline production-related equipment and services to Iran, and to restrict international banking relationships with Iran (among many provisions).

Legislative History and Provisions

Originally called the Iran and Libya Sanctions Act (ILSA), ISA was enacted to try to deny Iran the resources to further its nuclear program and to support terrorist organizations such as Hizbollah, Hamas, and Palestine Islamic Jihad. Iran's petroleum sector generates about 20% of Iran's GDP (which is about $870 billion), and 80% of its government revenue. Iran's oil sector is as old as the petroleum industry itself (early 20th century), and Iran's onshore oil fields and oil industry infrastructure are far past peak production and in need of substantial investment. Its large natural gas resources (940 trillion cubic feet, exceeded only by Russia) were virtually undeveloped when ISA was first enacted. Iran has 136.3 billion barrels of proven oil reserves, the third-largest after Saudi Arabia and Canada.

The opportunity for the United States to try to harm Iran's energy sector came in November 1995, when Iran opened the sector to foreign investment. To accommodate its insistence on retaining control of its national resources, Iran used a "buy-back" investment program in which foreign firms gradually recoup their investments as oil and gas is discovered and then produced. With input from the Administration, on September 8, 1995, Senator Alfonse D'Amato introduced the "Iran Foreign Oil Sanctions Act" to sanction foreign firms' exports to Iran of energy technology. A revised version instead sanctioning *investment* in Iran's energy sector passed the Senate on December 18, 1995 (voice vote). On December 20, 1995, the Senate passed a version applying the provisions to Libya, which was refusing to yield for trial the two intelligence agents suspected in the December 21, 1988, bombing of Pan Am 103. The House passed H.R. 3107, on June 19, 1996 (415-0), and then concurred on a Senate version adopted on July 16, 1996 (unanimous consent). The Iran and Libya Sanctions Act was signed on August 5, 1996 (P.L. 104-172).

Key "Triggers"

ISA consists of a number of "triggers"—transactions with Iran that would be considered violations of ISA and could cause a firm or entity to be sanctioned under ISA's provisions. When triggered, ISA provides a number of different sanctions that the President could impose that would harm a foreign firm's business opportunities in the United States. ISA does not, and probably could not practically, compel any foreign government to act against one of its firms.

Original Triggers

ISA primarily targets foreign firms, because American firms are already prohibited from investing in Iran under the 1995 trade and investment ban discussed earlier. The pre-2010 version of ISA requires the President to sanction companies (entities, persons) that make an "investment"[1] of more than $20 million[2] in one year in Iran's energy sector,[3] *or* that sell to

Iran weapons of mass destruction (WMD) technology or "destabilizing numbers and types" of advanced conventional weapons.[4]

Trigger Added by CISADA: Selling Gasoline and Refinery Equipment

ISA, as initially constituted, did not address Iran's gasoline dependency because selling Iran equipment with which it can build or expand its refineries using its own construction capabilities did not constitute "investment" under the original definition of ISA. Sales to Iran of gasoline were not sanctionable either. However, taking responsibility for constructing oil refineries or petrochemical plants in Iran did constitute sanctionable projects under the original version of ISA because ISA's definition of investment includes "responsibility for the development of petroleum resources located in Iran." *Table 3* provides some information on openly announced contracts to upgrade or refurbish Iranian oil refineries.) Nor did ISA clearly apply to Iranian investments in oil refineries in several other countries, such as Iranian investment to help build five oil refineries in Asia (China, Indonesia, Malaysia, and Singapore) and in Syria, reported in June 2007, would have constituted "investment" under ISA.

Many in the 111th Congress took exception to the limited of the original version of ISA, arguing that Iran was dependent on gasoline imports to meet about 40% of its gasoline needs. There have been a relatively limited group of major gasoline suppliers to Iran, and many in Congress believed that trying to stop such sells could put economic pressure on Iran's leaders. The ideas that became the core of CISADA were introduced as legislation in the 110th and 111th Congresses. In the 110th Congress, H.R. 2880 would have made sales to Iran of refined petroleum resources a violation of ISA.

To address this perceived weakness of the original version of ISA, CISADA (P.L. 111-195) added new triggers: selling to Iran (over specified threshold amounts) refined petroleum (gasoline, aviation fuel, and other fuels included in the definitions); and selling equipment or services for Iran to expand its own ability to produce refined petroleum. (Fuel oil, a petroleum by-product which is reportedly being sold to Iran by exporters in the Kurdish region of Iraq, is not included in the definition of refined petroleum.)

Pre-CISADA Efforts to Sanction Gasoline Sales to Iran

In the 111th Congress, a few initiatives were adopted prior to CSIDA. Using U.S. funds to fill the Strategic Petroleum Reserve with products from firms that sell over $1 million worth of gasoline to Iran is prevented by the FY2010 Energy and Water Appropriation (H.R. 3183, P.L. 111-85, signed October 28, 2009). A provision of the FY2010 consolidated appropriation (P.L. 111-117) would deny Ex-Im Bank credits to any firm that sells gasoline to Iran, provides equipment to Iran that it can use to expand its oil refinery capabilities, or performs gasoline production projects in Iran.

These initiatives did deter some gasoline sales to Iran. The Reliance Industries Ltd. of India decision to cease new sales of refined gasoline to Iran (as of December 31, 2008), mentioned above, came after several Members of Congress urged the Ex-Im Bank of the United States to suspend assistance to Reliance, on the grounds that it was assisting Iran's economy with the gas sales. The Ex-Im Bank, in August 2008, had extended a total of $900 million in financing guarantees to Reliance to help it expand.

CISADA Legislative History

CISADA had its origins in several bills introduced in April 2009 (H.R. 2194, S. 908, H.R. 1208, and H.R. 1985) that would amend ISA to make sanctionable efforts by foreign firms to supply refined gasoline to Iran or to supply equipment to Iran that could be used by Iran to expand or construct oil refineries. H.R. 2194 and S. 908 were both titled the Iran Refined Petroleum Sanctions Act of 2009 (IRPSA). H.R. 2194 passed the House on December 15, 2009, by a vote of 412-12, with four others voting "present" and six others not voting.

A bill in the Senate, the "Dodd-Shelby Comprehensive Iran Sanctions, Accountability, and Divestment Act," (S. 2799), was reported to the full Senate by the Senate Banking Committee on November 19, 2009, and passed the Senate, by voice vote, on January 28, 2010. It was adopted by the Senate under unanimous consent as a substitute amendment to H.R. 2194 on March 11, 2010, setting up conference action on the two versions of H.R. 2194. The Senate bill contained very similar provisions of the Iran Refined Petroleum Sanctions Act, but, as discussed in *Table 2* below, added provisions affecting U.S.-Iran trade and other issues.

A public meeting of the House-Senate conference, chaired by Representative Berman and Senator Dodd, was held on April 28, 2010. Obama Administration officials were said to be concerned by some provisions of H.R. 2194 because of the legislation's potential to weaken allied unity on Iran. The Administration sought successfully to persuade Members to delay passage of until a new U.N. sanctions resolution was adopted—for fear that some P5+1 countries might refuse to support the U.N. resolution if there is a chance their firms would be sanctioned by a new U.S. law. The U.N. Resolution was adopted on June 9, 2010. A conference report on H.R. 2194 was agreed on June 22, 2010, and was submitted on June 23, 2010. On June 24, 2010, the Senate passed it 99-0, and the House passed it 408-8, with one voting "present." President Obama welcomed the passage and signed it into law on July 1, 2010.

As widely predicted, and as shown in *Table 2* below, the final version contained many of the extensive provisions of the Senate version, and some of the efforts to compel sanctions represented in the House version. Administration concerns about angering U.S. partner countries were addressed in the provisions for waivers, delayed mandatory investigations of violations, and for the "special rule" exempting from sanctions companies that promise to end their business in Iran. As was widely predicted, the conference report contains provisions to sanction Iranian human rights abusers, including denial of visas for their travel to the United States and freezing of their assets.

Those who supported CISADA said it would strengthen President Obama's ability to obtain an agreement with Iran that might impose limitations on its nuclear program. It was argued that Iran's dependence on gasoline imports could, at the very least, cause Iran's government to have to spend more for such imports. Others, however, believed the Iranian government would have numerous ways to circumvent its effects, including rationing, reducing gasoline subsidies in an effort to reduce gasoline consumption; or offering premium prices to obscure gasoline suppliers. The effect on Iran's supplies are discussed later in this report.

Requirement and Time Frame to Investigate Violations

In the original version of ISA, there was no time frame for the Administration to determine that a firm has violated ISA's provisions. Some might argue that the amendments of P.L. 111-195 still do not set a binding determination deadline, although the parameters are narrowed significantly.

Earlier, P.L. 109-293, the "Iran Freedom Support Act" (signed September 30, 2006) amended ISA by calling for, *but not requiring*, a 180-day time limit for a violation determination (there is no time limit in the original law).[5]

In restricting the Administration's ability to choose not to act on information about potential violations, CISADA (P.L. 111-195), Section 102(g)(5), made mandatory that the Administration begin an investigation of potential ISA violations when there is "credible information" about a potential violation. The same section of CISADA made mandatory the 180 day time limit for a determination of violation (with the exception that the mandatory investigations and time limit go into effect one year after enactment, with respect to gasoline related sales to Iran). However, there is still lack of precision and potential differences of opinion over what constitutes "credible information" that an investment or sanctionable sale has been undertaken.

Earlier versions of legislation (H.R. 282, S. 333) that ultimately became P.L. 109-293 contained ISA amendment proposals that were viewed by the Bush Administration as too inflexible and restrictive, and potentially harmful to U.S. relations with its allies. These provisions included setting a mandatory 90-day time limit for the Administration to determine whether an investment is a violation; cutting U.S. foreign assistance to countries whose companies violate ISA; and applying the U.S.-Iran trade ban to foreign subsidiaries of U.S. firms.

Available Sanctions under ISA

Once a firm is determined to be a violator, the original version of ISA required the imposition of *two* of a menu of six sanctions on that firm. CISADA added three new possible sanctions and requires the imposition of at least *three out of the nine* against violators. The nine available sanctions against the sanctioned entity that the President can select from (Section 6) include

1) denial of Export-Import Bank loans, credits, or credit guarantees for U.S. exports to the sanctioned entity;
2) denial of licenses for the U.S. export of military or militarily useful technology to the entity;
3) denial of U.S. bank loans exceeding $10 million in one year to the entity;
4) if the entity is a financial institution, a prohibition on its service as a primary dealer in U.S. government bonds; and/or a prohibition on its serving as a repository for U.S. government funds (each counts as one sanction);
5) prohibition on U.S. government procurement from the entity;
6) restriction on imports from the violating entity, in accordance with the International Emergency Economic Powers Act (IEEPA, 50 U.S.C. 1701);
7) prohibitions in transactions in foreign exchange by the entity;
8) prohibition on any credit or payments between the entity and any U.S. financial institution;

9) prohibition of the sanctioned entity from acquiring, holding, or trading any U.S.-based property.

New Mandatory ISA Sanction Imposed by CISADA: Prohibition on Contracts with the U.S. Government

CISADA (Section 102(b)) added a provision to further incent foreign companies to comply with ISA. It requires companies, as a condition of obtaining a U.S. government contract, to certify to the relevant U.S. government agency, that the firm—and any companies it owns or controls—are not violating ISA, as amended. A contract may be terminated—and further penalties imposed—if it is determined that the company's certification of compliance was false. CISADA requires a revision of the Federal Acquisition Regulation (within 90 days of CISADA enactment on July 1, 2010) to reflect this requirement. This requirement has been imposed in regulations, as per an interim rule issued on September 29, 2010. H.R. 6296, introduced September 29, 2010, in the 111th Congress, would have authorized state and local governments to similarly ban such contracts.

Waivers, Exemptions, and Termination Authority

The President has had the authority under ISA to waive sanctions if he certifies that doing so is *important* to the U.S. national interest (Section 9(c)). CISADA (Section 102(c)), changed the 9(c) ISA waiver standard to "*necessary*" to the national interest. Under the original version of ISA, there was also waiver authority (Section 4(c)) if the parent country of the violating firm joined a sanctions regime against Iran, but this waiver provision was changed by P.L. 109-293 to allow for a waiver determination based on U.S. vital national security interests. The Section 4(c) waiver was altered by CISADA to provide for a six month (extendable) waiver if doing so is vital to the national interest and if the parent country of the violating entity is "closely cooperating" with U.S. efforts against Iran's WMD and advanced conventional weapons program. The criteria of "closely cooperating" are defined in the conference report, with primary focus on implementing all U.N. sanctions against Iran. However, it is not clear why an Administration would use a Section 4 waiver rather than a Section 9 waiver, although it could be argued that using a Section 4 waiver would support U.S. diplomacy with the parent country of the offending entity.

ISA (Section5(f)) also contains several exceptions such that the President is not required to impose sanctions that prevent procurement of defense articles and services under existing contracts, in cases where a firm is the sole source supplier of a particular defense article or service. The President also is not required to prevent procurement or importation of essential spare parts or component parts.

In the 110th Congress, several bills contained provisions that would have further amended ISA, but they were not adopted. H.R. 1400, which passed the House on September 25, 2007 (397-16), would have removed the Administration's ability to waive ISA sanctions under Section 9(c), national interest grounds, but it would not have imposed on the Administration a time limit to determine whether a project is sanctionable.

"Special Rule" Exempting Firms that End their Business with Iran

CISADA (Section 102(g)(5) also amended ISA to provide a means—a so-called "special rule"— for firms to avoid any possibility of U.S. sanctions by pledging to verifiably end their business with Iran and to forgo any sanctionable business with Iran in the future. Under the special rule, the Administration is not required to make a determination of sanctionability against a firm that makes such pledges. The special rule was invoked on September 30, 2010, and again on November 17, 2010.

Termination Requirements

In its entirety, ISA application to Iran would terminate if Iran is determined by the Administration to have ceased its efforts to acquire WMD; is removed from the U.S. list of state sponsors of terrorism; *and* no longer "poses a significant threat" to U.S. national security and U.S. allies.[6] The amendments to ISA made by P.L. 111-195 would terminate if the first two criteria are met.

ISA Sunset

ISA was to sunset on August 5, 2001, in a climate of lessening tensions with Iran (and Libya). During 1999 and 2000, the Clinton Administration had eased the trade ban on Iran somewhat to try to engage the relatively moderate Iranian President Mohammad Khatemi. However, some maintained that Iran would view its expiration as a concession, and renewal legislation was enacted (P.L. 107-24, August 3, 2001). This law required an Administration report on ISA's effectiveness within 24 to 30 months of enactment; that report was submitted to Congress in January 2004 and did not recommend that ISA be repealed. ISA was scheduled to sunset on December 31, 2011 (as provided by P.L. 109-293). The sunset is now December 31, 2016, as provided for in CISADA).

Interpretations and Implementation

Traditionally reticent to impose economic sanctions, the European Union opposed ISA, when it was first enacted, as an extraterritorial application of U.S. law and filed a formal complaint before the World Trade Organization (WTO). In April 1997, the United States and the EU agreed to avoid a trade confrontation over ISA and a separate Cuba sanctions law (P.L. 104-114). The agreement involved the dropping of the WTO complaint and the May 18, 1998, decision by the Clinton Administration to waive ISA sanctions ("national interest"—Section 9c—waiver) on the first project determined to be in violation. That project was a $2 billion[7] contract, signed in September 1997, for Total SA of France and its partners, Gazprom of Russia and Petronas of Malaysia, to develop phases 2 and 3 of the 25+ phase South Pars gas field. The EU, for its part, pledged to increase cooperation with the United States on non-proliferation and counterterrorism. Then-Secretary of State Albright, in a statement, indicated that similar future such projects by EU firms in Iran would not be sanctioned, provided overall EU cooperation against Iranian terrorism and proliferation continued.[8] (The EU sanctions against Iran, announced July 27 2010, might render this understanding moot because the EU sanctions ban EU investment in and supplies of equipment and services to Iran's energy sector.)

ISA Sanctions Determinations: September 2010 to the Present

Since the Total/Petronas/Gazprom project in 1998, no projects were determined as violations of ISA until a State Department announcement of September 30, 2010.[9] Prior to the passage of CISADA, several Members of Congress questioned why no penalties had been imposed for violations of ISA. State Department reports to Congress on ISA, required every six months, have routinely stated that U.S. diplomats raise U.S. policy concerns about Iran with investing companies and their parent countries. However, these reports have not specifically stated which foreign companies, if any, were being investigated for ISA violations. No publication of such deals has been placed in the *Federal Register,* as required by Section 5e of ISA. In an effort to address the congressional criticism, Under Secretary of State for Political Affairs William Burns testified on July 9, 2008 (House Foreign Affairs Committee), that the Statoil project (listed in *Table 3*) was under review for ISA sanctions. Statoil is incorporated in Norway, which is not an EU member and it would therefore not fall under the 1998 U.S.-EU agreement discussed above.

Possibly in response to the pending CISADA legislation, and to an October 2009 letter signed by 50 Members of Congress referencing the CRS table below, Assistant Secretary of State for Near Eastern Affairs Jeffrey Feltman testified before the House Foreign Affairs Committee on October 27 2009, that the Obama Administration would review investments in Iran for violations of ISA. Feltman testified that the preliminary review would be completed within 45 days (by December 11, 2009) to determine which projects, if any, require further investigation. He testified that some announced projects were for political purposes and did not result in actual investment.

On February 25, 2010, Secretary of State Clinton testified before the House Foreign Affairs Committee that the State Department's preliminary review was completed in early February and that some of the cases reviewed "deserve[] more consideration" and were undergoing additional scrutiny. The preliminary review, according to the testimony, was conducted, in part, through State Department officials' contacts with their counterpart officials abroad and corporation officials. The additional investigations of problematic investments would involve the intelligence community, according to Secretary Clinton. State Department officials told CRS in November 2009 that any projects that the State Department plan was to complete the additional investigation and determine violations within 180 days of the completion of the preliminary review. (The 180- day time frame was, according to the Department officials, consistent with the Iran Freedom Support Act amendments to ISA discussed above, even though the 180 day time frame was not a mandatory deadline before CISADA was adopted.) A final determination of sanctionability would therefore, according to the Administration, be issued in early August 2010 (180 days from "early February). On June 22, 2010, Assistant Secretary of State William Burns testified before the Senate Foreign Relations Committee that there were "less than 10" cases of possible ISA violations.

September 30, 2010 Sanctions Determinations

Several determinations of sanctionability were made on September 30, 2010. That day, a Swiss-based Iranian-owned oil trading company—Naftiran Intertrade Company (NICO)—became the first firm to be sanctioned under ISA. The three penalties selected were: a ban on Ex-Im Bank credits; a denial of dual use export licensing to the firm; and a denial of bank loans exceeding $10 million. The mandatory ban on receiving U.S. government contracts applies as well.

That same day, following a months-long Administration review discussed later, four major energy sector investing companies were deemed eligible to avoid sanctions, under the ISA "special rule," by pledging to end their business in Iran. They are:

- Total of France,
- Statoil of Norway,
- ENI of Italy, and
- Royal Dutch Shell of Britain and the Netherlands.
- Inpex of Japan was exempted from sanctions under the special rule on November 17, 2010, according to a State Department announcement. The firm announced on October 15, 2010, that it is shedding its stake in the Azadegan development project shown in the table.

There remained some difference of opinion on the Administration invocation of the special rule, as evident at a hearing of the House Foreign Affairs Committee on December 1, 2010. At the hearing, Under Secretary Burns stated that companies exempted under the special rule had pledged to end their existing investments in Iran "in the very near future." Some Members of Congress questioned the imprecision of that time frame and others question the process for determining whether a firm is adhering to its pledge to pursue no future business in Iran's energy sector. Observers provided reasons for why the energy firms insisted they needed time to wind down their investments in Iran—under the buy-back program used for investments in Iran, the energy firms are paid back their investment over time, making it highly costly for them to suddenly end operations in Iran.

March 29, 2011, Sanctions Determination against Belarusneft

As shown in *Table 3* below, several additional foreign investment agreements have been agreed with Iran not covered in the September 2010 determination. Some of these firms remained under Administration scrutiny, and the Administration stated that determinations will be made within 180 days (by April 1, 2011). On March 29, 2011, with that deadline approaching, the State Department announced that one additional firm would be sanctioned under ISA—Belarusneft, a subsidiary of the Belarus government owned Belneftekhim—for a $500 million contract with Naftiran (the company sanctioned in September 2010) to develop the Jofeir oil field discussed in *Table 3*. Other subsidiaries of Belneftekhim were sanctioned in 2007 under Executive Order 13405 related to U.S. policy on Belarus. The three ISA sanctions imposed on March 29, 2011, were denial of Exim Bank financing, denial of U.S. export licenses, and denial of U.S. loans above $10 million.

The Administration announcement did not indicate that some of the other investments in *Table 3* or other investments, for which no ISA determinations have been made to date, are still under investigation. In public statements, some Members of Congress have expressed concern that Chinese firms have not been sanctioned, indicating that the Administration might be emphasizing some policy goals with respect to China at the expense of implementing sanctions against Iran.

May 24, 2011 Sanctions Imposed on Gasoline Sellers

On May 24, 2011, the Administration issued its first sanctions determinations under the CISADAamended "trigger" that requires sanctions against sellers of gasoline and related equipment and services. The reasons for the sanctions, including size of gasoline shipments to Iran or characterization of sanctionable dealings with Iran, as well as the ISA-related sanctions selected, can be found at http://www.state.gov/r/pa/prs/ps/2011/05/164132.htm. The seven firms sanctioned are

- Petrochemical Commercial Company International (PCCI) of Bailiwick of Jersey and Iran
- Royal Oyster Group (UAE)
- Tanker Pacific (Singapore)
- Ofer Brothers Group (Israel)
- Speedy Ship (UAE/Iran)
- Associated Shipbroking (Monaco)
- Petroleos de Venezuela (PDVSA) of Venezuela

Many of the firms sanctioned on May 24, 2011 were subjected to the financial-related sanctions provided in ISA. With respect to PDVSA, the Administration made clear in its announcement that U.S.-based subsidiaries were not included in the determination and that U.S. purchases of Venezuelan oil would not be affected. The day prior to the sanctions announcement, President Obama issued an Executive order clarifying that it is the responsibility of the Treasury Department to implement those ISA sanctions that involve the financial sector, including bans on loans, credits, and foreign exchange for, or imports from the sanctioned entity, as well as blockage of property of the sanctioned entity (if these sanctions are selected by the Secretary of State, who makes the decision which penalties to impose on sanctioned entities).

Non-Application to Crude Oil or Natural Gas Purchases from Iran or to Sales of Most Energy Equipment or Services

Purchases of oil or natural gas from Iran are generally considered not to constitute violations of ISA, because ISA sanctions *investment* in Iran's energy sector and sales to Iran of gasoline or gasoline-related services or equipment. Some of the deals listed in the chart later in this report involve combinations of investment and purchase. In March 2008, Switzerland's EGL utility agreed to buy 194 trillion cubic feet per year of Iranian gas for 25 years, through a Trans-Adriatic Pipeline (TAP) to be built by 2010, a deal valued at over $15 billion. The United States criticized the deal as sending the "wrong message" to Iran. In August 2008, Germany's SteinerPrematechnik-Gastec Co. agreed to apply its method of turning gas into liquid fuel at three Iranian plants.

Nor does ISA sanction sales to Iran of equipment that Iran could use to explore or extract its own oil or gas resources, *unless such sales are structured to provide ongoing profits or royalties (and therefore meet the definition of investments as provided in ISA)*.[10] For example, selling Iran an oil or gas drill rig or motors or other gear that Iran will use to drill for oil or gas would not appear to be sanctionable, unless the sale is structured to provide the seller ongoing profits or royalties. In addition, as noted, CISADA made sanctionable sales of equipment to Iran to enhance or expand its oil refineries, or equipment with which Iran could import gasoline (such as tankers), and of equipment that Iran could use to construct an energy pipeline.

Table 1. Major Energy Buyers From Iran (2009)
amounts in millions of U.S. dollars
(includes mineral fuels, crude oil, natural gas, distillates, and the like)

China	10,529
France	1,340
Germany	400.79
Greece	309.99
Hong Kong	372.59
India	9,541
Indonesia	182.95
Italy	2,363
Japan	9,192
Malaysia	964.33
Netherlands	2,765
Portugal	214.52
Singapore	1,998
South Africa	21,973
South Korea	5,420
Spain	2,624
Sri Lanka	843.51
Taiwan	1,788
Thailand	127.49
Turkey	3,047
United Kingdom	174.46

Source: Adapted by CRS, Susan Chesser, from the World Trade Atlas.

Official credit guarantee agencies are not considered sanctionable entities under ISA. In the 110th Congress, several bills—including S. 970, S. 3227, S. 3445, H.R. 957 (passed the House on July 31, 2007), and H.R. 7112 (which passed the House on September 26, 2008)—would have expanded the definition of sanctionable entities to official credit guarantee agencies, such as France's COFACE and Germany's Hermes, and to financial institutions and insurers generally. Some versions of CISADA would have made these entities sanctionable but these provisions were not included in the final law, probably out of concern for alienating U.S. allies in Europe.

Application to Energy Pipelines

As noted earlier, ISA's definition of sanctionable "investment"—which specifies investment in Iran's petroleum resources, defined as petroleum and natural gas—has been interpreted by successive administrations to include construction of energy pipelines to or through Iran. That interpretation was reinforced by the amendments to ISA in P.L. 111-195, which include in the definition of petroleum resources "products used to construct or maintain pipelines used to transport oil or liquefied natural gas." The Clinton and Bush Administrations used the threat of ISA sanctions to deter oil routes involving Iran and thereby successfully promoted an alternate route from Azerbaijan (Baku) to Turkey (Ceyhan). The route became operational in 2005.

Only a few significant pipelines involving Iran have been constructed in recent years—a line built in 1997 to carry natural gas from Iran to Turkey. Each country constructed the pipeline on its side of their border. At the time the project was under construction, State Department testimony stated that Turkey would be importing gas originating in Turkmenistan, not Iran, under a swap arrangement. That was one reason given for why the State Department did not determine that the project was sanctionable under ISA. However, many believe the decision not to sanction the pipeline was because the line was viewed as crucial to Turkey, a key U.S. ally. That explanation was reinforced when direct Iranian gas exports to Turkey through the line began in 2001, and no determination of sanctionability has been made. In May 2009, Iran and Armenia inaugurated a natural gas pipeline between the two, built by Gazprom of Russia. No determination of sanctionability has been announced.

As shown in *Table 3,* in July 2007, a preliminary agreement was reached to build a second Iran-Turkey pipeline, through which Iranian gas would also flow to Europe. That agreement was not finalized during Iranian President Mahmoud Ahmadinejad's visit to Turkey in August 2008 because of Turkish commercial concerns, but the deal reportedly remains under discussion. On February 23, 2009, Iranian newspapers said Iran had formed a joint venture with a Turkish firm to export 35 billion cubic meters of gas per year to Europe; 50% of the venture would be owned by the National Iranian Gas Export Company (NIGEC).

Iran and Kuwait have held talks on the construction of a 350-mile pipeline that would bring Iranian gas to Kuwait. The two sides have apparently reached agreement on volumes (8.5 million cubic meters of gas would go to Kuwait each day) but not on price.[11] There are also discussions reported between Iran and Iraq on constructing pipelines to facilitate oil and gas swaps between the two, but no firm movement on these projects is evident.

Iran-India Pipeline

Another pending pipeline project would carry Iranian gas, by pipeline, to Pakistan. India had been a part of the $7 billion project, which would take about three years to complete, but India was reported in June 2010 to be largely out of the project. India did not sign a memorandum between Iran and Pakistan finalizing the deal on June 12, 2010. India reportedly has been concerned about the security of the pipeline, the location at which the gas would be officially transferred to India, pricing of the gas, tariffs, and the source in Iran of the gas to be sold.

During the Bush Administration, Secretary of State Rice on several occasions "expressed U.S. concern" about the pipeline deal or called it "unacceptable." Possibly contributing to India's hesitancy to move forward, the late Ambassador Richard Holbrooke, the Administration Special Representative on Pakistan and Afghanistan, during 2010 trips to Pakistan, raised the possibility that the project could be sanctioned if it is undertaken, citing enactment of CISADA. Other steps taken by India in late 2010 to prevent some banking transactions with Iran, discussed later, could suggest that India is now cautious about any expansion of energy or other commercial relations with Iran. Previously, the threat of imposition of U.S. sanctions had not dissuaded Indian firms from taking some equity stakes in various Iranian energy projects, as shown in *Table 3* below.

India may envision an alternative to the pipeline project, as a means of tapping into Iran's vast gas resources. During high-level economic talks in early July 2010, Iranian and Indian officials reportedly raised the issue of constructing an underwater natural gas pipeline, which would avoid going through Pakistani territory. However, such a route would presumably be much more expensive to construct than would be an overland route.

European Gas Pipeline Routes

Iran also is attempting to position itself as a gas exporter to Europe. The Obama Administration, like its predecessors, takes the view that Iran be excluded from gas pipeline projects to Europe, even though the projects might make Europe less dependent on Russian gas supplies. One potential project involving Iran is the Nabucco pipeline project, which would transport Iranian gas to western Europe. Iran, Turkey, and Austria reportedly have negotiated on that project. Another is the Trans-Adriatic Pipeline (TAP) although, as discussed below, partners in that project have announced that Iranian gas would not be involved. Iran's Energy Minister GholamHossein Nozari said on April 2, 2009, that Iran is considering negotiating a gas export route—the "Persian Pipeline"—that would send gas to Europe via Iraq, Syria, and the Mediterranean Sea.

Application to Iranian Firms or the Revolutionary Guard

Although ISA is widely understood to apply to firms around the world that reach an investment agreement with Iran, the provisions could also be applied to Iranian firms and entities subordinate to the National Iranian Oil Company (NIOC), which is supervised by the Oil Ministry. The firm that was sanctioned, Naftiran Interrade Company (NICO), is one such entity; it is a subsidiary of NIOC. However, such entities, including Naftiran, do not do business in the United States and would not likely be harmed by any of the penalties that could be imposed under ISA. Some of the other major components of NIOC are:

- The Iranian Offshore Oil Company;
- The National Iranian Gas Export Co.;
- National Iranian Tanker Company; and
- Petroleum Engineering and Development Co.

Actual construction and work is largely done through a series of contractors. Some of them, such as Khatam ol-Anbia and Oriental Kish, have been identified by the U.S. government as controlled by Iran's Revolutionary Guard and have been sanctioned under various executive orders, discussed below. The relationship of other Iranian contractors to the Guard, if any, is unclear.

Some of the Iranian contractor firms include Pasargad Oil Co, Zagros Petrochem. Co, Sazeh Consultants, Qeshm Energy, Sadid Industrial Group, and others.

Application to Liquefied Natural Gas

The original version of ISA did not apply to the development of liquefied natural gas. Iran has no LNG export terminals, in part because the technology for such terminals is patented by U.S. firms and unavailable for sale to Iran. However, CISADA, specifically includes LNG in the definition of petroleum resources and therefore makes investment in LNG (or supply of LNG tankers or pipelines) sanctionable.

Table 2. Comparison of Major Versions of H.R. 2194/P.L. 111-195

House Version	Senate Version	Final Law and Implementation Status
General Goals and Overview: Seeks to expand the authorities of the Iran Sanctions Act (ISA, P.L. 104- 172) to deter sales by foreign companies of gasoline to Iran.	Broader goals than House: sanctions sales of gasoline to Iran similar to House version of H.R. 2194, but also would affect several other U.S. sanctions against Iran already in place, including revoking some exemptions to the U.S. ban on imports from Iran.	Generally closer to the Senate version, but adds new provisions (not in either version) sanctioning Iranians determined to be involved in human rights abuses and prohibiting transactions with foreign banks that conduct business with Revolutionary Guard and U.N.-sanctioned Iranian entities.
Statement of U.S. Policy on Sanctioning Iran's Central Bank (Bank Markazi): Section2(c) and 3(a) state that it shall be U.S. policy to fully enforce ISA to encourage foreign governments: - to cease investing in Iran's energy sector. - to sanction Iran's Central Bank and other financial institutions that do business with the Iranian Central Bank (or any Iranian bank involved in proliferation or support of terrorist activities)	Section 108 urges the President to use existing U.S. authorities to impose U.S. sanctions against the Iranian Central Bank or other Iranian banks engaged in proliferation or support of terrorist groups. Such authorities could include Section 311 of the USA Patriot Act (31 U.S.C. 5318A), which authorizes designation of foreign banks as "of primary money laundering concern" and thereby cut off their relations with U.S. banks.	Section 104 (see below) contains sense of Congress urging U.S. sanctions against Iranian Central Bank and would prohibit U.S. bank dealings with any financial institution that helps the Central Bank facilitate circumvention of U.N. resolutions on Iran.

Table 2. (Continued)

House Version	Senate Version	Final Law and Implementation Status
Extension of ISA to Sales of Gasoline: Section 3(a) would amend ISA to make sanctionable: -the sale to Iran of equipment or services (of over $200,000 in value, or $500,000 combined sales in one year) that would enable Iran to maintain or expand its domestic production of refined petroleum. -or, the sale to Iran of refined petroleum products or ships, vehicles, or insurance or reinsurance to provide such gasoline to Iran (same dollar values as sale of equipment).	Section 102(a) contains similar provisions regarding both gasoline sales and sales of equipment and services for Iran to expand its own refinery capacity. However, sets the aggregate one-year sale value at $1 million—double the level of the House bill.	Section 102(a) contains provisions amending ISA to include sales of gasoline and refining services and equipment as sanctionable (similar to both versions). Sets dollar value "trigger" at $1 million transaction, or $5 million aggregate value (equipment or gasoline sales) in a one-year period. Specifies that what is sanctionable includes helping Iran develop its liquefied natural gas (LNG) sector. Products whose sales is sanctionable include LNG tankers and products to build pipelines used to transport oil or LNG. Includes aviation fuel in definition of refined petroleum. Formally reduces investment threshold to $20 million to trigger sanctionability.
Expansion of ISA Sanctions: Section 3(b) would mandate certain sanctions (not currently authorized by ISA) on sellers of the equipment, gasoline, or services described in Section 3(a) to include: - prohibition of any transactions in foreign exchange with sanctioned entity; - prohibition of credit or payments to the sanctioned entity; - and, prohibition on any transactions involving U.S.-based property of the sanctioned entity. (These sanctions would be imposed in addition to the required two out of six sanctions currently specified in ISA.)	Similar to House bill (Section 102(a)).	Section 102(b) amends ISA to add add three sanctions to the existing menu of six sanctions in ISA and requires the President to impose 3 out of the 9 specified sanctions on entities determined to be violators. (As it previously existed, ISA required the imposition of two out of six sanctions of the menu.)
U.S. Government Enforcement Mechanism:	Section 103(b)(4) contains a similar provision, but mandates	Section 102(b) amends ISA by adding a provision similar to the

House Version	Senate Version	Final Law and Implementation Status
Section 3(b) also requires the heads of U.S. Government agencies to ensure that their agencies contract with firms that certify to the U.S. agency that they are not selling any of the equipment, products, or services to Iran (gasoline and related equipment and services) specified in Section 3(a). The section contains certain penalties, such as prohibition on future bids for U.S. government contracts, to be imposed on any firm that makes a false certification about such activity.	that the head of a U.S. agency may not contract with a person who meets criteria of sanctionability in the act. Would not require the bidding/contracting firm to certify its own compliance, thereby placing the burden of verifying such compliance on the U.S. executive agency.	House version: requiring, within 90 days of enactment (by October 1, 2010) new Federal Acquisition Regulations that mandate that firms to certify that they are not in violating of ISA as a condition of receiving a U.S. government contract, and providing for penalties for any falsification. The Civilian Agency Acquisition Council issued the needed regulations (interim ruling) on September 29, 2010. Paperwork that firms must sign making that certification now included as part of their contract signature package.
Additional Sanctions Against Suppliers of Nuclear, Missile, or Advanced Conventional Weapons Technology to Iran: Section 3(c) provides an additional ISA sanction to be imposed on any country whose entity(ies) violate ISA by providing nuclear weapons-related technology or missile technology to Iran. The sanction to be imposed on such country is a ban on any nuclear cooperation agreement with the United States under the Atomic Energy Act of 1954, and a prohibition on U.S. sales to that country of nuclear technology in accordance with such an agreement. The sanction can be waived if the President certifies to Congress that the country in question is taking effective actions against its violating entities.	No equivalent, although, as noted below, the Senate bill does contain several proliferation-related provisions.	Section 102(a)(2) amends ISA by adding a prohibition on licensing of nuclear materials, facilities, or technology to any country which is the parent country of an entity determined to be sanctioned under ISA for providing WMD technology to Iran. Waiver is provided on vital national security interest grounds.

Table 2. (Continued)

House Version	Senate Version	Final Law and Implementation Status
Alterations to Waiver and Implementation Provisions: Section 3(d)(1) imposes a requirement (rather than an non-binding exhortation in the existing law) that the Administration "immediately" initiate an investigation of any potentially sanctionable activity under ISA. Section 3(d)(2) would require the President to certify that a waiver of penalties on violating entities described above is "vital to the national security interest of the United States." rather than, as currently stipulated in ISA, is "important to the national interest of the United States.	No similar provisions	Implementation and waiver provisions closer to House version. Section 102(g) amends ISA to make mandatory the beginning of an investigation of potentially sanctionable activity, and makes mandatory a decision on sanctionability within 180 days of the beginning of such an investigation. (Previously, 180 day period was nonbinding.) Mandatory investigation (which goes into effect July 1, 2011) of gasoline sales to Iran can be delayed for 180 days subject to a report—by June 1, 2011—certifying that there has been a substantial reduction in gasoline sales to Iran as a result of CISADA. Section 102(c) sets 9(c) waiver standard as "necessary to the national interest" Section 102(g) also alters existing 4(c) ISA waiver to delay sanctions on firms of countries that are "closely cooperating" with U.S. efforts against Iran's WMD programs. (This is not an automatic "carve out" for cooperating countries.) Section 102(g)(3) adds to ISA a "special rule" that no investigation of a potential violation need be started if a firm has ended or pledged to end its violating activity in/with Iran. "Special rule" invoked twice, as discussed above.
Required Reports: Section 3(e) would amend ISA's current Administration reporting requirements to also include an assessment of Iran's support for militant movements and to	Section 107 contains a provision similar to the new reporting requirement of the House bill with regard to firms that sold gasoline and related equipment and services to Iran, and	Various reporting requirements throughout (separate from those required to trigger or justify the various sanctions or waivers). These reporting requirements are:

House Version	Senate Version	Final Law and Implementation Status
acquire weapons of mass destruction technology. A new reporting requirement would be created (every six months) on firms providing Iran gasoline and related equipment and services specified above, as well as the names and dates of such activity, and any contracts such entities have with U.S. Government agencies. The required report is to include information on persons the President determines is affiliated with Iran's Islamic Revolutionary Guard Corp (IRGC), as well as persons providing material support to the IRGC or conducting financial transactions with the IRGC or its affiliates. Also required is an Administration report, within one year of enactment, on trade between Iran and countries in the G-20.	invested in Iran's energy sector. The Senate bill does not require reporting on the IRGC that is stipulated in the House bill, or the report on Iran-G-20 trade. However, the Senate bill (Section 109) expresses the sense of Congress that the United States "continue to target" the IRGC for supporting terrorism, its role in proliferation, and its oppressive activities against the people of Iran.	- Amendment of section 10 of ISA to include a report, within 90 days of enactment, and annual thereafter, on trade between Iran and the countries of the Group of 20 Finance Ministers and Central Bank Governors. (From House version) - Section 110 of the law (not an amendment to ISA) requires a report within 90 days, and every 180 days hence, on investments made in Iran's energy sector since January 1, 2006. The report must include significant joint ventures outside Iran in which Iranian entities are involved. - The Section 110 report is to include an estimate of the value of ethanol imported by Iran during the reporting period. - Section 111 (not an ISA amendment) requires a report within 90 days on the activities of export credit agencies of foreign countries in guaranteeing financing for trade with Iran).
Expansion of ISA Definitions: Section 3(f) would expand the definitions of investing entities, or persons, contained in ISA, to include: - export credit agencies. (Such a provision is widely considered controversial because export credit agencies are arms of their governments, and therefore sanctioning such agencies is considered a sanction against a government.)	Similar provision contained in Section 102(d).	Does not include export credit agencies as a sanctionable entity under ISA (as amended). (However, a report is required on export credit agency activity, as discussed above.) Does include LNG as petroleum resources.

Table 2. (Continued)

House Version	Senate Version	Final Law and Implementation Status
Termination Provisions: Section 3(g) would terminate the bill's sanctions against persons who are sanctioned, under the act, for sales of WMD-related technology, if the President certifies that Iran has ceased activities to acquire a nuclear device and has ceased enrichment of uranium and other nuclear activities.	Title IV would terminate the act's provisions 30 days after the President certifies that Iran has: - ceased support for international terrorism and qualifies for removal from the U.S. "terrorism list" - and, has ceased the pursuit and development of WMD and ballistic missile technology.	Same as Senate version, which means that the amendments to ISA in this law terminate if the President certifies that Iran has ceased WMD development, and has qualified for removal from the U.S. terrorism list. However, the pre-existing version of ISA would continue to apply until the President also certifies that Iran poses no significant threat to U.S. national security, interests, or allies.
ISA Sunset: Section 3(h) would extend all provisions of ISA until December 31, 2016. It is currently scheduled to "sunset" on December 31, 2011, as amended by the Iran Freedom Support Act (P.L. 109-293).	No similar provision.	Sunset provision same as House version ISA to sunset December 31, 2016.
Additional Provisions That Are Not Amendments to ISA		
Modification to U.S. Ban on Trade With and Investment in Iran:		
No provision	Section 103(b)(1) would ban all imports of Iranian origin from the United States, with the exception of informational material. Currently, modifications to the U.S. trade ban with Iran (Executive Order 12959 of May 6, 1995) that became effective in 2000 permit imports of Iranian luxury goods, such as carpets, caviar, nuts, and dried fruits. - Section 103(b)(2)) generally reiterates/codifies current provisions of U.S. trade ban related to U.S. exports to	Same as Senate version. However, contains a new section that the existing U.S. ban (by Executive order) on most exports to Iran not include the exportation of services for Internet communications. Provision also states that the ban on most exports should not include goods or services needed to help non-governmental organizations support democracy in Iran. Both provisions designed to support opposition protesters linked to

House Version	Senate Version	Final Law and Implementation Status
	Iran. Provision would prohibit exports to Iran of all goods except food and medical devices, informational material, articles used for humanitarian assistance to Iran, or goods needed to ensure safe operation of civilian aircraft.	Iran's "Green movement." Implementation: In July 2010, Treasury Office of Foreign Assets Control issued a statement that, effective September 29, 2010, the general license for imports of Iranian luxury goods will be eliminated (no such imports allowed). This went into effect that day.
Freezing of Assets/Travel Restriction on Revolutionary Guard and Related Entities and Persons: No provision	Section 103(b)(3) mandates the President to freeze the assets of Iranian diplomats, IRGC, or other Iranian official personnel deemed a threat to U.S. national security under the International Emergency Economic Powers Act (50 U.S.C. 1701 et seq.). Provision would require freezing of assets of families and associates of persons so designated. Section 109 calls for a ban on travel of IRGC and affiliated persons.	Similar to Senate version
Application of U.S. Trade Ban to Subsidiaries: No provision	Section 104 would apply the provisions of the U.S. trade ban with Iran (Executive Order 12959) to subsidiaries of U.S. firms if the subsidiary is established or maintained for the purpose of avoiding the U.S. ban on trade with Iran . The definition of subsidiary, under the provision, is any entity that is more than 50% owned or is directed by a U.S. person or firm.	No provision

Table 2. (Continued)

House Version	Senate Version	Final Law and Implementation Status
Mandatory Sanctions on Financial Institutions that Help Iran's Sanctioned Entities: No provision	No provision	Section 104(c) requires the Treasury Department to develop regulations (within 90 days of enactment) to prohibit and specify penalties for any U.S. financial transactions with any foreign financial institution that - facilitates efforts by the Revolutionary Guard to acquire WMD or fund terrorism - facilitate the activities of any person sanctioned under U.N. resolutions on Iran. - facilitates the efforts by Iran's Central Bank to support the Guard's WMD acquisition efforts or support any U.N.- sanctioned entity Section 104(d) requires penalties to be specified in regulations within 90 days. Section 104(e) requires regulations (no date specified) to make this requirement retroactive to existing accounts, pending an audit by the U.S. banks involved. Implementation: Treasury Department regulations implementing Section 104(c) and (d) provisions issued August 16, 2010. Regulations to implement 104(e) were proposed by Treasury Department's Financial Crimes Enforcement Network (FINCEN) on April 27, 2011.
Sanctions on Iranian Human Rights Abusers: No provision	No provision	Section 105 requires, within 90 days, a report listing Iranian officials (or affiliates) determined responsible for or complicit in serious human rights abuses since the June 12, 2009, Iranian election. Those listed are ineligible for a U.S. visa, their U.S, property is to be blocked, and transactions with

House Version	Senate Version	Final Law and Implementation Status
		those listed are prohibited. On September 29, 2010, President Obama issued Executive Order 13553 providing for these sanctions. See human rights section of this paper for Iranians sanctioned.
Sanctioning Certain Information Technology Sales to Iran: No provision	Section 105 prohibits U.S. executive agencies from contracting with firms that export sensitive technology to Iran. "Sensitive technology" is defined as hardware, software, telecommunications equipment, or other technology that restricts the free flow of information in Iran or which monitor or restrict "speech" of the people of Iran.	Section 106 of the conference report is similar to Senate version. The contracting restriction is to be imposed "pursuant to such regulations as the President may prescribe." The contracting regulations issued September 29, 2010, "partially" implement this requirement, with further regulations to be issued.
Treasury Department Authorization to prevent misuse of the U.S. financial system by Iran or other countries: No provision	Section 106(b) authorizes $64.611 million for FY2010 (and "such sums as may be necessary" for FY2011 and 2012) for the Treasury Department's Office of Terrorism and Financial Intelligence. The funds are authorized to ensure that countries such as Iran are not misusing the international financial system for illicit purposes. Iran is not mentioned specifically. $104.26 million is authorized by the section for FY2010 for the Department's Financial Crimes Enforcement Network.	Section 109 authorizes $102 million for FY2011 and "sums as may be necessary" for FY2012 and 2013 to the Treasury Department Office of Terrorism and Financial Intelligence. Another $100 million is authorized for FY2011 for the Financial Crimes Enforcement Network, and $113 million for FY2011 for the Bureau of Industry and Security for the Department of Commerce

Table 2. (Continued)

House Version	Senate Version	Final Law and Implementation Status
Hezbollah: No specific provision, although, as noted above, the House bill does expand ISA reporting requirements to include Iran's activities to support terrorist movements. Lebanese Hezbollah is named as a Foreign Terrorist Organization (FTO) by the U.S. State Department.	Section 110 contains a sense of Congress that the President impose the full range of sanctions under the International Emergency Economic Powers Act (50 U.S.C. 1701) on Hezbollah, and that the President renew international efforts to disarm Hezbollah in Lebanon (as called for by U.N. Security Council Resolutions 1559 and 1701).	Section 113 similar to Senate version.
Divestment: No provisions	Title II of the Senate bill (Section 203) prevents criminal, civil, or administrative action against any investment firm or officer or adviser based on its decision to divest from securities that - have investments or operations in Sudan described in the Sudan Accountability and Divestment Act of 2007 - or, engage in investments in Iran that would be considered sanctionable by the Senate bill.	Similar to Senate version
Prevention of Transshipment, Reexportation, or Diversion of Sensitive Items to Iran: No provision	Section 302 requires a report by the Director of National Intelligence that identifies all countries considered a concern to allow transshipment or diversion of WMD-related technology to Iran (technically: "items subject to the provision of the Export Administration Regulations"). Section 303 requires the Secretary of Commerce to designate a country as a "Destination of Possible Diversion Concern" if such country is considered to have inadequate export controls or is unwilling to prevent the diversion of U.S. technology to Iran. The provision stipulates	Similar to Senate version, but does not provide for prior negotiations before designating a country as a "Destination of Possible Diversion Concern." List of countries that are believed to be allowing diversion of specified goods or technology to Iran to be named in a report provided within 180 days of enactment.

House Version	Senate Version	Final Law and Implementation Status
	government-to- government discussions are to take place to improve that country's export control systems. If such efforts did not lead to improvement, the section would mandate designation of that country as a "Destination of Diversion Concern" and would set up a strict licensing requirement for U.S. exports of sensitive technologies to that country.	

Table 3. Post-1999 Major Investments/Major Development Projects in Iran's Energy Sector

Date	Field/Project	Company(ies)/Status (If Known)	Value	Output/Goal
February 1999	Doroud (oil) (Energy Information Agency, Department of Energy, August 2006.) Total and ENI exempted from sanctions on September 30 because of pledge to exit Iran market	Total (France)/ENI(Italy)	$1 billion	205,000 bpd
April 1999	Balal (oil) ("Balal Field Development in Iran Completed," World Market Research Centre, May 17, 2004.)	Total/ Bow Valley (Canada)/ENI	$300 million	40,000 bpd
Nov. 1999	Soroush and Nowruz (oil) ("News in Brief: Iran." Middle East Economic Digest, (MEED) January 24, 2003.) Royal Dutch exempted from sanctions on 9/30 because of pledge to exit Iran market	Royal Dutch Shell (Netherlands)/Japex (Japan)	$800 million	190,000 bpd
April 2000	Anaran bloc (oil) (MEED Special Report, December 16, 2005, pp. 48-50.)	Norsk Hydro and Statoil (Norway) and Gazprom and Lukoil (Russia) No production to date; Statoil and Norsk have left project.	$105 million	65,000
July 2000	Phase 4 and 5, South Pars (gas) (Petroleum Economist, December 1, 2004.) ENI exempted 9/30 based on pledge to exit Iran market	ENI Gas onstream as of Dec. 2004	$1.9 billion	2 billion cu.ft./day (cfd)
March 2001	Caspian Sea oil exploration—construction of submersible drilling rig for Iranian partner (IPR Strategic Business Information Database, March 11, 2001.)	GVA Consultants (Sweden)	$225 million	NA

Table 3. (Continued)

Date	Field/Project	Company(ies)/Status (If Known)	Value	Output/Goal
June 2001	Darkhovin (oil) ("Darkhovin Production Doubles." Gulf Daily News, May 1, 2008.) ENI told CRS in April 2010 it would close out all Iran operations by 2013. ENI exempted from sanctions on 9/30, as discussed above	ENI Field in production	$1 billion	100,000 bpd
May 2002	Masjid-e-Soleyman (oil) ("CNPC Gains Upstream Foothold." MEED, September 3, 2004.)	Sheer Energy(Canada)/China National Petroleum Company (CNPC). Local partner is Naftgaran Engineering	$80 million	25,000 bpd
Sept. 2002	Phase 9 + 10, South Pars (gas) ("OIEC Surpasses South Korean Company in South Pars." IPR Strategic Business Information Database, November 15, 2004.)	LG Engineering and Construction Corp. (now known as GS Engineering and Construction Corp., South Korea) On stream as of early2009	$1.6 billion	2 billion cfd
October 2002	Phase 6, 7, 8, South Pars (gas) (Source: Statoil, May 2011) Field began producing late 2008; operational control handed to NIOC in 2009. Statoil exempted from sanctions on 9/30/2010 because Statoil pledged to exit Iran market.	Statoil (Norway)	$750 million	3 billion cfd
January 2004	Azadegan (oil) "Japan Mulls Azadegan Options." (APS Review Oil Market Trends, November 27, 2006.) October 15, 2010: Inpex announced it would exit the project by selling its stake; "special rule" exempting it from ISA investigation invoked November 17, 2010.	Inpex (Japan) 10% stake. CNPC agreed to develop "north Azadegan" in Jan. 2009	$200 million(Inpex stake); China $1.76 billion	260,000 bpd
August 2004	Tusan Block Oil found in block in Feb. 2009, but not in commercial quantity, according to the firm. ("Iran-Petrobras Operations." APS Review Gas Market Trends, April 6, 2009; "Brazil's Petrobras Sees Few Prospects for Iran Oil," (http://www.reuters.com/article/idUSN0317110720090703.)	Petrobras (Brazil)	$178 million	No production
October 2004	Yadavaran (oil) ("Iran, China's Sinopec Ink Yadavaran Oilfield	Sinopec (China), deal finalized December 9,	$2 billion	300,000 bpd

Date	Field/Project	Company(ies)/Status (If Known)	Value	Output/Goal
	Development Contract." Payvand's Iran News, December 9, 2009.)	2007		
2005	Saveh bloc (oil) GAO report, cited below	PTT (Thailand)	?	?
June 2006	Garmsar bloc (oil) Deal finalized in June 2009("China's Sinopec signs a deal to develop oil block in Iran—report," Forbes, 20 June 2009, http://www.forbes.com/feeds/afx/2006/ 06/20/afx2829188.html.)	Sinopec (China)	$20 million	?
July 2006	Arak Refinery expansion (GAO report; Fimco FZE Machinery website; http://www.fimco.org /index.php? option=com_content& task=view&id=70& Itemid=78.)	Sinopec (China); JGC (Japan)	$959 million	Expansion to produce 250,000 bpd
Sept. 2006	Khorramabad block (oil) Seismic data gathered, but no production is planned. (Statoil factsheet, May 2011)	Norsk Hydro and Statoil (Norway).	$49 million	?
Feb. 2007	LNG Tanks at Tombak Port Contract to build three LNG tanks at Tombak, 30 miles north of Assaluyeh Port. (May not constitute "investment" as defined in pre-2010 version of ISA, because that definition did not specify LNG as "petroleum resource" of Iran.) "Central Bank Approves $900 Million for Iran LNG Project." Tehran Times, June 13, 2009.	Daelim (S. Korea)	$320 million	200,000 ton capacity
March 2007	Esfahan refinery upgrade ("Daelim, Others to Upgrade Iran's Esfahan Refinery." Chemical News and Intelligence, March 19, 2007.)	Daelim (S. Korea)	$16 billion	NA
Dec. 2007	Golshan and Ferdows onshore and offshore gas fields and LNG plant contract modified but reaffirmed December 2008 (GAO report; Oil Daily, January 14, 2008.)	SKS Ventures, Petrofield Subsidiary(Malaysia)		3.4 billion cfd
2007(unspec.)	Jofeir Field (oil) GAO report cited below. Belarusneft, a subsidiary of Belneftekhim, sanctioned under ISA on March 29, 2011. Naftiran sanctioned on September 29, 2010 for this and other activities.	Belarusneft (Belarus) under contract to Naftiran. No production to date	$500 million	40,000 bpd
2008	Dayyer Bloc (Persian Gulf, offshore, oil) GAO report cited below	Edison (Italy)	$44 million	?
February 2008	Lavan field (offshore natural gas) GAO report cited below	PGNiG (Poland) Status unclear	$2 billion	

Table 3. (Continued)

Date	Field/Project	Company(ies)/Status (If Known)	Value	Output/Goal
March 2008	Danan Field (on-shore oil) "PVEP Wins Bid to Develop Danan Field." Iran Press TV, March 11, 2008	Petro Vietnam Exploration and Production Co. (Vietnam)	?	?
April 2008	Moghan 2 (onshore oil and gas, Ardebil province) GAO report cited below	INA (Croatia)	$40-$140 million(dispute over size)	?
?	Kermanshah petrochemical plant (new construction) GAO report cited below	Uhde (Germany)		300,000 metric tons/yr
January 2009	"North Azadegan" (Chinadaily.com. "CNPC to Develop Azadegan Oilfield," http://www.chinadaily.com.cn/bizchina/2009-01/16/content_7403699.htm.)	CNPC (China)	$1.75 billion	75,000 bpd
Oct. 2009	South Pars Gas Field—Phases 6-8, Gas Sweetening Plant CRS conversation with Embassy of S. Korea in Washington, D.C, July 2010 Contract signed but then abrogated by S. Korean firm	G and S Engineering and Construction(South Korea)	$1.4 billion	
Nov. 2009	South Pars: Phase 12—Part 2 and Part 3 ("Italy, South Korea To Develop South Pars Phase 12." Press TV (Iran), November 3, 2009, http://www.presstv.com/pop/Print/?id = 110308.)	Daelim (S. Korea)—Part 2; Tecnimont (Italy)—Part 3	$4 billion ($2 bn each part)	
February 2010	South Pars: Phase 11 Drilling to Begin in March 2010("CNPC in Gas Deal, Beefs Up Tehran Team—Source," Reuters India, February 10, 2010, http://in.reuters.com.articlePrint?articleId=INTOE61909U20100210.)	CNPC (China)	$4.7 billion	
Totals: $41 billion investment				
Other Pending/Preliminary Deals				
North Pars Gas Field (offshore gas). Includes gas purchases (December 2006) (http://english.peopledaily.com.cn/200705/19/print20070519_376139.html.)		China National Offshore Oil Co.	$16 billion	3.6 billion cfd
Phase 13, 14—South Pars (gas); (Feb. 2007). Deadline to finalize as May 20, 2009, apparently not met; firms submitted revised proposals to Iran in June 2009. (http://www.rigzone.com/news/article.asp?a_id=77040& hmpn=1.) State Department said on September 30, 2010, that Royal Dutch Shell and Repsol have ended negotiations with Iran and will not pursue this project any further		Royal Dutch Shell, Repsol (Spain)	$4.3 billion	?

Date	Field/Project	Company(ies)/Status (If Known)	Value	Output/Goal
Phase 22, 23, 24—South Pars (gas), incl. transport Iranian gas to Turkey, and on to Europe and building three power plants in Iran. Initialed July 2007; not finalized to date.		Turkish Petroleum Company (TPAO)	$12. billion	2 billion cfd
Iran's Kish gas field (April 2008) Includes pipeline from Iran to Oman (http://www.presstv.ir/detail.aspx?id=112062&sectionid=351020103.		Oman (co-financing of project)	$7 billion	1 billion cfd
Phase 12 South Pars (gas)—part 1. Incl. LNG terminal construction and Farzad-B natural gas bloc (March 2009). Financing stalled due to sanctions; Tehran gave ONGC and Hinduja until January 31, 2011, to line up financing or the bid will be considered abandoned.		Taken over by Indian firms (ONGC, Oil India Ltd., Hinduja, Petronet in 2007)	$8 billion+	20 million tonnes of LNG annually by 2012
South Pars gas field (September 2009)		Petroleos de Venezuela S.A.; 10% stake in venture	$760 million	
Abadan refinery Upgrade and expansion; building a new refinery at Hormuz on the Persian Gulf coast (August 2009)		Sinopec	up to $6 billion if new refinery is built	

Sources: As noted in table, as well as CRS conversations with officials of the State Department Bureau of Economics, and officials of embassies of the parent government of some of the listed companies (2005-2009). Some information comes from a March 2010 GAO report, "Firms Reported in Open Sources as Having Commercial Activity in Iran's Oil, Gas, and Petrochemical Sectors." GAO-10-515R Iran's Oil, Gas, and Petrochemical Sectors. http://www.gao.gov/new.items/d10515r.pdf. The GAO report lists 41 firms with "commercial activity in Iran's energy sector; several of the listed agreements do not appear to constitute "investment," as defined in ISA.

Note: CRS has neither the mandate, the authority, nor the means to determine which of these projects, if any, might constitute a violation of the Iran Sanctions Act. CRS has no way to confirm the precise status of any of the announced investments, and some investments may have been resold to other firms or terms altered since agreement. In virtually all cases, such investments and contracts represent private agreements between Iran and its instruments and the investing firms, and firms are not necessarily required to confirm or publicly release the terms of their arrangements with Iran. Reported $20 million+ investments in oil and gas fields, refinery upgrades, and major project leadership are included in this table. Responsibility for a project to develop Iran's energy sector is part of ISA investment definition.

BAN ON U.S. TRADE AND INVESTMENT WITH IRAN

A ban on U.S. trade with and investment in Iran was imposed on May 6, 1995, by President Clinton, through Executive Order 12959.[12] This followed an earlier March 1995 executive order barring U.S. investment in Iran's energy sector. The trade and investment ban was intended to blunt criticism that U.S. trade with Iran made U.S. appeals for multilateral containment of Iran less credible. Each March since 1995 (and most recently on March 10,

2010), the U.S. Administration has renewed a declaration of a state of emergency that triggered the investment ban; it is likely to be renewed again in March 2011. The operation of the trade regulations is stipulated in Section 560 of the Code of Federal Regulations (Iranian Transactions Regulations, ITR's). As noted above, in accordance with CISADA, the strict ban on imports from Iran was restored on September 29, 2010; the ban on exports to Iran was altered only slightly by CISADA.

Some modifications to the trade ban since 1999 account for the fact that trade between the United States and Iran is minimal. Total U.S.-Iran trade was about $300 million in 2010 ($208 million in exports to Iran, and $94 million in imports). Trade was about $350 million worth of goods for all of 2009 ($281 million in exports to Iran, and $67 million in imports from Iran). That is about half the value of the bilateral trade in 2008.

The following conditions and modifications, as administered by the Office of Foreign Assets Control (OFAC) of the Treasury Department, apply:

- Some goods related to the safe operation of civilian aircraft may be licensed for export to Iran (Section 560.528 of Title 31, C.F.R.). As recently as September 2006, the George W. Bush Administration, in the interests of safe operations of civilian aircraft, permitted a sale by General Electric of Airbus engine spare parts to be installed on several Iran Air passenger aircraft (by European airline contractors). (A provision of H.R. 6296, a bill introduced in the 111th Congress, sought to prevent these sales to Iran.) An Administration intent to sell Iran data to repair certain GE engines for its legacy American-made aircraft, in order to ensure safe operation, was notified to Congress on March 16, 2011.
- U.S. firms may not negotiate with Iran or to trade Iranian oil overseas, but U.S. companies may apply for licenses to conduct "swaps" of Caspian Sea oil with Iran. A Mobil Corporation application to do so was denied in April 1999.
- According to the Iranian Transactions Regulations (ITR's), the ban does not apply to personal communications (phone calls, e-mails), or to humanitarian donations. U.S. non-government organizations (NGOs) require a specific license to operate in Iran, and some NGOs say the licensing requirements are too onerous to make work in Iran practical.
- Since April 1999, commercial sales of food and medical products to Iran have been allowed, on a case-by-case basis and subject to OFAC licensing. According to OFAC in April 2007, licenses for exports of medicines to treat HIV and leukemia are routinely expedited for sale to Iran, and license applications are viewed favorably for business school exchanges, earthquake safety seminars, plant and animal conservation, and medical training in Iran.
- OFAC generally declines to discuss export licenses approved, and a press account on December 24, 2010,[13] paints a picture of broad export approvals to Iran of such condiments as ice cream sprinkles, chewing gum, food additives, hot sauces, body-building supplements, and other goods that appear to have uses other than those that are purely humanitarian or nutritive. U.S. exporters widely mentioned include Mars Co. (candy manufacturer); Kraft Foods; Wrigley's (gum); and McCormick and Co. (spices). Some goods were sold through a Revolutionary Guard-owned chains of stores in Iran called Qods; as well as a government owned Shahrvand store and a

chain called Refah. OFAC officials indicated in the press accounts that such licenses were not in contradiction with U.S. law or policy, although there might have been less than full scrutiny of some Iranian end users and that such scrutiny might be increased in future licensing decisions.

- As far as financing of approved U.S. sales to Iran, private letters of credit can be used to finance approved transactions, but no U.S. government credit guarantees are available, and U.S. exporters are not permitted to deal directly with Iranian banks. The FY2001 agriculture appropriations law (P.L. 106-387) contained a provision banning the use of official credit guarantees for food and medical sales to Iran and other countries on the U.S. terrorism list, except Cuba, although allowing for a presidential waiver to permit such credit guarantees. No U.S. Administration has authorized credit guarantees, to date. In December 2004, the trade ban was further modified to allow Americans to freely engage in ordinary publishing activities with entities in Iran (and Cuba and Sudan).
- In April 2000, the trade ban was further eased to allow U.S. importation of Iranian nuts, dried fruits, carpets, and caviar. Financing was permitted for U.S. importers of these goods. The United States was the largest market for Iranian carpets before the 1979 revolution, but U.S. anti-dumping tariffs imposed on Iranian products in 1986 dampened of many Iranian products. As discussed above, CISADA ended approval of such imports as of October 1, 2010. Prior to the entry into force of this CISADA provision, the number one U.S. import from Iran was pomegranate juice concentrate. Iranian carpets were another popular import, despite a U.S. tariff of about 3%-6%. Imports of Iranian caviar carried a duty of about 15%.

Application to Foreign Subsidiaries of U.S. Firms

The U.S. trade ban does not bar subsidiaries of U.S. firms from dealing with Iran, as long as the subsidiary has no operational relationship to the parent company. Foreign subsidiaries are generally considered foreign persons, not U.S. persons. The March 7, 2010, *New York Times* article, cited above, discusses some subsidiaries of U.S. firms that have been active in Iran and which have also received U.S. government contracts, grants, loans, or loan guarantees. Among major foreign subsidiaries of U.S. firms that have traded with Iran are the following:

- U.S. energy equipment firms. Some subsidiaries of such firms may still be in the Iranian market, according to their "10-K" filings with the Securities and Exchange Commission. These include Natco Group,[14] Overseas Shipholding Group,[15] UOP (United Oil Products, a Honeywell subsidiary based in Britain),[16] Itron[17], Fluor,[18] Flowserve,[19] Parker Drilling, Vantage Energy Services,[20] Weatherford,[21]and a few others. UOP reportedly sells refinery equipment to Iran; new such sales are now potentially sanctionable under ISA, as modified by CISADA.
- An Irish subsidiary of the Coca Cola company provides syrup for the U.S.-brand soft drink to an Iranian distributor, Khoshgovar. Local versions of both Coke and of Pepsi

(with Iranian-made syrups) are also marketed in Iran by distributors who licensed the recipes for those soft drinks before the Islamic revolution and before the trade ban was imposed on Iran.

- Transammonia Corp., via a Swiss-based subsidiary, is said to be conducting business with Iran to help it export ammonia, a growth export for Iran.

Subsidiaries Exiting Iran

As international sanctions against Iran have increased in recent years, many foreign subsidiaries have decided that the risks of continuing to do business with Iran outweigh the benefits:

- Chemical manufacturer Huntsman announced in January 2010 its subsidiaries would halt sales to Iran.
- Halliburton. On January 11, 2005, Iran said it had contracted with U.S. company Halliburton, and an Iranian company, Oriental Kish, to drill for gas in Phases 9 and 10 of South Pars. Halliburton reportedly provided $30 million to $35 million worth of services per year through Oriental Kish, leaving unclear whether Halliburton would be considered in violation of the U.S. trade and investment ban or the Iran Sanctions Act (ISA)[22]—because the deals involved a subsidiary of Halliburton (Cayman Islands-registered Halliburton Products and Service, Ltd., based in Dubai). On April 10, 2007, Halliburton announced that its subsidiaries were, as promised in January 2005, no longer operating in Iran.
- General Electric (GE). The firm announced in February 2005 that it would seek no new business in Iran, and it reportedly wound down preexisting contracts by July 2008. GE was selling Iran equipment and services for hydroelectric, oil and gas services, and medical diagnostic projects through Italian, Canadian, and French subsidiaries.
- Oilfield services firm Smith International said on March 1, 2010, it would stop sales to Iran by its subsidiaries.
- On March 1, 2010, Caterpillar Corp. said it had altered its policies to prevent foreign subsidiaries from selling equipment to independent dealers that have been reselling the equipment to Iran.[23] Ingersoll Rand, maker of air compressors and cooling systems, followed suit.[24]
- In April 2010, it was reported that foreign partners of several U.S. or other multinational accounting firms had cut their ties with Iran, including KPMG of the Netherlands, and local affiliates of U.S. firms PricewaterhouseCoopers and Ernst and Young.[25]

In the 110th Congress, S. 970, S. 3227, S. 3445, and three House-passed bills (H.R. 1400, H.R. 7112, and H.R. 957)—would have applied sanctions to the parent companies of U.S. subsidiaries if those subsidiaries are directed by the parent company to trade with Iran. The Senate version of CISADA contained a similar provision, but it was taken out in conference action. A provision of H.R. 6296, the bill introduced in the 111th Congress, would apply this sanction, and there reportedly is consideration of introducing similar legislation in the 112th Congress.

BANKING AND FINANCE: TREASURY DEPARTMENT FINANCIAL MEASURES AND CISADA

U.S. efforts to shut Iran out of the international banking system—gaining strength as other countries have joined the effort—have been implemented by the Treasury Department (office of then-Under Secretary of the Treasury Stuart Levey) through "targeted financial measures." Since 2006, strengthened by leverage provided in five U.N. Security Council Resolutions, Levey and other officials have been able to convince at least 80 foreign banks that dealing with Iran entails financial risk and furthers terrorism and proliferation. Treasury Secretary Timothy Geithner has described Levey as having "led the design of a remarkably successful program"[26] with regard to targeting Iran's proliferation networks. Some fear that U.S. sanctions may not be as vigorously enforced now that Levey has left office as of April 2011. His replacement is Daniel Cohen.

In earlier action intended to cut Iran off from the U.S. banking system, on September 6, 2006, the Treasury Department barred U.S. banks from handling any indirect transactions ("U-turn transactions," meaning transactions with non-Iranian foreign banks that are handling transactions on behalf of an Iranian bank) with Iran's Bank Saderat (see above), which the Administration accuses of providing funds to Hezbollah.[27] Bank Sepah is subject to asset freezes and transactions limitations as a result of Resolutions 1737 and 1747. The Treasury Department extended that U-Turn restriction to all Iranian banks on November 6, 2008.

Thus far, the Treasury Department has not designated any bank as a "money laundering entity" for Iran-related transactions (under Section 311 of the USA Patriot Act). Nor has Treasury imposed any specific sanctions against Bank Markazi (Central Bank) which, according to a February 25, 2008, *Wall Street Journal* story, is helping other Iranian banks circumvent the U.S. and U.N. banking pressure. Several European countries reportedly still oppose such a sanction as an extreme step with potential humanitarian consequences, for example by preventing Iran from keeping its currency stable. S. 3445, a Senate bill in the 110th Congress, and a counterpart passed by the House on September 26, 2008 (H.R. 7112), called for this sanction. The Senate version of H.R. 2194 had a similar provision, which was included in conference action. Resolution 1929 references the need for vigilance in dealing with Iran's Central Bank but does not mandate any new sanctions against it.

The Treasury Department has also used punishments to pressure firms to cease doing business with Iran. In 2004, the Treasury Department fined UBS $100 million for the unauthorized movement of U.S. dollars to Iran and other sanctioned countries, and in December 2005, the Treasury Department fined Dutch bank ABN Amro $80 million for failing to fully report the processing of financial transactions involving Iran's Bank Melli (and another bank partially owned by Libya). In the biggest such instance, on December 16, 2009, the Treasury Department announced that Credit Suisse would pay a $536 million settlement to the United States for illicitly processing Iranian transactions with U.S. banks. Credit Suisse, according to the Treasury Department, saw business opportunity by picking up the transactions business from a competitor who had, in accordance with U.S. regulations discussed below, ceased processing dollar transactions for Iranian banks. Credit Suisse also pledged to cease doing business with Iran.

On December 17, 2008, the U.S. Attorney for the Southern District of New York filed a civil action seeking to seize the assets of the Assa Company, a UK-chartered entity. Assa allegedly was maintaining the interests of Bank Melli in an office building in New York City. An Iranian foundation, the Alavi Foundation, allegedly is an investor in the building.

Banking Provisions of CISADA

Section 104 of CISADA is a section of that law that, in the aggregate, would seek to exclude foreign banks from operating in the United States if these banks conduct transactions with Iranian entities that are subject to international or U.S. sanctions. The premise of the provision was that cutting off Iran's access to the international financial system would make it more difficult for Iran to move its money. The binding provisions of Section 104 require the Secretary of the Treasury to prescribe several sets of regulations. Section 104 states that these regulations must forbid U.S. banks from opening new "correspondent accounts" or "payable through accounts"—or force the cancellation of existing such accounts—with foreign banks that process "significant transactions" with several categories of Iranian (or other) entities. Foreign banks that do not have operations in the United States typically establish such accounts with U.S. banks as a means of accessing the U.S. financial system and financial industry. The entities with which transactions would trigger the sanctions are:

- The Islamic Revolutionary Guard Corps (IRGC) or any of its agents or affiliates that are sanctioned under U.S. executive orders. The two executive orders that have served as the principal source of U.S. sanctions against Iranian firms and organizations are Executive Order 13224 (September 23, 2001) and 13382 (June 28, 2005), discussed elsewhere in this paper.
- Any entity that is sanctioned by U.S. executive orders such as the two mentioned above. To date, over 125 entities (including individuals), almost all of them Iran-based or of Iranian origin, have been designated for Iran-related proliferation or terrorism activities under these orders.
- Any entity designated under the various U.N. Security Council resolutions adopted to impose sanctions on Iran.
- Any entity that assists Iran's Central Bank in efforts to help the IRGC acquire weapons of mass destruction or support international terrorism.

Terrorism List Designation-Related Sanctions

Several U.S. sanctions are in effect as a result of Iran's presence on the U.S. "terrorism list." The list was established by Section 6(j) of the Export Administration Act of 1979 (P.L. 96-72, as amended), sanctioning countries determined to have provided repeated support for acts of international terrorism. Iran was added to the list in January 1984, following the October 1983 bombing of the U.S. Marine barracks in Lebanon (believed perpetrated by Hezbollah). Sanctions imposed as a consequence include a ban on U.S. foreign aid to Iran;

restrictions on U.S. exports to Iran of dual use items; and requires the United States to vote against international loans to Iran.

- The terrorism list designation restricts sales of U.S. dual use items (Export Administration Act, as continued through presidential authorities under the International Emergency Economic Powers Act, IEEPA, as implemented by executive orders), and, under other laws, bans direct U.S. financial assistance (Section 620A of the Foreign Assistance Act, FAA, P.L. 87-195) and arms sales (Section 40 of the Arms Export Control Act, P.L. 95-92, as amended), and requires the United States to vote to oppose multilateral lending to the designated countries (Section 327 of the Anti-Terrorism and Effective Death Penalty Act of 1996, P.L. 104-132). Waivers are provided under these laws, but successive foreign aid appropriations laws since the late 1980s ban direct assistance to Iran (loans, credits, insurance, Ex-Im Bank credits) without providing for a waiver.
- Section 307 of the FAA (added in 1985) names Iran as unable to benefit from U.S. contributions to international organizations, and require proportionate cuts if these institutions work in Iran. No waiver is provided for.
- The Anti-Terrorism and Effective Death Penalty Act (Sections 325 and 326 of P.L. 104-132) requires the President to withhold U.S. foreign assistance to any country that provides to a terrorism list country foreign assistance or arms. Waivers are provided.

U.S. sanctions laws do not bar disaster aid. The United States donated $125,000, through relief agencies, to help victims of two earthquakes in Iran (February and May 1997), and another $350,000 worth of aid to the victims of a June 22, 2002, earthquake. (The World Bank provided some earthquake related lending as well.) The United States provided $5.7 million in assistance (out of total governmental pledges of about $32 million, of which $17 million have been remitted) to the victims of the December 2003 earthquake in Bam, Iran, which killed as many as 40,000 people and destroyed 90% of Bam's buildings. The United States military flew in 68,000 kilograms of supplies to Bam. In the Bam case, there was also a temporary exemption made in the regulations to allow for a general licensing (no need for a specific license) for donations to Iran of humanitarian goods by American citizens and organizations. Those exemptions were extended several times but expired in March 2004. When that expiration occurred, the policy reverted to a requirement for specific licensing (application to OFAC) and approval process for donations and operations in Iran of U.S.-based humanitarian NGO's.

Executive Order 13224

The separate, but related, Executive Order 13324 (September 23, 2001) authorizes the President to freeze the assets of and bar U.S. transactions with entities determined to be supporting international terrorism. This order, issued two weeks after the September 11 attacks, under the authority of the IEEPA, the National Emergencies Act, the U.N. Participation Act of 1945, and Section 301 of the U.S. Code, was intended to primarily target

Al Qaeda-related entities. However, it has increasingly been applied to Iranian entities. Such Iran-related entities named and sanctioned under this order are in *Table 6* at the end of this report, which also contains the names of Iranian entities sanctioned under other orders and under United Nations resolutions pertaining to Iran's nuclear program.

PROLIFERATION-RELATED U.S. SANCTIONS

Iran is prevented from receiving advanced technology from the United States under relevant and Iran-specific anti-proliferation laws[28] and by Executive Order 13382 (June 28, 2005). Some of these laws and executive measures seek to penalize foreign firms and countries that provide equipment to Iran's WMD programs.

Iran-Iraq Arms Nonproliferation Act

The Iran-Iraq Arms Nonproliferation Act (P.L. 102-484) imposes a number of sanctions on foreign entities that supply Iran with WMD technology or "destabilizing numbers and types of conventional weapons." Sanctions imposed on violating entities include a ban, for two years, on U.S. government procurement from that entity, and a two-year ban on licensing U.S. exports to that entity. A sanction to ban imports to the United States from the entity is authorized.

If the violator is determined to be a foreign country, sanctions to be imposed are a one-year ban on U.S. assistance to that country; a one-year requirement that the United States vote against international lending to it; a one-year suspension of U.S. co-production agreements with the country; a one-year suspension of technical exchanges with the country in military or dual use technology; and a one-year ban on sales of U.S. arms to the country. The President is also authorized to deny the country most-favored-nation trade status; and to impose a ban on U.S. trade with the country.

The Iran-Iraq Arms Nonproliferation Act (Section 1603) also provides for a "presumption of denial" for all dual use exports to Iran (which would include computer software). A waiver to permit such exports, on a case-by-case basis, is provided for.

Iran-Syria-North Korea Nonproliferation Act

The Iran Nonproliferation Act (P.L. 106-178), now called the Iran-Syria-North Korea Non-Proliferation Act) authorizes sanctions on foreign *persons* (individuals or corporations, not countries or governments) that are determined by the Administration to have assisted Iran's WMD programs. It bans U.S. extraordinary payments to the Russian Aviation and Space Agency in connection with the international space station unless the President can certify that the agency or entities under its control had not transferred any WMD or missile technology to Iran within the year prior.[29] (A Continuing Resolution for FY2009, which funded the U.S. government through March 2009, waived this law to allow NASA to continue to use Russian vehicles to access the International Space Station.)

Executive Order 13382

Executive Order 13382 (June 28, 2005) allows the President to block the assets of proliferators of weapons of mass destruction (WMD) and their supporters under the authority granted by the International Emergency Economic Powers Act (IEEPA, 50 U.S.C. 1701 et seq.), the National Emergencies Act (50 U.S.C. 1601 et seq.), and Section 301 of Title 3, United States Code. *Table 6* lists Iran-related entities sanctioned under the order.

Foreign Aid Restrictions for Suppliers of Iran

In addition, successive foreign aid appropriations punish the Russian Federation for assisting Iran by withholding 60% of any U.S. assistance to the Russian Federation unless it terminates technical assistance to Iran's nuclear and ballistic missiles programs.

U.S. Efforts to Promote Divestment

A growing trend not only in Congress but in several states is to require or call for or require divestment of shares of firms that have invested in Iran's energy sector (at the same levels considered sanctionable under the Iran Sanctions Act).[30] The concept of these sanctions is to express the view of Western and other democracies that Iran is an outcast internationally.

Legislation in the 110th Congress, H.R. 1400, did not require divestment, but would have required a presidential report on firms that have invested in Iran's energy sector. Another bill, H.R. 1357, required government pension funds to divest of shares in firms that have made ISA-sanctionable investments in Iran's energy sector and bar government and private pension funds from future investments in such firms. Two other bills, H.R. 2347 (passed by the House on July 31, 2007) and S. 1430, would protect mutual fund and other investment companies from shareholder action for any losses that would occur from divesting in firms that have investing in Iran's energy sector.

In the 111th Congress, H.R. 1327 (Iran Sanctions Enabling Act), a bill similar to H.R. 2347 of the 110th Congress, was reported by the Financial Services Committee on April 28, 2009. It passed the House on October 14, 2009, by a vote of 414-6. A similar bill. S. 1065, was introduced in the Senate. Provisions along these lines was contained in CISADA (P.L. 111-195)—in particular providing a "safe harbor" for investment managers who sell shares of firms that invest in Iran's energy sector (as defined by ISA, as amended by CISADA).

U.S. Sanctions Intended to Support Democratic Change in Iran

A trend since the June 2009 Iran election dispute has been to promote the prospects for the domestic opposition in Iran. Proposals to target the Revolutionary Guard for sanctions, discussed throughout, represent one facet of the trend toward measures that undermine the legitimacy of Iran's regime and support Iran's domestic opposition. The Revolutionary Guard is involved in Iran's WMD programs but it is also the key instrument through which the regime has suppressed the pro-democracy movement. Several measures to support the opposition's ability to communicate, to reduce the regime's ability to monitor or censor Internet communications, and to identify and sanction Iranian human rights abusers were included in CISADA.

Earlier legislation, the Iran Freedom Support Act (IFSA, P.L. 109-293), represented a congressional effort to promote the prospects for opponents of the regime. That law authorized "sums as may be necessary" to assist Iranians who are "dedicated" to "democratic values ... and the adoption of a democratic form of government in Iran"; and "advocates the adherence by Iran to nonproliferation regimes...."

Expanding Internet and Communications Freedoms

Some Members have focused on expanding Internet freedom in Iran or preventing the Iranian government from using the Internet to identify opponents. Subtitle D of the FY2010 Defense Authorization Act (P.L. 111-84), called the "VOICE" (Victims of Iranian Censorship) Act contains several provisions to increase U.S. broadcasting to Iran and to identify (in a report to be submitted 180 days after enactment, or April 25, 2009) companies that are selling Iran technology equipment that it can use to suppress or monitor the internet usage of Iranians. The VOICE Act authorized funds to document Iranian human rights abuses since the June 12, 2009, presidential election. Another provision of P.L. 111-84 (Section 1241) required an Administration report, not later than January 31, 2010, on U.S. enforcement of sanctions against Iran, and the effect of those sanctions on Iran.

In the 111th Congress, the "Reduce Iranian Cyber-Suppression Act," (S. 1475 and H.R. 3284) was incorporated into CISADA. It authorizes the President to ban U.S. government contracts with foreign companies that sell technology that Iran could use to monitor or control Iranian usage of the internet. Another provision of CISADA exempts from the U.S. export ban on Iran equipment to help Iranians communicate and use the Internet. The provisions were directed, in part, against firms, including a joint venture between Nokia (Finland) and Siemens (Germany), reportedly sold Internet monitoring and censorship technology to Iran in 2008.[31] Perhaps to avoid further embarrassment, Siemens announced on January 27, 2010, that it would stop signing new business deals in Iran as of mid-2010.[32]

Also in line with this trend, on March 8, 2010, OFAC amended the Iran Transactions Regulations that implement the U.S.-Iran trade ban to provide for a general license for providing to Iranians free mass market software in order to facilitate internet communications. The ruling appeared to incorporate the major features of a proposal in the

111th Congress, H.R. 4301, the "Iran Digital Empowerment Act." The OFAC determination required a waiver of the provision of the Iran-Iraq Arms Nonproliferation Act (Section 1606 waiver provision) discussed above.

Measures to Sanction Human Rights Abuses and Promote the Opposition

Another part of the effort to help Iran's opposition has been legislation to sanction regime officials involved in suppressing the domestic opposition in Iran. Senator John McCain proposed to offer amendments to S. 2799 (the Senate version of what became H.R. 2194) to focus on banning travel and freezing assets of those Iranians determined to be human rights abusers. These provisions were included in the conference report on CISADA. The provisions were similar to those of Senator McCain's earlier stand alone bill, S. 3022, the "Iran Human Rights Sanctions Act." Companion measures in the House were H.R. 4647 and H.R. 4649.

On September 29, 2010, the Administration implemented the CISADA provision when President Obama signed an Executive Order (13553) providing for the CISADA sanctions against Iranians determined to be responsible for or complicit in post-2009 Iran election human rights abuses. Along with the order, an initial group of eight Iranian officials were penalized, including Mohammad Ali Jafari, the commander-in-chief of the IRGC, and several other officials who were in key security or judicial positions at the time of the June 2009 election and aftermath. On February 23, 2011, the State Department added two Iranian officials to the list of those sanctioned (Tehran Prosecutor General Abbas Dowlatabai and Basij Commander Mohammad Reza Naqdi). On June 9, 2011, the Administration added to the designation list three entities – the Revolutionary Guard, Basij, and Law Enforcement Forces (LEF) - and one person – LEF commander Ismail Ahmad Moghadam. Under State Department interpretations of the Executive Order, if an entity is designated, all members of that entity are ineligible for visas to enter the United States.[33] Similar sanctions against many of these same officials—as well as several others—were imposed by the European Union (a total of 32 Iranians sanctioned by the EU) on April 14, 2011.

BLOCKED IRANIAN PROPERTY AND ASSETS

Iranian leaders continue to assert that the United States is holding Iranian assets, and that this is an impediment to improved relations. A U.S.-Iran Claims Tribunal at the Hague continues to arbitrate cases resulting from the 1980 break in relations and freezing of some of Iran's assets. Major cases yet to be decided center on hundreds of Foreign Military Sales (FMS) cases between the United States and the Shah's regime, which Iran claims it paid for but were unfulfilled. About $400 million in proceeds from the resale of that equipment was placed in a DOD FMS account, and about $22 million in Iranian diplomatic property remains blocked, although U.S. funds have been disbursed—credited against the DOD FMS account—to pay judgments against Iran for past acts of terrorism against Americans. Other disputes include the mistaken U.S. shoot-down on July 3, 1988, of an Iranian Airbus passenger jet (Iran Air flight 655), for which the United States, in accordance with an ICJ judgment, paid Iran $61.8 million in compensation ($300,000 per wage earning victim, $150,000 per non-wage earner) for the 248 Iranians killed. The United States has not compensated Iran for the airplane itself. As it has in past similar cases, the Bush Administration opposed a terrorism lawsuit against Iran by victims of the U.S. Embassy Tehran seizure on the grounds of diplomatic obligation.[34]

U.N. Sanctions

The U.S. sanctions discussed in this report are more comprehensive than those imposed, to date, by the United Nations Security Council or by individual foreign countries or groups of countries, such as the European Union. However, there is increasing convergence among all these varying sets of sanctions.

As part of a multilateral process of attempting to convince Iran to choose the path of negotiations or face further penalty, during 2006-2008, three U.N. Security Council resolutions—1737, 1747, and 1803—imposed sanctions primarily on Iran's weapons of mass destruction (WMD) infrastructure. The multilateral group negotiation with Iran ("P5+1:" the Security Council permanent members, plus Germany) at the same time offered Iran incentives to suspend uranium enrichment. After failed negotiations with Iran during 2009, Resolution 1929 was adopted on June 9, 2010, by a vote of 12-2 (Turkey and Brazil), with one abstention (Lebanon). (Iranian entities and persons sanctioned by the United Nations are in *Table 6*.)

The main points of Resolution 1929 are:[35]

- It adds several firms affiliated with the Revolutionary Guard firms to the list of sanctioned entities.
- It makes mandatory a ban on travel for Iranian persons named in it and in previous resolutions—including those Iranians for whom there was a nonbinding travel ban in previous resolutions.
- It gives countries the authorization to inspect any shipments—and to dispose of its cargo—if the shipments are suspected to carry contraband items. However, inspections on the high seas are subject to concurrence by the country that owns that ship. This provision is modeled after a similar provision imposed on North Korea, which did cause that country to reverse some of its shipments.
- It prohibits countries from allowing Iran to invest in uranium mining and related nuclear technologies, or nuclear-capable ballistic missile technology.
- It bans sales to Iran of most categories of heavy arms to Iran and requests restraint in sales of light arms, but does not bar sales of missiles not on the "U.N. Registry of Conventional Arms."
- It requires countries to insist that their companies refrain from doing business with Iran *if* there is reason to believe that such business could further Iran's WMD programs.
- It requests, but does not mandate, that countries prohibit Iranian banks to open in their countries, or for their banks to open in Iran, *if* doing so could contribute to Iran's WMD activities.

- It authorizes the establishment of a "panel of experts," which is chaired by senior State Department arms control and proliferation adviser Robert Einhorn, to assess the effect of the resolution and previous Iran resolutions and suggest ways of more effective implementation.
- The resolution did not make mandatory some measures that reportedly were considered, including barring any foreign investment in Iranian bond offerings; banning insurance for transport contracts for shipments involving Iran; banning international investment in Iran's energy sector; banning the provision of trade credits to Iran, or banning all financial dealings with Iranian banks.

Table 4. Summary of Provisions of U.N. Resolutions on Iran Nuclear Program (1737, 1747, 1803, and 1929)

Require Iran to suspend uranium enrichment, and to refrain from any development of ballistic missiles that are nuclear capable (1929)
Prohibit transfer to Iran of nuclear, missile, and dual use items to Iran, except for use in light-water reactors Prohibit Iran from exporting arms or WMD-useful technology
Prohibit Iran from investing abroad in uranium mining, related nuclear technologies or nuclear capable ballistic missile technology
Freeze the assets of over 80 named Iranian persons and entities, including Bank Sepah, and several corporate affiliates of the Revolutionary Guard.
Require that countries ban the travel of over 40 named Iranians Mandates that countries not export major combat systems to Iran
Calls for "vigilance" (a non-binding call to cut off business) with respect to all Iranian banks, particularly Bank Melli and Bank Saderat.
Calls for vigilance (voluntary restraint) with respect to providing international lending to Iran and providing trade credits and other financing and financial interactions.
Calls on countries to inspect cargoes carried by Iran Air Cargo and Islamic Republic of Iran Shipping Lines—or by any ships in national or international waters—if there are indications they carry cargo banned for carriage to Iran. Searches in international waters would require concurrence of the country where the ship is registered.
A Sanctions Committee, composed of the 15 members of the Security Council, monitors Implementation of all Iran sanctions and collects and disseminates information on Iranian violations and other entities involved in banned activities. A "panel of experts" is empowered by 1929 to make recommendations for improved enforcement.

Source: Text of U.N. Security Council resolutions 1737, 1747, 1803, and 1929. http://www.un.org. More information on specific provisions of each of these resolutions and the nuclear negotiations with Iran is in CRS Report. CRS Report RL32048, Iran: U.S. Concerns and Policy Responses, by Kenneth Katzman.

International Implementation and Compliance

U.S. allies have supported the Obama Administration's sanctions toward Iran, in part because the approach is perceived as not purely punitive, and in part because concerns about Iran's nuclear advancement have increased. U.S. and European/allied approaches have been gradually converging since 2002, when the nuclear issue came to the fore, but as of 2010, an unprecedented degree of global consensus has emerged on how to deal with Iran. There is a degree of consensus among experts that many countries, not only allies of the United States, are complying with the provisions of U.N. sanctions, but there are selected exceptions (discussed below). Implementation appears to be somewhat less complete in Iran's immediate region, perhaps because its neighbors do not want confrontation with Iran and are hesitant to disrupt traditional relationships among traders and businessmen in the region.

European Union and other Western States

In its July 27, 2010, sanctions measures, the product of consensus among the EU states, the EU countries imposed sanctions on Iran that exceed those mandated in Security Council resolutions. Concurrent with the EU announcement, not only Norway (not an EU member) but also Canada and Australia announced similar, although less sweeping, Iran sanctions. A comparison between U.S., U.N., and EU sanctions against Iran is contained in the chart below, although noting that there are differing legal bases and authorities for these sanctions. A U.S. President cannot mandate a foreign company take any particular action; however, the U.S. government can penalize or reward foreign firms who take action that supports U.S. objectives. U.N. Security Council resolutions are considered binding on U.N. Member states. The EU clarified in late October 2010, that its sanctions against Iran do not ban importation of Iranian oil and gas, nor do they ban exports of gasoline to Iran.

Japan and South Korea

In early September 2010, Japan and then South Korea announced Iran sanctions similar to those of the EU. Both countries adopted measures limiting trade financing for Iran, limiting new banking relations with Iran, sanctioning numerous named Iranian entities, and restricting new projects in Iran's energy sector. The sanctions adopted by both were far more extensive than was expected by U.S. officials.

India/Asian Clearing Union

India has generally been considered friendly toward Iran and unlikely to impose any national sanctions on that country. Therefore, many experts were surprised when India's central bank, in late December 2010, announced that it would no longer use a regional body, the Asian Clearing Union, to handle transactions with Iran. The Asian Clearing Union, based in Tehran, was set up in the 1970s by the United Nations to ease commerce among Asian nations. There have been allegations in recent years that Iran might be using the Clearing Union to handle transactions so as to avoid limitations imposed by European and other banks.

The Indian move complicated India's purchases of about 350,000-400,000 barrels per day of Iranian oil, and Indian officials subsequently undertook negotiations with Iran to find an alternate mechanism to clear Indian payments for that oil and other Iranian goods. Still, the Indian move— and the reported difficulty in agreeing to a replacement payments mechanism—appeared to signal that India was taking steps to join U.S./European-led efforts to shut Iran out of the international financial system. The Indian move followed President Obama's visit there in November 2010.

Several banks considered as replacement mechanisms were either under U.N. sanctions or fear fallout (restrictions in the U.S. banking system) from transacting banking business for Iran. In mid-February 2010, India and Iran agreed to use Europaisch-Iranische Handelsbank (EIH) to clear the payments. EIH has accounts with National Iranian Oil Company as well as with the Central Bank of Germany, rendering the bank able to process the Indian payments to Iran. Some Members of Congress have previously characterized that bank as one of Iran's few remaining access points to the European financial system and had asked the German government to order it closed.[36] On May 23, 2011, the EU named EIH and about 100 other entities as Iran proliferation-related activities, meaning the bank might be forced to close and India and Iran will again have to seek an alternative payments mechanism.

China, Russia, and others

The position of Russia, China, and several other countries on the issue of Iran sanctions has been of concern to several Members of Congress. The formal position of both Russia and China is that they will impose only those sanctions required by applicable U.N. Security Council resolutions, but not impose sanctions beyond those specifically mandated. As noted below, some Members and outside experts express concern that Chinese firms, in particular, are moving to fill the void left by vacating European firms ("backfill"), but Administration officials say they have not seen evidence of such a trend.

An even more significant concern is that these and other countries are refusing or failing to prevent Iran from acquiring weapons and WMD technology. Secretary of State Clinton singled out China on January 19, 2011, as not enforcing all aspects of international sanctions that bar sales of most nuclear-related equipment to Iran; the comment came of the eve of the state visit to the United States by President Hu Jintao. On March 9, 2011, State Department Special Adviser for Non-Proliferation and Arms Control, Robert Einhorn, said Iran may be working with Chinese firms to obtain sensitive technology useful for nuclear weapons development. In some cases, Iran has been able, according to some reports, to obtain sophisticated technology even from U.S. firms.[37]

A related issue is Iran's efforts to use the high seas or the territory of other countries to supply weapons to groups it supports (such shipments are barred by U.N. resolutions; see above). In March 2011, Israel intercepted a freighter, the Victoria, that it said was carrying Iranian weapons to Palestinian militant groups. Also in March 2011, Turkey, generally considered friendly toward Iran, complied with U.N. requirements by twice forcing the landing in Turkey of Iranian cargo aircraft. In both cases, the aircraft were searched, and in one instance, weapons were removed, allegedly bound for Syria, before the aircraft were allowed to proceed.

Contrast with Previous Periods

The emerging consensus on Iran sanctions differs from early periods when there was far more disagreement. Reflecting the traditional European preference for providing incentives rather than enacting economic punishments, during 2002-2005, there were active negotiations between the European Union and Iran on a "Trade and Cooperation Agreement" (TCA). Such an agreement would have lowered the tariffs or increased quotas for Iranian exports to the EU countries.[38] However, negotiations were discontinued after the election of Ahmadinejad in June 2005, at which time Iran's position on its nuclear program hardened. Similarly, there is insufficient international support to grant Iran membership in the World Trade Organization (WTO) until there is progress on the nuclear issue. Iran first attempted to apply to join the WTO in July 1996. On 22 occasions after that, representatives of the Clinton and then the George W. Bush Administration blocked Iran from applying (applications must be by consensus of the 148 members). As discussed above, as part of an effort to assist the EU-3 nuclear talks with Iran, at a WTO meeting in May 2005, no opposition to Iran's application was registered, and Iran formally began accession talks.

Earlier, during the 1990s, EU countries maintained a policy of "critical dialogue" with Iran, and the EU and Japan refused to join the 1995 U.S. trade and investment ban on Iran. The European dialogue with Iran was suspended in April 1997 in response to the German terrorism trial ("Mykonos trial") that found high-level Iranian involvement in killing Iranian dissidents in Germany, but resumed in May 1998 during Khatemi's presidency. In the 1990s, European and Japanese creditors—over U.S. objections—rescheduled about $16 billion in Iranian debt. These countries (governments and private creditors) rescheduled the debt bilaterally, in spite of Paris Club rules that call for multilateral rescheduling. In July 2002, Iran tapped international capital markets for the first time since the Islamic revolution, selling $500 million in bonds to European banks. (A provision of H.R. 6296 would make sanctionable under ISA the purchase of Iranian sovereign debt).

World Bank Loans

The July 27, 2010, EU measures appear to narrow substantially the prior differences between the EU and the United States over international lending to Iran. As noted above, the United States representative to international financial institutions is required to vote against international lending, but that vote, although weighted, is not sufficient to block international lending. In 1993 the United States voted its 16.5% share of the World Bank against loans to Iran of $460 million for electricity, health, and irrigation projects, but the loans were approved. To block that lending, the FY1994-FY1996 foreign aid appropriations (P.L. 103-87, P.L. 103-306, and P.L. 104-107) cut the amount appropriated for the U.S. contribution to the bank by the amount of those loans. The legislation contributed to a temporary halt in new bank lending to Iran. (In the 111th Congress, a provision of H.R. 6296—Title VII—cut off U.S. contributions to the World Bank, International Finance Corp., and the Multilateral

Investment Guarantee Corp. if the World Bank approves a new Country Assistance Strategy for Iran or makes a loan to Iran.)

During 1999-2005, Iran's moderating image had led the World Bank to consider new loans over U.S. opposition. In May 2000, the United States' allies outvoted the United States to approve $232 million in loans for health and sewage projects. During April 2003-May 2005, a total of $725 million in loans were approved for environmental management, housing reform, water and sanitation projects, and land management projects, in addition to $400 million in loans for earthquake relief.

Table 5. Points of Comparison Between U.S., U.N., and EU Sanctions Against Iran

U.S. Sanctions	U.N. Sanctions	Implementation by EU (July 27, 2010) and Some Allied Countries
General Observation: Most sweeping sanctions on Iran of virtually any country in the world	Increasingly sweeping, but still intended to primarily target Iran's nuclear and other WMD programs. No mandatory sanctions on Iran's energy sector.	EU abides by all U.N. sanctions on Iran, but new package of Iran sanctions announced July 27, 2010, more closely aligns EU sanctions with those of the U.S. than ever before. Japan and South Korean sanctions (September 2010) similar to EU.
Ban on U.S. Trade with and Investment in Iran: Executive order 12959 bans (with limited exceptions) U.S. firms from exporting to Iran, importing from Iran, or investing in Iran. There is an exemption for sales to Iran of food and medical products, but no trade financing or financing guarantees are permitted.	U.N. sanctions do not ban civilian trade with Iran or general civilian sector investment in Iran. Nor do U.N. sanctions mandate restrictions on provision of trade financing or financing guarantees by national export credit guarantee agencies.	No general EU ban on trade in civilian goods with Iran, although the July 27, 2010, sanctions ban sales of energy related equipment and services. On May 23, 2011, the EU named about 100 entities as Iran proliferation-related entities which EU entities would be unable to do business with. EU, Japan, and South Korea measures ban "medium and long term" trade financing and financing guarantees. Short term financing is permitted, but there is a call for EU states to "exercise restraint" on that.
Sanctions on Foreign Firms that Do Business With Iran's Energy Sector: The Iran Sanctions Act, P.L. 104-172 (as amended most recently by the Comprehensive Iran Sanctions, Accountability, and Divestment Act of 2010, P.L. 111-195) mandates specified sanctions on foreign firms that invest threshold amounts in Iran's Energy Sector or that sell certain threshold amounts of refined petroleum or refinery related equipment or services to Iran.	No U.N. equivalent exists. However, preambular language in Resolution 1929 "not[es] the potential connection between Iran's revenues derived from its energy sector and the funding of Iran's proliferation-sensitive nuclear activities." This wording is interpreted by most observers as providing U.N. support for countries who want to ban their companies from investing in Iran's energy sector.	July 27, 2010, EU sanctions prohibit EU companies from financing energy sector projects in Iran (a de-facto ban on energy sector investment) and ban sales to Iran of equipment or services for its energy sector, including projects outside Iran. No ban on buying oil or gas from Iran or selling gasoline to Iran. Japan and South Korean measures ban new energy projects in Iran and call for restraint on ongoing projects.

Table 5. (Continued)

U.S. Sanctions	U.N. Sanctions	Implementation by EU (July 27, 2010) and Some Allied Countries
Ban on Foreign Assistance: U.S. foreign assistance to Iran—other than purely humanitarian aid—is banned under Section 620A of the Foreign Assistance Act . That section bans U.S. assistance to countries on the U.S. list of "state sponsors of terrorism." Iran has been on this "terrorism list" since January 1984. Iran is also routinely denied direct U.S. foreign aid under the annual foreign operations appropriations acts (most recently in Section 7007 of division H of P.L. 111-8).	No U.N. equivalent	EU measures of July 27, 2010, ban grants, aid, and concessional loans to Iran. Also prohibit financing of enterprises involved in Iran's energy sector. Japan and South Korea measures did not specifically ban aid or lending to Iran.
Ban on Arms Exports to Iran: Because Iran is on the "terrorism list," it is ineligible for U.S. arms exports pursuant to Section 40 of the Arms Export Control Act (AECA, P.L. 95-92). The International Trafficking in Arms Regulations (ITAR, 22 CFR Part 126.1) also cite the President's authority to control arms exports, and to comply with U.N. Security Council Resolutions as a justification to ban arms exports and imports.	Resolution 1929 (operative paragraph 8) bans all U.N. member states from selling or supplying to Iran major weapons systems, including tanks, armored vehicles, combat aircraft, warships, and most missile systems, or related spare parts or advisory services for such weapons systems.	EU sanctions include a comprehensive ban on sale to Iran of all types of military equipment, not just major combat systems. No similar Japan and South Korean measures announced, but neither has exported arms to Iran.
Restriction on Exports to Iran of "Dual Use Items": Primarily under Section 6(j) of the Export Administration Act (P.L. 96-72) and Section 38 of the Arms Export Control Act, there is a denial of license applications to sell Iran goods that could have military applications.	The U.N. Resolutions on Iran, cumulatively, ban the export of almost all dual-use items to Iran.	EU bans the sales of dual use items to Iran, in line with U.N. resolutions. Japan announced full adherence to strict export control regimes when evaluating sales to Iran.
Sanctions Against International Lending to Iran: Under Section 1621 of the International Financial Institutions Act (P.L. 95-118), U.S. representatives to international financial institutions, such as the World Bank, are required to vote against loans to Iran by those institutions.	Resolution 1747 (oper. paragraph 7) requests, but does not mandate, that countries and international financial institutions refrain from making grants or loans to Iran, except for development and humanitarian purposes.	The July 27, 2010, measures prohibit EU members from providing grants, aid, and concessional loans to Iran, including through international financial institutions. No specific similar Japan or South Korea measures announced.

U.S. Sanctions	U.N. Sanctions	Implementation by EU (July 27, 2010) and Some Allied Countries
Sanctions Against Foreign Firms that Sell Weapons of Mass Destruction-Related Technology to Iran: Several laws and regulations, including the Iran-Syria North Korea Nonproliferation Act (P.L. 106-178), the Iran-Iraq Arms Nonproliferation Act (P.L. 102-484) and Executive Order 13382 provide for sanctions against entities, Iranian or otherwise, that are determined to be involved in or supplying Iran's WMD programs (asset freezing, ban on transaction with the entity).	Resolution 1737 (oper. paragraph 12) imposes a worldwide freeze on the assets and property of Iranian entities named in an Annex to the Resolution. Each subsequent Resolution has expanded the list of Iranian entities subject to these sanctions.	The EU measures imposed July 27, 2010, commit the EU to freezing the assets of entities named in the U.N. resolutions, as well as numerous other named Iranian entities. Japan and South Korea froze assets of U.N.-sanctioned entities.
Ban on Transactions With Terrorism Supporting Entities: Executive Order 13224 bans transactions with entities determined by the Administration to be supporting international terrorism. Numerous entities, including some of Iranian origin, have been so designated.	No direct equivalent The U.N. Resolutions against Iran are intended primarily to slow or halt Iran's nuclear and other WMD programs. However, Resolution 1747 (oper. paragraph 5) bans Iran from exporting any arms—a provision widely interpreted as trying to reduce Iran's material support to groups such as Lebanese Hizbollah, Hamas, Shiite militias in Iraq, and insurgents in Afghanistan.	No direct equivalent, but EU measures taken July 27, 2010, include some IRGC Qods Force and related persons and entities as subject to a freeze on EU-based assets.
Travel Ban on Named Iranians: The Comprehensive Iran Sanctions, Accountability, and Divestment Act of 2010 (P.L. 111-195) provides for a prohibition on travel to the U.S. , blocking of U.S.-based property, and ban on transactions with Iranians determined to be involved in serious human rights abuses against Iranians since the June 12, 2009, presidential election there.	Resolution 1803 imposed a binding ban on international travel by several Iranians named in an Annex to the Resolution. Resolution 1929 extended that ban to additional Iranians, and forty Iranians are now subject to the ban. However, the Iranians subject to the travel ban are so subjected because of their involvement in Iran's WMD programs, not because of involvement in human rights abuses.	The EU sanctions announced July 27, 2010, contains an Annex of named Iranians subject to a ban on travel to the EU countries. An additional 32 Iranians involved in human rights abuses were subjected to EU sanctions on April 14, 2011. Japan and South Korea announced bans on named Iranians.
Restrictions on Iranian Shipping: Under Executive Order 13382, the U.S. Treasury Department has named Islamic Republic of Iran Shipping Lines and several affiliated entities as entities whose U.S.-based property is to be frozen.	Resolution 1803 and 1929 authorize countries to inspect cargoes carried by Iran Air and Islamic Republic of Iran Shipping Lines (IRISL)—or any ships in national or international waters—if there is an indication that the shipments include goods whose export to Iran is banned.	The EU measures announced July 27, 2010, bans Iran Air Cargo from access to EU airports. The measures also freeze the EU-based assets of IRISL and its affiliates. Insurance and re-insurance for Iranian firms is banned. Japan and South Korean measures take similar actions against IRISL and Iran Air.

Table 5. (Continued)

U.S. Sanctions	U.N. Sanctions	Implementation by EU (July 27, 2010) and Some Allied Countries
Banking Sanctions: A number or provisions and policies have been employed to persuade foreign banks to end their relationships with Iranian banks. Several Iranian banks have been named as proliferation or terrorism supporting entities under Executive Orders 13382 and 13224, respectively. P.L. 111-195 contains a provision that prohibits banking relationships with U.S. banks for any foreign bank that conducts transactions with Iran's Revolutionary Guard or with Iranian entities sanctioned under the various U.N. resolutions.	No direct equivalent However, two Iranian banks are named as sanctioned entities under the U.N. Security Council resolutions.	The EU announcement on July 27, 2010, prohibit the opening in EU countries of any new branches or offices of Iranian banks. The measures also prohibit EU banks from offices or accounts in Iran. In addition, the transfer of funds exceeding 40,000 Euros (about $50,000) between and Iranian bank and an EU bank require prior authorization by EU bank regulators. Japan and South Korea measures similar to the above, with South Korea adhering to the same 40,000 Euro authorization requirement. Japan and S. Korea froze the assets of 15 Iranian banks; South Korea targeted Bank Mellat for freeze.
No direct equivalent, although, as discussed above, U.S. proliferations laws provide for sanctions against foreign entities that help Iran with its nuclear and ballistic missile programs.	Resolution 1929 (oper. paragraph 7) prohibits Iran from acquiring an interest in any country involving uranium mining, production, or use of nuclear materials, or technology related to nuclear-capable ballistic missiles. Operative Paragraph 9 of Resolution 1929 prohibits Iran from undertaking "any activity" related to ballistic missiles capable of delivering a nuclear weapon.	EU measures on July 27, 2010, require adherence to this provision of Resolution 1929.

EFFECTS OF SANCTIONS ON IRAN

The effectiveness of U.S. and international sanctions on Iran is often difficult to measure and may vary depending upon which goals are being examined. U.S. officials acknowledge that the sanctions have not achieved the fundamental goal of altering Iran's commitment to its nuclear program, but they and others believe that the sanctions may be possibly be achieving the related goal of slowing the advancement of Iran's nuclear program. Most outside experts agree that the sanctions are compounding the mismanagement and other structural inadequacies of Iran's economy and that the sanctions are only beginning to apply pressure on Iran's economy as worldwide enforcement and understanding of Iran's evasions ramps up. At the same time, there is a view that high oil prices are helping Iran weather the economic effects of the sanctions.

At various conferences, some Administration officials have urged to allow time for the existing sanctions to work but have not ruled out new international sanctions. Still, as of late

May 2011, there do not appear to be active discussions among the P5+1 contact group on Iran's nuclear program to draw up a new U.N. Security Council sanctions resolution. Most experts believe that the most effective sanction would be a mandated, worldwide embargo on the purchase of Iranian crude oil, although there are no indications that such a step is to be proposed at the United Nations in the near term or that doing so would achieve consensus. With the United States and Europe seeking to boost economic growth, a sanction that would result in a further increase in oil prices would appear unlikely to attract broad support. Specific sanctions effects are discussed below.

Effect on Nuclear Negotiations

There is a consensus that U.S. and U.N. sanctions have not, to date, accomplished their core strategic objective of causing a demonstrable shift in Iran's commitment to its nuclear program. Most experts assess that the optimal means for sanctions to affect the nuclear program is by contributing to a decision by Iran to a compromise that would limit Iran's nuclear development. In late November 2010, Iran accepted new nuclear talks in Geneva. However, during two days of talks (December 6 and 7), Iran did not agree to curbs on its enrichment of uranium, the core U.S. demand. There was an agreement to have new talks in Turkey, which took place during January 21-22, 2011. However, the talks, by all accounts, made little progress as Iran refused to discuss details of various proposals for nuclear confidence building measures. The talks were said to have nearly broken down at the end of the first day and an exchange of letters between Iran and the EU foreign policy representative (acting on behalf of the P5+1) during February–May 2011 did not indicate sufficient Iranian flexibility to prompt the P5+1 to seek to schedule new talks with Iran.

Counter-Proliferation Effects

A related issue is whether the cumulative sanctions have, in and of themselves, added bottlenecks to Iran's nuclear efforts by making it difficult for Iran to import needed materials or skills. In a statement in the UAE on January 10, 2011, Secretary of State Clinton said that "The sanctions are working.... Their program, from our best estimate, has been slowed down."[39] Others, however, say that there is not clear evidence that sanctions are slowing Iran's program in that International Atomic Energy Agency (IAEA) reports—including the latest one issued May 24, 2011—say that Iran's stockpile of low-enriched uranium continues to expand.[40] The lack of clear evidence that Iran is trying to acquire a nuclear weapons capability could be caused by Iranian decisions rather than the effect of sanctions.

General Political Effects

It has been hoped that international sanctions might widen splits in Iran's leadership and cause its leaders to reconsider major foreign policy decisions, particularly the nuclear program. There are growing indications of splits in the Iranian leadership - particularly between Ahmadinejad and the Supreme Leader – but this split does not appear to be driven primarily by differences over how to react to international sanctions. In September 2010, a senior leader, Ali Akbar Hashemi- Rafsanjani, criticized Ahmadinejad for dismissing the effect of the burgeoning sanctions on Iran's economy. Possibly in retaliation, in March 2011 Ahmadinejad succeeded in ousting Rafsanjani from a key position—chairman of the powerful "Assembly of Experts."

At the broader level, in February 2011, the opposition Green movement began returning to the streets with significant protests. However, the protests have not been sustained since and there is no evidence that international sanctions are affecting the strength of the domestic opposition either positively or negatively. The opposition is driven by long-standing political grievances and has not, to date, been joined by labor groups or other protesters articulating purely economic demands.

While the Green movement has not necessarily broadened, anecdotal reports suggest that many Iranians, particularly in the middle class are blaming the regime for economic difficulties. There has been unrest among small and large merchants who are having trouble obtaining trade financing, insurance, and shipping availability, which is driving up their costs by an estimated 40%, even if the merchants can complete desired transactions at all.[41] A substantial portion of the Iranian economy depends on import-export activity, so the damage to that sector from international sanctions has been considerable.

Economic Effects

An IMF statement issued June 13, 2011 casts some doubt that international sanctions are seriously harming Iran's economy. The statement, based on a May 28-June 9 study visit, indicated that Iran's GDP is growing at a rate of about 3.5%, and that the government has brought inflation down from 25% in 2008 to about 12% in 2010/2011. The IMF also credits positive economic effects to the government's privatization program. Many believe that the economic effects of international sanctions can be tolerated by the regime as long as world oil prices remain high, at nearly $100 per barrel in June 2011.

U.S. officials believe that Iran's economy will inevitably begin to suffer as U.S. and partner strategy shuts Iran out of the global financial system, raises the costs for Iran of financing its transactions, and causes international firms to exit Iran:

- During 2006 and 2010, Treasury and State Departments officials say they persuaded at least 80 banks not to process transactions for Iranian banks. Among those that have pulled out of Iran are UBS (Switzerland), HSBC (Britain), Germany's Commerzbank A.G., and Deutsche Bank AG. U.S. financial diplomacy has reportedly convinced Kuwaiti banks to stop transactions with Iranian accounts,[42] and some banks in Asia (primarily South Korea and Japan) and the rest of the Middle East have done the same. Then-Under Secretary Levey said on September 20, 2010, that "today, Iran is effectively unable to access financial services from reputable banks and is increasingly unable to conduct major transactions in dollars or Euros."[43]
- In late September 2010, the value of Iran's currency, the rial, fell by about 15% when the UAE, a major financial hub for Iran, began restricting transactions with Iranian banks sanctioned by U.N. resolutions and by the United States.

- Treasury Department's designations of affiliates and ships belong to Islamic Republic of Iran Shipping Lines (IRISL) reportedly are harming Iran's ability to ship goods and raised the prices of goods to Iranian import-export dealers. Some ships have been impounded by various countries for non-payment of debts due on them.

Foreign Companies Exiting the Iran Market

Many experts believe that, over time, the efficiency and output of Iran's economy will decline as foreign expertise departs and Iran invites in or makes purchases from less capable foreign companies. Neither the U.S. ban on trade and investment with Iran, nor U.N. sanctions, nor European Union sanctions on Iran, ban trade with Iran in all civilian goods. Still, because the international community has sought to isolate Iran economically, companies all over the world have come to a decision to end their business with Iran, even when such business would not appear to violate any U.N. or national sanction.

- ABB of Switzerland said in January 2010 it would cease doing business with Iran.
- Siemens of Germany was active in the Iran telecommunications infrastructure market, but announced in February 2010 that it would cease pursuing business in Iran. Finemeccanica, a defense and transportation conglomerate of Italy, followed suit, as did Thyssen-Krupp, a German steelmaker.
- Germany's Daimler (Mercedes-Benz maker) said in April 2010 it would freeze planned exports to Iran of cars and trucks.
- In August-September 2010, Japan and South Korea announced that their automakers Toyota, Hyundai, and Kia Motors would cease selling automobiles to Iran.

Foreign Firms Remaining in the Iran Market

Some firms continue to run the financial risk of doing business with Iran. Some of the well-known firms that continue to do so include Alcatel-Lucent of France; Bank of Tokyo-Mitsubishi UFJ; BNP Paribas of France; Bosch of Germany; Canon of Japan; Fiat SPA of Italy; Ericsson of Sweden; ING Group of the Netherlands; Mercedes of Germany; Renault of France; Samsung of South Korea; Sony of Japan; Volkswagen of Germany; Volvo of Sweden; and numerous others. Some of the foreign firms that trade with Iran, such as Mitsui and Co. of Japan, Alstom of France, and Schneider Electric of France, are discussed in the March 7, 2010, *New York Times* article on foreign firms that do business with Iran and also receive U.S. contracts or financing. The *Times* article does not claim that these firms have violated any U.S. sanctions laws.

Other questions have arisen over how U.S. sanctions might apply to business with foreign firms that Iran might acquire a full or partial interest in. Such firms include Daewoo Electronics of South Korea, where an Iranian firm—Entekhab Industrial Corp.—is a leading bidder to take over that firm. Another example is Adabank of Turkey, which reportedly might be sold to Iran.

Subsidy Phase-out Issue

A larger issue, which may have been affected by sanctions, but perhaps positively for Iran, is a long-delayed plan to phase out state subsidies on staple goods such staples as gasoline and some foods over the next five years. International sanctions might have helped Ahmadinejad convince the Majles (parliament) that passing the subsidy reduction plan was urgent if Iran was to parry the effects of burgeoning international sanctions. After several delays, the program started on December 19, 2010, with a reduction in subsidies of gasoline and bread. The price of traditional bread immediately escalated to 40 cents, from 15 cents, when the program began. Gasoline prices now run on a tiered system in which a small increment is available at the subsidized price of about 1.60 per gallon, but amounts above that threshold are available only at a price of about $2.60 per gallon, close to the world price. The lower and lower middle class is being compensated with direct cash payments of about $40 per month.[44]

The IMF statement of June 13, 2011, discussed above, said that the program removed about $60 billion in subsidies. The statement also credits the regime with successfully containing initial impact of the rise in domestic energy prices on inflation.

Nor has the subsidy phase out produced major additional unrest. When the plan went into effect in December 2010, some Iranian truckers simply stopped working on the grounds that their work was no longer profitable (because the government limited the amount of extra fees that can be charged to make up for the increase in costs). However, the subsidy phase out did not produce new Green movement demonstrations or other indicators of opposition.

Effect on the Energy Sector

As noted throughout, the U.S. objective has been to target sanctions against Iran's energy sector, considered the engine of Iran's economy and source of most of its revenue. Depriving the regime of revenue, it is believed, will reduce its ability to enlist and maintain the loyalty of security personnel or to buy off key interest groups. There are clear indications that the sanctions— coupled with the overall sense that Iran is isolated from the international community—are causing substantial injury to this sector. State Department Special Advisor Einhorn testified on July 29, 2010, that about $50 billion in investment in Iran's energy sector had been deterred by sanctions and other forms of pressure. Some U.S. officials in 2011 put the figure closer to $60 billion in lost investment. As noted above, several major European firms have either announced pullouts from some of their Iran projects, declined to make further investments, or resold their investments to other companies. Observers at key energy fields in Iran say there is little evidence of foreign investment activity and little new development activity sighted, including at the large South Pars gas field that Iran has focused on for at least 10 years. It is highly unlikely that Iran will attract the $145 billion in new investment by 2018 that Iran's deputy Oil Minister said in November 2008 that Iran needs.

Possibly or partly as a result, Iran's oil production has fallen slightly to about 3.8 million barrels per day (mbd) from about 4.1 million barrels per day (mbd) in the mid-2000s, and is projected to fall to about 3.3 mbd by 2015.[45] Others maintain that Iran's gas sector can more than compensate for declining oil exports, although it needs gas to reinject into its oil fields and remains a relatively minor gas exporter. It exports about 3.6 trillion cubic feet of gas, primarily to Turkey. Some Members of Congress believe that ISA would have been even more effective if successive administrations had imposed sanctions available in U.S. law, and have expressed frustration that the executive branch has imposed few, if any, actual sanctions under ISA.

The EU sanctions apparently have also derailed a BP-NIOC joint venture in the Rhum gas field, 200 miles off the coast of Scotland. BP announced in November 2010 that it would stop production there to ensure compliance with the EU sanctions. In addition, partners in the Trans-Adriatic Pipeline (TAP) said in September 2010 that the pipeline would not be used to transport Iranian gas to Europe.

Some believe that a key to further harming Iran's energy sector is to persuade remaining oil services firms to pull out of Iran. In press articles and in the December 1, 2010, House Foreign Affairs Committee hearing discussed above, the large oil services firm Schlumberger, which in incorporated in the Netherlands Antilles, has said it will wind down its business with Iran. However, press reports citing company documents say all contracts with Iran might not be terminated until at least 2013.[46]

Concerns about "Backfill"

There has been a concern that some of the investment void might be "backfilled," at least partly, by Asian firms such as those from China, Malaysia, Vietnam, and countries in Eastern Europe. Russian firms are said to be in talks with Iran on new energy projects. However, many such deals are said to be in preliminary stages, and clear examples of "backfilling" are few, to date. Most of the potential backfilling companies are perceived as not being as technically capable as those that have withdrawn from Iran. In July 2010, after the enactment of Resolution 1929 and CISADA, the Revolutionary Guard's main construction affiliate, Khatem ol-Anbiya, announced it had withdrawn from developing Phases 15 and 16 of South Pars—a project worth $2 billion.[47] Khatem ol-Anbiya took over that project in 2006 when Norway's Kvaerner pulled out of it. It is likely that the IRGC perceived its involvement as likely to scare away foreign participation in the work because U.S. and U.N. sanctions are targeting the IRGC and its corporate affiliates.

Effect on Gasoline Availability and Importation

In March 2010, well before the passage of CSIDA on June 24, 2010, several gas suppliers to Iran, anticipating this legislation, announced that they had stopped or would stop supplying gasoline to Iran.[48] Others have ceased since the enactment of CISADA, and some observers say that gasoline deliveries to Iran have fallen from about 3.5 million barrels per day before CISADA to about 900,000 barrels per day.[49] That is a decline of nearly 75%, a reduction that most experts continue to view as valid. As noted in a *New York Times* report of March 7, 2010,[50] and a Government Accountability Office study released September 3, 2010,[51] some firms that have supplied Iran have received U.S. credit guarantees or contracts.

The main suppliers to Iran over the past few years, and the GAO-reported status of their sales to Iran are listed below (with the caveat that some reports say that partners or affiliates of these firms may still sell to Iran in cases where the corporate headquarters have announced a halt):

- Vitol of Switzerland (notified GAO it stopped selling to Iran in early 2010);

- Trafigura of Switzerland (notified GAO it stopped selling to Iran in November 2009);
- Glencore of Switzerland (notified GAO it stopped selling in September 2009);
- Total of France (notified GAO it stopped sales to Iran in May 2010);
- Reliance Industries of India (notified GAO it stopped sales to Iran in May 2009). Reliance has also told press outlets on April 1, 2010 that it would not import Iranian crude oil in 2010;
- Petronas of Malaysia (said on April 15, 2010, it had stopped sales to Iran);[52]
- Lukoil of Russia (reportedly to have ended sales to Iran in in April 2010,[53] although some reports continue that Lukoil affiliates are supplying Iran);
- Royal Dutch Shell of the Netherlands (notified GAO it stopped sales in October 2009);
- Kuwait's Independent Petroleum Group told U.S. officials it is no longer selling gasoline to Iran, as of September 2010; [54]
- Tupras of Turkey (according to the State Department on May 24, 2011);
- British Petroleum of United Kingdom, Shell, Q8, Total, and OMV are no longer selling aviation fuel to Iran Air, according to U.S. State Department officials on May 24, 2011;
- One UAE firm, Dragon Oil, has not renewed a deal with Iran, which expired in July 2010, to swap oil with Iran via Turkmenistan. Another UAE firm, Golden Crown Petroleum FZE, told the author in April 2011 that, as of June 29, 2010, it no longer leases vessels for the purpose of shipping petroleum products from or through Iran;
- Munich Re, Allianz, Hannover Re (Germany) were providing insurance and re-insurance for gasoline shipments to Iran. However, they reportedly have exited the market for insuring gasoline shipments for Iran;[55]
- Lloyd's (Britain). The major insurer had been the main company insuring Iranian gas (and other) shipping, but reportedly has ended that business as of July 2010

According to the State Department, key shipping associations have created clauses in their contracts that enable ship owners to refuse to deliver gasoline to Iran;

- The State Department reported on September 30, 2010, that Hong Kong company NYK Line Ltd. had ended shipping business with Iran (on any goods, not just gasoline);
- According to the State Department on May 24, 2011, Linde of Germany has said it had stopped supplying gas liquefaction technology to Iran, contributing to Iran's decision to suspend its LNG program.

Firms Believed to Still Be Supplying Gasoline or Related Equipment

- The firms sanctioned by the Administration on May 24, 2011 (discussed above): PCCI (Jersey/Iran); Royal Oyster Group (UAE); Speedy Ship (UAE/Iran); Tanker Pacific (Singapore); Ofer Brothers Group (Israel); Associated Shipbroking (Monaco); and Petroleos de Venezuela (Venezuela);

- Zhuhai Zhenrong, Unipec, and China Oil of China are said by GAO to still be selling to Iran and have not denied continuing sales to the GAO;
- Emirates National Oil Company of UAE was reported by GAO to still be selling to Iran;
- Hin Leong Trading of Singapore was reported by GAO to still be selling gasoline to Iran;
- Some refiners in Bahrain reportedly may still be selling gasoline to Iran.

Despite the large reduction in gasoline sales to Iran, as of late 2010, Iranian officials have said they have largely coped with the reduction in gasoline imports. The phaseout of gasoline subsidies discussed above has already reportedly begun to reduce demand for gasoline. Still, in December 2010 Iran slowed gasoline shipments to Afghanistan under a long-standing arrangement, possible to have gasoline available inside Iran to cope with any unrest that might result from real or perceived gas shortages.

Even before the subsidy reduction, there had not been gasoline shortages or gasoline rationing, although some Iranian oppositionists have reported otherwise. Iran has coped by converting at least two petrochemical plants to gasoline production, through a generally inferior process that initially produces benzene. The gasoline produced reportedly has led to a large increase in air pollution in Tehran, which was expected. Iran also says it has accelerated renovations and other improvements to existing gasoline refineries, allocating $2.2 billion for that purpose.

Building new refining capacity appears to be Iran's long term effort to reduce its vulnerability to gasoline supply reductions. Iran's deputy oil minister said in July 2010 Iran would try to invest $46 billion to upgrade its nine refineries and build seven new ones, a far larger amount than Iran had previously allocated to oil refining capacity.

Recent or Pending Legislation to Impose Additional Sanctions

Some in the 112th Congress believe that the cumulative effect of U.S. and international sanctions remain insufficient to accomplish key U.S. policy goals toward Iran, and are advocating further steps. However, in June 2011, outgoing Deputy Secretary of State Jim Steinberg told journalists ("The Cable") that the Administration does not support new legislation because the Administration is already implementing and expanding sanctions against Iran.[56]

Among specific recent proposals for new sanctions, in the 111th Congress, Representative Sherman introduced H.R. 6296, which, in Section 202, would amend ISA to make sanctionable "long term agreements" to buy oil from Iran—agreements that would involve large, up-front payments to Iran for purchases of oil over a long period of time. A provision of that bill would have extended ISA sanctionability to any energy project conducted with NIOC, anywhere in the world. An amended version of the bill was introduced in the 112th Congress (H.R. 1655, introduced April 15, 2011).

Another bill, H.R. 1905, contains language restating the provisions of ISA and would:

- Add two sanctions to the available ISA menu: a ban on visas for the principal officers or controlling shareholders of sanctioned firms (and their subsidiaries, parents, and affiliates); and application of any ISA sanction to these persons.
- Require the President to impose at least six out of the expanded ISA menu of 11 available sanctions.
- Would subject to ISA sanctions any purchases of Iranian oil or gas if the Revolutionary Guard is involved in the transaction (production or sale of that gas or oil).
- States that it is U.S. policy to support those in Iran seeking democracy.
- Would require an Administration report listing all persons who are members of named Iranian government institutions, including high ranking Revolutionary Guard officers – and ban visas for the named individuals.
- Contains elements similar to H.R. 740 on Securities and Exchange Commission (SEC) disclosures.

Another bill that focuses primarily on economic sanctions and proliferation sanctions is S.1048, introduced May 23, 2011. (A companion measure, H.R. 2105, was introduced in the House on June 3, 2011.) Among other provisions, this bill:

- States (Section 101) that it is the policy of the United States to prevent Iran from acquiring a nuclear weapons capability.
- Primarily targets affiliates of the Revolutionary Guard for sanctions, and expands the list of sanctions (adding a ban on financing, aid, or investment) to be imposed on violators named under the Iran, Syria, North Korea Non-Proliferation Act, discussed above.
- Like H.R. 1905, subjects to ISA sanctions purchases of Iranian oil or gas in which the Revolutionary Guard or its affiliates are involved.
- Would sanction foreign firms that participate in energy-related joint ventures with Iran outside Iranian territory.
- Would prohibit ships to put into port in the United States if the vessel entered a port in Iran, North Korea, or Syria any time 180 days prior.
- Like H.R. 1905, would deny visas to senior officials of Iran, but extends that to North Korea and Syria, and does not define specific government agencies in Iran whose members shall be named by the Administration.
- Provides for sanctions against any person determined to be providing or acquiring militarily useful equipment to/from Iran, North Korea, or Syria.
- Contains Iran human rights-related and SEC disclosure provisions similar to bills discussed below.

Other economic sanctions-related measures introduced in the 112th Congress include S. 366 and H.R. 740. These bills would require firms to declare in their required filings with the Securities and Exchange Commission whether that firm had undertaken activity that could violate ISA, CISADA, or executive orders (13224 or 13382) and regulations that bar dealings with designated Iranian entities.

Another apparent trend in the 112th Congress, based on introduced legislation, is to expand the sanctioning of Iranians named as human rights abusers. This builds on the human rights provisions of CISADA and the earlier Iran Freedom Support Act. In particular, the Iran Human Rights and Democracy Promotion Act of 2011 (S.879 and H.R. 1714) would: make mandatory investigations of Iranian human rights abusers; sanction the sale to Iran of equipment that could be used to suppress demonstrations; reauthorize the Iran Freedom Support Act (see below); and create a "Special Representative" position at the Department of State to focus on highlighting Iran's human rights abuses and coordinate U.S. and international responses. As noted, portions of H.R. 1905 and S. 1048, which mainly focus on economic sanctions, also contain measures to further penalize Iranian human rights abusers or otherwise promote Internet freedom and democracy in Iran.

Table 6. Entities Sanctioned Under U.N. Resolutions and U.S. Laws and Executive Orders (Persons listed are identified by the positions they held when designated; some have since changed)

Entities Named for Sanctions under Resolution 1737

Atomic Energy Organization of Iran (AEIO) Mesbah Energy Company (Arak supplier)
Kalaye Electric (Natanz supplier)
Pars Trash Company (centrifuge program) Farayand Technique (centrifuge program) Defense Industries Organization (DIO)
7th of Tir (DIO subordinate)
Shahid Hemmat Industrial Group (SHIG)—missile program
Shahid Bagheri Industrial Group (SBIG)—missile program
Fajr Industrial Group (missile program)
Mohammad Qanadi, AEIO Vice President
Behman Asgarpour (Arak manager)
Ehsan Monajemi (Natanz construction manager)
Jafar Mohammadi (Adviser to AEIO)
Gen. Hosein Salimi (Commander, IRGC Air Force)
Dawood Agha Jani (Natanz official)
Ali Hajinia Leilabadi (director of Mesbah Energy)
Lt. Gen. Mohammad Mehdi Nejad Nouri (Malak Ashtar University of Defence Technology rector)
Bahmanyar Morteza Bahmanyar (AIO official)
Reza Gholi Esmaeli (AIO official)
Ahmad Vahid Dastjerdi (head of Aerospace Industries Org., AIO)
Maj. Gen. Yahya Rahim Safavi (Commander in Chief, IRGC)

Entities/Persons Added by Resolution 1747

Ammunition and Metallurgy Industries Group (controls 7th of Tir)
Parchin Chemical Industries (branch of DIO)
Karaj Nuclear Research Center
Novin Energy Company
Cruise Missile Industry Group

Sanam Industrial Group (subordinate to AIO)
Ya Mahdi Industries Group
Kavoshyar Company (subsidiary of AEIO)
Sho'a Aviation (produces IRGC light aircraft for asymmetric warfare)
Bank Sepah (funds AIO and subordinate entities)
Esfahan Nuclear Fuel Research and Production Center and Esfahan Nuclear Technology Center
Qods Aeronautics Industries (produces UAV's, para-gliders for IRGC asymmetric warfare)
Pars Aviation Services Company (maintains IRGC Air Force equipment)
Gen. Mohammad Baqr Zolqadr (IRGC officer serving as deputy Interior Minister
Gen. Qasem Soleimani (Qods Force commander)
Fereidoun Abbasi-Davani (senior defense scientist)
Mohasen Fakrizadeh-Mahabai (defense scientist)
Seyed Jaber Safdari (Natanz manager)
Mohsen Hojati (head of Fajr Industrial Group)
Ahmad Derakshandeh (head of Bank Sepah)
Brig. Gen. Mohammad Reza Zahedi (IRGC ground forces commander)
Amir Rahimi (head of Esfahan nuclear facilities)
Mehrdada Akhlaghi Ketabachi (head of SBIG)
Naser Maleki (head of SHIG)
Brig. Gen. Morteza Reza'i (Deputy commander-in-chief, IRGC)
Vice Admiral Ali Akbar Ahmadiyan (chief of IRGC Joint Staff)
Brig. Gen. Mohammad Hejazi (Basij commander)

Entities Added by Resolution 1803

Thirteen Iranians named in Annex 1 to Resolution 1803; all reputedly involved in various aspects of nuclear program. Bans travel
for five named Iranians.
Electro Sanam Co.
Abzar Boresh Kaveh Co. (centrifuge production)
Barzaganin Tejaral Tavanmad Saccal
Jabber Ibn Hayan
Khorasan Metallurgy Industries
Niru Battery Manufacturing Co. (Makes batteries for Iranian military and missile systems)
Ettehad Technical Group (AIO front co.)
Industrial Factories of Precision
Joza Industrial Co.
Pshgam (Pioneer) Energy Industries
Tamas Co. (involved in uranium enrichment)
Safety Equipment Procurement (AIO front, involved in missiles)

Entities Added by Resolution 1929

Over 40 entities added; makes mandatory a previously non-binding travel ban on most named Iranians of previous resolutions.
Adds one individual banned for travel—AEIO head Javad Rahiqi
Amin Industrial Complex
Armament Industries Group

Defense Technology and Science Research Center (owned or controlled by Ministry of Defense)
Doostan International Company
Farasakht Industries
First East Export Bank, PLC (only bank added by 1929)
Kaveh Cutting Tools Company
M. Babaie Industries
Malek Ashtar University (subordinate of Defense Technology and Science Research Center, above)
Ministry of Defense Logistics Export (sells Iranian made arms to customers worldwide)
Mizan Machinery Manufacturing Modern Industries Technique Company
Nuclear Research Center for Agriculture and Medicine (research component of the AEIO)
Pejman Industrial Services Corp. Sabalan Company
Sahand Aluminum Parts Industrial Company
Shahid Karrazi Industries
Shahid Sattari Industries
Shahid Sayyade Shirazi Industries (acts on behalf of the DIO)
Special Industries Group (another subordinate of DIO)
Tiz Pars (cover name for SHIG) Yazd Metallurgy Industries
The following are Revolutionary Guard affiliated firms, several are subsidiaries of Khatam ol-Anbiya, the main Guard construction
affiliate:
Fater Institute
Garaghe Sazendegi Ghaem Gorb Karbala
Gorb Nooh
Hara Company
Imensazan Consultant Engineers Institute
Khatam ol-Anbiya
Makin
Omran Sahel
Oriental Oil Kish
Rah Sahel
Rahab Engineering Institute Sahel Consultant Engineers Sepanir
Sepasad Engineering Company
The following are entities owned or controlled by Islamic Republic of Iran Shipping Lines (IRISL):
Irano Hind Shipping Company IRISL Benelux
South Shipping Line Iran

Entities Designated Under U.S. Executive Order 13382 (many designations coincident with designations under U.N. resolutions)

Entity	Date Named
Shahid Hemmat Industrial Group (Iran)	June 2005, September 2007
Shahid Bakeri Industrial Group (Iran)	June 2005, February 2009
Atomic Energy Organization of Iran	June 2005
Novin Energy Company (Iran)	January 2006
Mesbah Energy Company (Iran)	January 2006

Four Chinese entities: Beijing Alite Technologies, LIMMT Economic and Trading Company, China Great Wall Industry Corp, and China National Precision Machinery Import/Export Corp.	June 2006
Sanam Industrial Group (Iran)	July 2006
Ya Mahdi Industries Group (Iran)	July 2006
Bank Sepah (Iran)	January 2007
Defense Industries Organization (Iran)	March 2007
Pars Trash (Iran, nuclear program)	June 2007
Farayand Technique (Iran, nuclear program)	June 2007
Fajr Industries Group (Iran, missile program)	June 2007
Mizan Machine Manufacturing Group (Iran, missile prog.)	June 2007
Aerospace Industries Organization (AIO) (Iran)	September 2007
Korea Mining and Development Corp. (N. Korea)	September 2007
Islamic Revolutionary Guard Corps (IRGC)	October 21, 2007
Ministry of Defense and Armed Forces Logistics	October 21, 2007
Bank Melli (Iran's largest bank, widely used by Guard); Bank Melli Iran Zao (Moscow); Melli Bank PC (U.K.)	October 21, 2007
Bank Kargoshaee	October 21, 2007
Arian Bank (joint venture between Melli and Bank Saderat). Based in Afghanistan	October 21, 2007
Bank Mellat (provides banking services to Iran's nuclear sector); Mellat Bank SB CJSC (Armenia). Reportedly has $1.4 billion in assets in UAE	October 21, 2007
Persia International Bank PLC (U.K.)	October 21, 2007
Khatam ol Anbiya Ghorargah Sazendegi Nooh (main IRGC construction and contracting arm, with $7 billion in oil, gas deals)	October 21, 2007
Oriental Oil Kish (Iranian oil exploration firm)	October 21, 2007
Ghorb Karbala; Ghorb Nooh (synonymous with Khatam ol Anbiya)	October 21, 2007
Sepasad Engineering Company (Guard construction affiliate)	October 21, 2007
Omran Sahel (Guard construction affiliate)	October 21, 2007
Sahel Consultant Engineering (Guard construction affiliate)	October 21, 2007
Hara Company	October 21, 2007
Ghorargahe Sazandegi Ghaem	October 21, 2007
Bahmanyar Morteza Bahmanyar (AIO, Iran missile official, see above under Resolution 1737)	October 21, 2007
Ahmad Vahid Dastjerdi (AIO head, Iran missile program)	October 21, 2007
Reza Gholi Esmaeli (AIO, see under Resolution 1737)	October 21, 2007

Morteza Reza'i (deputy commander, IRGC) See also Resolution 1747	October 21, 2007
Mohammad Hejazi (Basij commander). Also, Resolution 1747	October 21, 2007
Ali Akbar Ahmadian (Chief of IRGC Joint Staff). Resolution 1747	October 21, 2007
Hosein Salimi (IRGC Air Force commander). Resolution 1737	October 21, 2007
Qasem Soleimani (Qods Force commander). Resolution 1747	October 21, 2007
Future Bank (Bahrain-based but allegedly controlled by Bank Melli)	March 12, 2008
Yahya Rahim Safavi (former IRGC Commander in Chief	July 8, 2008
Mohsen Fakrizadeh-Mahabadi (senior Defense Ministry scientist)	July 8, 2008
Dawood Agha-Jani (head of Natanz enrichment site)	July 8, 2008
Mohsen Hojati (head of Fajr Industries, involved in missile program)	July 8, 2008
Mehrdada Akhlaghi Ketabachi (heads Shahid Bakeri Industrial Group)	July 8, 2008
Naser Maliki (heads Shahid Hemmat Industrial Group)	July 8, 2008
Tamas Company (involved in uranium enrichment)	July 8, 2008
Shahid Sattari Industries (makes equipment for Shahid Bakeri)	July 8, 2008
7th of Tir (involved in developing centrifuge technology)	July 8, 2008
Ammunition and Metallurgy Industries Group (partner of 7th of Tir)	July 8, 2008
Parchin Chemical Industries (deals in chemicals used in ballistic missile programs)	July 8, 2008
Karaj Nuclear Research Center	August 12, 2008
Esfahan Nuclear Fuel Research and Production Center (NFRPC)	August 12, 2008
Jabber Ibn Hayyan (reports to Atomic Energy Org. of Iran, AEIO)	August 12, 2008
Safety Equipment Procurement Company	August 12, 2008
Joza Industrial Company (front company for Shahid Hemmat Industrial Group, SHIG)	August 12, 2008
Islamic Republic of Iran Shipping Lines (IRISL) and 18 affiliates, including Val Fajr 8; Kazar; Irinvestship; Shipping Computer Services; Iran o Misr Shipping; Iran o Hind; IRISL Marine Services; Iriatal Shipping; South Shipping; IRISL Multimodal; Oasis; IRISL Europe; IRISL Benelux; IRISL China; Asia Marine Network; CISCO Shipping; and IRISL Malta	September 10, 2008

Firms affiliated to the Ministry of Defense, including Armament Industries Group; Farasakht Industries; Iran Aircraft Manufacturing Industrial Co.; Iran Communications Industries; Iran Electronics Industries; and Shiraz Electronics Industries	September 17, 2008
Export Development Bank of Iran. Provides financial services to Iran's Ministry of Defense and Armed Forces Logistics	October 22, 2008
Banco Internacional de Desarollo, C.A., Venezuelan-based Iranian bank, sanctioned as an affiliate of the Export Development Bank.	
Assa Corporation (alleged front for Bank Melli involved in managing property in New York City on behalf of Iran)	December 17, 2008
11 Entities Tied to Bank Melli: Bank Melli Iran Investment (BMIIC); Bank Melli Printing and Publishing; Melli Investment Holding; Mehr Cayman Ltd.; Cement Investment and Development; Mazandaran Cement Co.; Shomal Cement; Mazandaran Textile; Melli Agrochemical; First Persian Equity Fund; BMIIC Intel. General Trading	March 3, 2009
IRGC General Rostam Qasemi, head of Khatem ol-Anbiya Construction Headquarters (key corporate arm of the IRGC)	February 10, 2010 (see also October 21, 2007)
Fater Engineering Institute (linked to Khatem ol-Anbiya)	February 10, 2010
Imensazen Consultant Engineers Institute (linked to Khatem ol-Anbiya)	February 10, 2010
Makin Institute (linked to Khatem ol-Anbiya)	February 10, 2010
Rahab Institute (linked to Khatem on-Anbiya)	February 10, 2010
Entities sanctioned on June 16, 2010	

Entities sanctioned on June 16, 2010

- Post Bank of Iran
- IRGC Air Force
- IRGC Missile Command
- Rah Sahel and Sepanir Oil and Gas Engineering (for ties to Khatem ol-Anibya IRGC construction affiliate) - Mohammad Ali Jafari—IRGC Commander-in-Chief since September 2007
- Mohammad Reza Naqdi—Head of the IRGC's Basij militia force that suppresses dissent (since October 2009) - Ahmad Vahedi—Defense Minister
- javedan Mehr Toos, Javad Karimi Sabet (procurement brokers or atomic energy managers)
- Naval Defense Missile Industry Group (controlled by the Aircraft Industries Org that manages Iran's missile programs)
- Five front companies for IRISL: Hafiz Darya Shipping Co.; Soroush Sarzamin Asatir Ship Management Co.; Safiran Payam Darya; and Hong Kong-based Seibow Limited and Seibow Logistics.

Also identified on June 16 were 27 vessels linked to IRISKL and 71 new names of already designated IRISL ships.

Several Iranian entities were also designated as owned or controlled by Iran for purposes of the ban on U.S. trade with Iran. Entities sanctioned on November 30, 2010

- Pearl Energy Company (formed by First East Export Bank , a subsidiary of Bank Mellat
- Pearl Energy Services, SA
- Ali Afzali (high official of First East Export Bank)
- IRISL front companies: Ashtead Shipping, Byfleet Shipping, Cobham Shipping, Dorking Shipping, Effingham Shipping, Farnham Shipping, Gomshall Shipping, and Horsham Shipping (all located in the Isle of Man).
- IRISL and affiliate officials: Mohammad Hosein Dajmar, Gholamhossein Golpavar, Hassan Jalil Zadeh, and Mohammad Haji Pajand. Entities sanctioned on December 21, 2010:
- Bonyad (foundation) Taavon Sepah, for providing services to the IRGC
- Ansar Bank (for providing financial services to the IRGC)
- Mehr Bank (same justification as above)
- Moallem Insurance Company (for providing marine insurance to IRISL, Islamic Republic of Iran Shipping Lines)

Entities Sanctioned Under Executive Order 13224
(Terrorism Entities)

Qods Force	October 21, 2007
Bank Saderat (allegedly used to funnel Iranian money to Hezbollah, Hamas, PIJ, and other Iranian supported terrorist groups)	October 21, 2007
Al Qaeda Operatives in Iran: Saad bin Laden; Mustafa Hamid; Muhammad Rab'a al-Bahtiyti; Alis Saleh Husain	January 16, 2009
Qods Force senior officers: Hushang Allahdad, Hossein Musavi,Hasan Mortezavi, and Mohammad Reza Zahedi	August 3, 2010
Iranian Committee for the Reconstruction of Lebanon, and its director Hesam Khoshnevis, for supporting Lebanese Hizballah	August 3, 2010
Imam Khomeini Relief Committee Lebanon branch, and its director Ali Zuraik, for providing support to Hizballah	August 3, 2010
Razi Musavi, a Syrian based Iranian official allegedly providing support to Hizballah	August 3, 2010
Liner Transport Kish (for providing shipping services to transport weapons to Lebanese Hizballah)	December 21, 2010

Entities Sanctioned Under the Iran North Korea Syria Non-Proliferation Act or Executive Order 12938
The designations are under the Iran, North Korea, Syria Non-Proliferation Act (INKSNA) unless specified. These designations expire after two years, unless re-designated

Baltic State Technical University and Glavkosmos, both of Russia	July 30, 1998 (E.O. 12938). Both removed in 2010—Baltic on Jan. 29, 2010, and Glavkosmos on March 4, 2010
D. Mendeleyev University of Chemical Technology of Russia and Moscow Aviation Institute	January 8, 1999 (E.O. 12938). Both removed

	on May 21, 2010
Norinco (China). For alleged missile technology sale to Iran.	May 2003
Taiwan Foreign Trade General Corporation (Taiwan)	July 4, 2003
Tula Instrument Design Bureau (Russia). For alleged sales of laser-guided artillery shells to Iran.	September 17, 2003 (also designated under Executive Order 12938), removed May 21, 2010
13 entities sanctioned including companies from Russia, China, Belarus, Macedonia, North Korea, UAE, and Taiwan.	April 7, 2004
14 entities from China, North Korea, Belarus, India (two nuclear scientists, Dr. Surendar and Dr. Y.S.R. Prasad), Russia, Spain, and Ukraine.	September 29, 2004
14 entities, mostly from China, for alleged supplying of Iran's missile program. Many, such as North Korea's Changgwang Sinyong and China's Norinco and Great Wall Industry Corp, have been sanctioned several times previously. Newly sanctioned entities included North Korea's Paeksan Associated Corporation, and Taiwan's Ecoma Enterprise Co.	December 2004 and January 2005
9 entities, including those from China (Norinco yet again), India (two chemical companies), and Austria. Sanctions against Dr. Surendar of India (see September 29, 2004) were ended, presumably because of information exonerating him.	December 26, 2005
7 entities. Two Indian chemical companies (Balaji Amines and Prachi Poly Products); two Russian firms (Rosoboronexport and aircraft manufacturer Sukhoi); two North Korean entities (Korean Mining and Industrial Development, and Korea Pugang Trading); and one Cuban entity (Center for Genetic Engineering and Biotechnology).	August 4, 2006 (see below for Rosoboronexport removal)
9 entities. Rosoboronexport, Tula Design, and Komna Design Office of Machine Building, and Alexei Safonov (Russia); Zibo Chemical, China National Aerotechnology, and China National Electrical (China). Korean Mining and Industrial Development (North Korea) for WMD or advanced weapons sales to Iran (and Syria).	January 2007 (see below for Tula and Rosoboronexport removal)
14 entities, including Lebanese Hezbollah. Some were penalized for transactions with Syria. Among the new entities sanctioned for assisting Iran were Shanghai Non-Ferrous Metals Pudong Development Trade Company (China); Iran's Defense Industries Organization; Sokkia Company (Singapore); Challenger Corporation (Malaysia); Target Airfreight (Malaysia); Aerospace Logistics Services(Mexico); and Arif Durrani (Pakistani national).	April 23, 2007
13 entities: China Xinshidai Co.; China Shipbuilding and Offshore International Corp.; Huazhong CNC (China); IRGC; Korea Mining Development Corp. (North Korea); Korea Taesong Trading Co. NK); Yolin/Yullin Tech, Inc. (South Korea); (Rosoboronexport (Russia sate arms export agency); Sudan Master Technology;	October 23, 2008. Rosoboronexport removed May 21, 2010.

Sudan Technical Center Co; Army Supply Bureau (Syria); R and M International FZCO (UAE); Venezuelan Military Industries Co. (CAVIM);	
16 entities: Belarus: Belarusian Optical Mechanical Association; Beltech Export; China: Karl Lee; Dalian Sunny Industries; Dalian Zhongbang Chemical Industries Co.; Xian Junyun Electronic; Iran: Milad Jafari; DIO; IRISL; Qods Force; SAD Import-Export; SBIG; North Korea: Tangun Trading; Syria: Industrial Establishment of Defense; Scientific Studies and Research Center; Venezuela: CAVIM.	May 23, 2011

Entities Designated as Threats to Iraqi Stability under Executive Order 13438

Ahmad Forouzandeh. Commander of the Qods Force Ramazan Headquarters, accused of fomenting sectarian violence in Iraq and of organizing training in Iran for Iraqi Shiite militia fighters	January 9, 2008
Abu Mustafa al-Sheibani. Iran based leader of network that funnels Iranian arms to Shiite militias in Iraq.	January 9, 2008
Isma'il al-Lami (Abu Dura). Shiite militia leader, breakaway from Sadr Mahdi Army, alleged to have committed mass kidnapings and planned assassination attempts against Iraqi Sunni politicians	January 9, 2008
Mishan al-Jabburi. Financier of Sunni insurgents, owner of pro- insurgent Al-Zawra television, now banned	January 9, 2008
Al Zawra Television Station	January 9, 2008
Khata'ib Hezbollah (pro-Iranian Mahdi splinter group)	July 2, 2009
Abu Mahdi al-Muhandis	July 2, 2009

Iranians Sanctioned Under September 29, 2010, Executive Order 13553 on Human Rights Abusers

1. IRGC Commander Mohammad Ali Jafari	All sanctioned on September 29, 2010
2. Minister of Interior at time of June 2009 elections Sadeq Mahsouli	
3. Minister of Intelligence at time of elections Qolam Hossein Mohseni-Ejei	
4. Tehran Prosecutor General at time of elections Saeed Mortazavi	
5. Minister of Intelligence Heydar Moslehi	
6. Former Defense Minister Mostafa Mohammad Najjar	
7. Deputy National Police Chief Ahmad Reza Radan	
8. Basij (security militia) Commander at time of elections Hossein Taeb	

9. Tehran Prosecutor General Abbas Dowlatabadi (appointed August 2009). Has indicted large numbers of Green movement protesters.	Sanctioned on February 23, 2011
10. Basij forces commander (since October 2009) Mohammad Reza Naqdi (was head of Basij intelligence during post 2009 election crackdown)	
11. Islamic Revolutionary Guad Corps (IRGC)	Sanctioned on June 9, 2011.
12. Basij Resistance Force	
13. Law Enforcement Forces (LEF)	
14. LEF Commander Ismail Ahmad Moghadam	

End Notes

[1] The definition of "investment" in ISA (Section 14 (9)) includes not only equity and royalty arrangements (including additions to existing investment, as added by P.L. 107-24) but any contract that includes "responsibility for the development of petroleum resources" of Iran. As amended by CISADA (P.L. 111-195), these definitions include pipelines to or through Iran, as well as contracts to lead the construction, upgrading, or expansions of energy projects. CISADA also changes the definition of investment to eliminate the exemption from sanctions for sales of energyrelated equipment to Iran, if such sales are structured as investments or ongoing profit-earning ventures.

[2] Under Section 4(d) of the original act, for Iran, the threshold dropped to $20 million, from $40 million, one year after enactment, when U.S. allies did not join a multilateral sanctions regime against Iran. However, P.L. 111-195 explicit sets the threshold investment level at $20 million. For Libya, the threshold was $40 million, and sanctionable activity included export to Libya of technology banned by Pan Am 103-related Security Council Resolutions 748 (March 31, 1992) and 883 (November 11, 1993).

[3] The definition of energy sector had included oil and natural gas, but now, as a consequence of the enactment of P.L. 111-195, also includes liquefied natural gas (LNG), oil or LNG tankers, and products to make or transport pipelines that transport oil or LNG.

[4] This latter "trigger" was added by P.L. 109-293.

[5] Other ISA amendments under that law included recommending against U.S. nuclear agreements with countries that supply nuclear technology to Iran and expanding provisions of the USA Patriot Act (P.L. 107-56) to curb moneylaundering for use to further WMD programs.

[6] This latter termination requirement added by P.L. 109-293. This law also removed Libya from the act, although application to Libya effectively terminated when the President determined on April 23, 2004, that Libya had fulfilled the requirements of all U.N. resolutions on Pan Am 103.

[7] Dollar figures for investments in Iran represent public estimates of the amounts investing firms are expected to spend over the life of a project, which might in some cases be several decades.

[8] Text of announcement of waiver decision by then Secretary of State Madeleine Albright, containing expectation of similar waivers in the future. http://www.parstimes.com/law/albright_southpars.html.

[9] Much of this section is derived from a meeting between the CRS author and officials of the State Department's Economics Bureau, which is tasked with the referenced review of investment projects. November 24, 2009.

[10] Prior to CISADA, the definition of investment in ISA specifically exempted sales of equipment or services under that definition. CISADA omitted that exclusion.

[11] http://www.kuwaittimes.net/read_news.php?newsid=NDQ0OTY1NTU4; http://english.farsnews.com/ newstext. php? nn=8901181055.

[12] The executive order was issued under the authority of: The International Emergency Economic Powers Act (IEEPA, 50 U.S.C. 1701 et seq.; the National Emergencies Act (50 U.S.C. 1601 et seq.; Section 505 of the International Security and Development Cooperation Act of 1985 (22 U.S.C. 2349aa-9) and Section 301 of Title 3, United States Code. An August 1997 amendment to the trade ban (Executive Order 13059) prevented

U.S. companies from knowingly exporting goods to a third country for incorporation into products destined for Iran.

[13] The information in this bullet is taken from: Becker, Jo. "With U.S. Leave, Companies Skirt Iran Sanctions." *New York Times*, December 24, 2010.

[14] Form 10-K Filed for fiscal year ended December 31, 2008.

[15] Prada, Paulo, and Betsy McKay. Trading Outcry Intensifies. *Wall Street Journal*, March 27, 2007; Brush, Michael. Are You Investing in Terrorism? MSN Money, July 9, 2007.

[16] New York Times, March 7, 2010, cited previously.

[17] Subsidiaries of the Registrant at December 31, 2009. http://www.sec.gov/Archives/edgar/data/ 780571/ 000078057110000007/ex_21-1.htm.

[18] "Exhibit to 10-K Filed February 25, 2009." Officials of Fluor claim that their only dealings with Iran involve property in Iran owned by a Fluor subsidiary, which the subsidiary has been unable to dispose of. CRS conversation with Fluor, December 2009.

[19] Form 10-K for Fiscal year ended December 31, 2009.

[20] Form 10-K for Fiscal year ended December 31, 2007.

[21] Form 10-K for Fiscal year ended December 31, 2008, claims firm directed its subsidiaries to cease new business in Iran and Cuba, Syria, and Sudan as of September 2007.

[22] "Iran Says Halliburton Won Drilling Contract." *Washington Times*, January 11, 2005.

[23] "Caterpillar Says Tightens 'No-Iran' Business Policy." Reuters, March 1, 2010.

[24] Nixon, Ron. "2 Corporations Say Business With Tehran Will Be Curbed." *New York Times*, March 11, 2010.

[25] Baker, Peter. "U.S. and Foreign Companies Feeling Pressure to Sever Ties With Iran." New York Times, April 24, 2010.

[26] Hearing of the Financial Services and General Government Subcommittee of the House Appropriations Committee, *Federal News Service*, May 21, 2009.

[27] Kessler, Glenn. "U.S. Moves to Isolate Iranian Banks." *Washington Post*, September 9, 2006.

[28] Such laws include the Atomic Energy Act of 1954 and the Energy Policy Act of 2005 (P.L. 109-58).

[29] The provision contains certain exceptions to ensure the safety of astronauts, but it nonetheless threatened to limit U.S. access to the international space station after April 2006, when Russia started charging the United States for transportation on its Soyuz spacecraft. Legislation in the 109th Congress (S. 1713, P.L. 109-112) amended the provision in order to facilitate continued U.S. access and extended INA sanctions provisions to Syria.

[30] For information on the steps taken by individual states, see National Conference of State Legislatures. State Divestment Legislation.

[31] Rhoads, Christopher. "Iran's Web Spying Aided by Western Technology." Wall Street Journal, June 22, 2009.

[32] End, Aurelia. "Siemens Quits Iran Amid Mounting Diplomatic Tensions." Agence France Press, January 27, 2010.

[33] U.S. Department of Treasury, Office of Public Affairs. Treasury Sanctions Iranian Security Forces for Human Rights Abuses, June 9, 2011.

[34] See CRS Report RL31258, *Suits Against Terrorist States by Victims of Terrorism*, by Jennifer K. Elsea.

[35] Text of the resolution is at http://www.isis-online.org/uploads/isis-reports/documents/Draft_resolution_on_ Iran_annexes.pdf.

[36] Letter signed by eleven U.S. Senators to German Foreign Minister Guido Westerwelle. February 1, 2011.

[37] Warrick, Joby. "Iran Using Fronts to Get Bomb Parts From U.S." *Washington Post*, January 11, 2009; Institute for Science and International Security. "Iranian Entities' Illicit Military Procurement Networks." David Albright, Paul Brannan, and Andrea Scheel. January 12, 2009.

[38] During the active period of talks, which began in December 2002, there were working groups focused not only on the TCA terms and proliferation issues but also on Iran's human rights record, Iran's efforts to derail the Middle East peace process, Iranian-sponsored terrorism, counter-narcotics, refugees, migration issues, and the Iranian opposition PMOI.

[39] Landler, Mark. "Clinton Says Sanctions Have Stalled Iran's Effort to Make Nuclear Weapons." *New York Times*, January 11, 2011.

[40] The text of the report is at http://www.isis-online.org/uploads/isis-reports/documents/Iran_24May2011.pdf.

[41] "Iran's Gateway in Dubai Highlights Sanctions Bite." *Associated Press*, February 1, 2011.

[42] Mufson, Steven and Robin Wright. "Iran Adapts to Economic Pressure." *Washington Post*, October 29, 2007.

[43] Speech by Stuart Levey before the Center for Strategic and International Studies. September 20, 2010.

[44] Erdbink, Thomas. "Leaving Iran's Middle Class Behind." *Washington Post*, November 7, 2010.

[45] http://online.wsj.com/article/SB10001424052748704569204575328851816763476.html.

[46] Stockman, Farah. "Oil Firm Says It Will Withdraw From Iran." Boston Globe, November 12, 2010.
[47] "Iran Revolutionary Guards Pull Out of Gas Deal Over Sanctions." *Platts*, July 19, 2010.
[48] Information in this section derived from, Blas, Javier. "Traders Cut Iran Petrol Line." Financial Times, March 8, 2010.
[49] Information provided at Foundation for Defense of Democracies conference on Iran. December 9, 2010.
[50] Becker, Jo and Ron Nixon. "U.S. Enriches Companies Defying Its Policy on Iran." *New York Times*, March 7, 2010.
[51] GAO-10-967R. Exporters of Refined Petroleum Products to Iran. September 3, 2010.
[52] http://www.ft.com/cms/s/0/009370f0-486e-11df-9a5d-00144feab49a.html.
[53] http://www.defenddemocracy.org/index.php?option=com_content&task=view&id=11788115&Itemid=105.
[54] http://www.defenddemocracy.org/index.php?option=com_content&task=view&id=11788115&Itemid=105.
[55] http://www.defenddemocracy.org/index.php?option=com_content&task=view&id=11788115&Itemid=105.
[56] Josh Rogin. "Steinberg: No Need for Another Iran Sanctions Bill." Foreign Policy: The Cable. June 15, 2011.

In: U.S. Led Sanctions on Iran
Editors: Robert K. Figg and Danielle A. Wilson ISBN: 978-1-62100-414-1

Chapter 2

IRAN SANCTIONS: NEW ACT UNDERSCORES IMPORTANCE OF COMPREHENSIVE ASSESSMENT OF SANCTIONS' EFFECTIVENESS*

United States Government Accountability Office

Statement of Joseph A. Christoff, Director
International Affairs and Trade

Mr. Chairman and Members of the Committee:

I am pleased to be here today to discuss our work on the implementation of U.S. sanctions against Iran. My testimony will discuss the continuing challenges the United States faces in (1) deterring the illegal transshipment of U.S. goods to Iran, (2) restricting foreign investment in Iran's energy sector, and (3) assessing the overall effectiveness of U.S. sanctions. In addition, I will discuss how the Comprehensive Iran Sanctions, Accountability, and Divestment Act of 2010 (signed into law on July 1, 2010) addresses these challenges.

The United States has imposed multiple sanctions against Iran to deter it from developing its nuclear program, supporting terrorism, and abusing human rights. The United States has banned most U.S. trade and investment with Iran and prohibited firms from knowingly transshipping U.S. goods to Iran through other nations. The United States has also acted to limit Iran's ability to explore for, extract, refine, or transport its petroleum resources. The Comprehensive Iran Sanctions, Accountability, and Divestment Act of 2010 expands existing sanctions against Iran and requires the Administration to report on information related to the sanctions.

My statement is drawn from prior GAO work related to sanctions against Iran.[1] We conducted this work in accordance with all sections of GAO's Quality Assurance Framework and generally accepting government auditing standards, as appropriate. Those standards

* This is an edited, reformatted and augmented version of the United States Government Accountability Office publication GAO-10-928T, dated July 29, 2010.

require that we plan and perform the audits to obtain sufficient, appropriate evidence to provide a reasonable basis for our findings and conclusions based on our audit objectives. We believe the evidence obtained provides a reasonable basis for our findings and conclusions based on our audit objectives.

SUMMARY

Iran is obtaining U.S. military and dual-use goods (civilian goods with potential military applications) that are illegally transshipped through intermediaries in third-party nations, most notably the United Arab Emirates, Malaysia, and Singapore. U.S. agencies have conducted investigations to uncover Iranian procurement networks and prosecuted at least 30 firms and individuals between 2007 and 2009. The Comprehensive Iran Sanctions, Accountability, and Divestment Act of 2010 requires the President to designate a country as a Destination of Diversion Concern if certain criteria are met. Moreover, the President shall impose a licensing requirement upon certain U.S. exports to the designated country unless the President makes a number of determinations, including determining that it is appropriate to provide technical assistance to strengthen the country's export control systems.

At least 41 foreign firms had commercial activity in Iran's energy sector between 2005 and 2009. Of these firms, seven had contracts with the U.S. government valued at almost $880 million. The Iran Sanctions Act of 1996 (ISA) provides for sanctions against persons (firms and individuals) who invest more than $20 million in Iran's energy sector in any 12-month period. However, the United States has not sanctioned firms under the ISA for investing in Iran's energy sector. The Comprehensive Iran Sanctions, Accountability, and Divestment Act of 2010 requires the President to investigate reports of certain sanctionable activity where credible evidence is received and make a determination in writing to Congress whether such activity has indeed occurred. The President would then be expected either to impose or waive sanctions.

We previously recommended that the Administration improve the disparate data collected on Iran sanctions, establish a baseline of information on Iran sanctions, and conduct an overall assessment of the sanctions' impact in achieving U.S. foreign policy goals. Recent congressional action has expanded sanctions against Iran and imposed new reporting requirements on the Administration. These actions underscore the importance of comprehensive assessments of the effectiveness of U.S. sanctions against Iran.

BACKGROUND

U.S. exports to Iran are severely restricted by U.S. laws and regulations.[2] The U.S. trade ban generally prohibits exports of U.S. goods (including dual-use goods) to countries other than Iran without a Treasury Department license if the exporter has reason to know the goods are specifically intended for transshipment to Iran.[3] Foreign firms are generally prohibited from knowingly re-exporting goods on the Commerce Department's list of controlled dual-use goods to Iran even if those goods were originally legally exported from the United States to a third country under a Commerce license.[4] For example, dual-use U.S. goods exported to countries other than Iran under a Commerce license may not be subsequently transshipped to Iran without a Treasury license if the exporter knew or had reason to know that such goods were intended for Iran. The Departments of Commerce, Defense, Homeland Security, Justice, and the Treasury investigate allegations of illegal transshipment of U.S. goods to Iran. Exporters who knowingly ship U.S. goods to Iran through other countries without a Treasury license are subject to prosecution by the Department of Justice.

Iran has the world's third largest oil reserves, or about 140 billion barrels, and produces about 4.2 million barrels per day. However, Iran's oil production has remained virtually flat in recent years and will likely stagnate in the medium term due to insufficient investment, according to the International Monetary Fund. Iran requires increasingly modern and advanced oil recovery technologies to stop natural declines of oil production, but has found advanced technology difficult to import due to international sanctions and high costs. According to the Department of Energy (DOE), Iran does not currently have sufficient refining capacity to meet its domestic demand for gasoline. Iran imported approximately 130,000 barrels of gasoline per day in 2009, as well as other refined products such as diesel fuel. Iran's nine refineries are operated by the National Iranian Oil Refining and Distribution Company, according to DOE. With the potential participation of foreign companies, Iran plans to add capacity at eight refineries to fully meet domestic demand for gasoline by 2013 or 2014, according to DOE officials.

Iran Obtains Illegal Transshipments of U.S. Military and Dual-Use Goods through other Countries; New Act Calls for Identification of Destinations of Diversion Concern

The United States banned nearly all trade and investment with Iran in 1995 after banning imports from that country in 1987. According to a Treasury official, the trade and investment ban is aimed at making it more difficult for Iran to procure U.S. goods, services, and technology, including those that could be used for terrorism or proliferation. However, as we have reported, attempts have been made to circumvent the trade ban through the transshipment of U.S. exports through third countries. U.S officials identified several locations that serve as transshipment points for military and dual-use goods destined for Iran, including the United Arab Emirates (UAE), Malaysia, Singapore, Thailand, Australia, Canada, Colombia, Brazil, Austria, France, Germany, Luxembourg, The Netherlands, and the United Kingdom (see figure 1).

A 2009 Justice Department report cited 30 cases that involved the use of intermediaries in these countries. More than half of the cases listed involved the use of intermediaries in the UAE for transshipment. About 20 percent involved the use of intermediaries in Malaysia and Singapore. U.S. goods involved in these cases included U.S. military aircraft components, laboratory equipment, specialty alloy pipes, night vision goggles, and sensitive technologies sent to Iranian missile and nuclear entities.

U.S. officials stated that the UAE has taken steps to address the use of its territory for transshipment. They noted that the UAE has increased cooperation with U.S. enforcement entities and enacted new export control legislation in 2007.

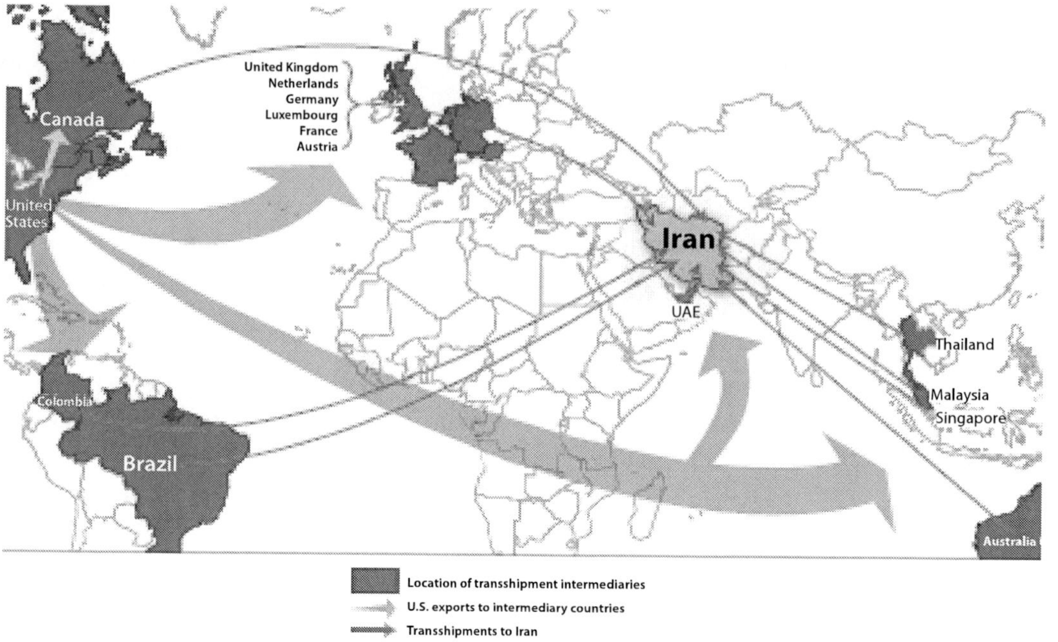

Sources: GAO analysis of Justice Department data; Map Resources (map).

Figure 1. Illegal Transshipment Routes to Iran.

According to the UAE government, the new law bans the export/re-export of strategic goods (including arms and military hardware, chemical and biological materials, and dual-use goods) without a special license, and specifies penalties that include imprisonment or fines.

Commerce officials stated that the law contains the basic elements of an export control regime to combat transshipment. However, Commerce officials have reported a high rate of unfavorable end-use checks for U.S. items exported to the UAE and U.S. officials note the potential shift of illegal transshipment operations to other nations, such as Malaysia and Singapore.

The Comprehensive Iran Sanctions, Accountability, and Divestment Act of 2010 addresses the use of intermediaries to transship military and dual-use items to Iran. Under the Act, the Director of National Intelligence must identify to the President, relevant agency heads, and appropriate congressional committees the countries whose governments the Director believes allow the transshipment or diversion to Iran of certain U.S. goods, services or technologies. Moreover, the President shall designate a country as a Destination of Diversion Concern if the President determines that the government of the country allows substantial diversion of specified U.S. goods, services, or technologies through the country to Iranian end-users or Iranian intermediaries. Upon designation, the President must submit to the appropriate congressional committees a report identifying the countries of concern and listing the items that are being diverted through each respective country. After designation, the President shall require a license to export to the designated country the specified U.S. goods, services, or technologies. This licensing requirement may be delayed if the President makes a number of determinations including determining that it is appropriate to provide technical assistance to strengthen the country's export control systems.

Foreign Firms Maintain Commercial Ties to Iran's Energy Sector; New Act Requires President to Begin Investigations and Report on Firms' Investments in Iran's Energy Sector

Iran's energy sector is vital to its economy and government. In recent years, oil export revenues have accounted for 50 to 76 percent of the Iranian government's revenues and 24 percent of Iran's gross domestic product. However, Iran has not reached peak crude oil production levels since 1978, does not produce sufficient natural gas for domestic use, and lacks the refining capacity to meet domestic demand for gasoline. Accordingly, Iran is seeking the participation of foreign firms in providing financing and technical assistance in numerous energy projects.

Based on our review of open source information, we identified 41 firms that had commercial activity in the Iranian energy sector between 2005 and 2009 (see app. 1). Open source information stated that these firms supported activities throughout Iran that involved the exploration and development of oil and gas, petroleum refining, or petrochemicals, including the construction of pipelines and tankers for the transport of oil or gas (see fig. 2).

Source: GAO analysis of U.S. Department of Energy data.

Figure 2. Map of Iranian Oil, Gas, and Petrochemical Activities.

Of the 41 firms, seven had contracts with the U.S. government (see app. II for these firms). From fiscal years 2005 through 2009, the U.S. government obligated almost $880 million in contracts to these seven firms. U.S. agencies obligated almost 90 percent of these funds for purchases of fuel and petroleum products overseas.

ISA provides for sanctions against persons who invest more than $20 million in Iran's energy sector in any 12-month period. ISA authorizes the President, who delegated authority to the Secretary of State, to ban such persons from U.S. government procurement. However, the Secretary of State has not determined that a firm's activities have met the legal criteria for sanctions under the Iran Sanctions Act since 1998. At that time, the Secretary waived the imposition of sanctions upon three foreign energy firms—Total (France), Gazprom (Russia), and Petronas (Malaysia). In waiving the sanctions, the Secretary cited the European Union's cooperation on counterterrorism efforts involving Iran and the possibility that the Union would take the issue to the World Trade Organization.

The Comprehensive Iran Sanctions, Accountability, and Divestment Act of 2010 requires additional action on the part of the President. The new act requires, rather than authorizes, the President to initiate an investigation upon receipt of credible evidence that a person is engaged in certain prohibited activities such as investment in the development of Iran's petroleum sector.[5] The President is also required to make a determination in writing to Congress about whether such activity has indeed occurred. The President would then be expected either to impose or waive sanctions. The Act also requires the President to submit a report to Congress on investments in Iraq's energy sector since January 2006, including a list of all significant energy related joint ventures, investments, and partnerships Iran has with entities from other countries and an estimate of the value of these investments.

Our list of 41 firms with commercial activity in Iran's energy sector has prompted reaction from the cited firms. Upon request, 13 of the 41 firms provided comments on a draft of the report. Since the report was released, four firms have provided additional comments. Tecnimont (Italy) stated that it had canceled its involvement in an Iranian energy project due to lack of financing. Statoil (Norway) confirmed that it had frozen new investments in Iran's South Pars natural gas field and halted oil exploration and development activities in Iran. Repsol (Spain) provided us a copy of its May 2010 letter to the Iranian government discontinuing its participation in a $10 billion project to develop Iran's Persian LNG project. Repsol's withdrawal from the project will be effective July 31, 2010. We also received a letter from Ashok Leyland Project Services of India stating that it had not made binding agreements regarding the cited projects and would not take actions that violate laws or expose it to U.S .sanctions.[6]

New Act Underscores Importance of Comprehensive Assessment of Sanctions' Effectiveness

Additional sanctions in the Comprehensive Iran Sanctions, Accountability, and Divestment Act of 2010 and new reporting requirements underscore the importance of comprehensive assessments of U.S. sanctions' effectiveness in deterring Iran's support for terrorism and continued nuclear proliferation. In December 2007, we recommended that the

Administration complete such an assessment. We found that U.S. agencies—State, Treasury, Commerce, Homeland Security, and others— collected disparate data on the multiple sanctions they implemented.

Accordingly, we recommended that U.S. agencies consider collecting and analyzing data on, but not limited to,

- the number of goods seized, penalties imposed, and convictions obtained under the trade ban (Homeland Security, Treasury, Commerce, Justice);
- sensitive items diverted to Iran through transshipment points (Commerce and the intelligence community);
- the amount of assets frozen resulting from financial sanctions (Treasury and the intelligence community); and
- the extent of delays in foreign investment in Iran's energy sector (State, Energy, and the intelligence community).

The data should then be used to establish baseline information for continuous monitoring and periodic reporting on what U.S. sanctions have achieved.

The Comprehensive Iran Sanctions, Accountability, and Divestment Act of 2010 expands the number of activities that are sanctionable. For example, the Act requires the President to impose sanctions against persons or entities that

- export at least a certain value of refined petroleum products to Iran,
- sell at least a certain value of services and technology to maintain or expand Iran's refinery capacity
- export sensitive technologies that the Iranian government can use to monitor or jam its citizens communications, and
- commit human rights abuses against Iranian citizens.
- The Act also adds reporting requirements that increase the transparency of the Administration's actions, but also underscore the importance of having a framework to utilize the reports' data and provide a comprehensive assessment. For example, the Administration must report on investments in Iran's energy sector, the activities of foreign export credit agencies, and the number of countries of diversion concern.
- These expanded sanctions and reporting requirements underscore the importance of improving data collection, establishing a baseline, and comprehensively assessing the impact of sanctions on Iran. Such assessments are important because they provide the Administration and Congress with important information on the impact of existing and new sanctions and the extent to which these collective sanctions further the achievement of U.S. foreign policy and security goals toward Iran.

Mr. Chairman, this concludes my statement. I would be pleased to answer any questions that you or other members may have at this time.

STAFF ACKNOWLEDGMENTS

Individuals who made key contributions to this statement include Tet Miyabara (Assistant Director), Pierre Toureille, Grace Lui, Jon Fremont, Jennifer Bryant, and Debbie Chung.

APPENDIX I. FOREIGN FIRMS PUBLICLY REPORTED TO HAVE COMMERCIAL ACTIVITY IN THE IRANIAN OIL, GAS, OR PETROCHEMICAL SECTORS AS OF MARCH 2010

	Firm [a]	Country [b]	Sector
1	ABB Lummus	Not applicable	Refining, petrochemicals
2	Amona	Malaysia	Oil exploration and production
3	Belneftekhim	Belarus	Oil exploration and production
4	China National Offshore Oil Corporation	China	Natural gas
5	China National Petroleum Corporation	China	Oil exploration and production, natural gas
6	Costain Oil, Gas & Process Ltd.	United Kingdom	Natural gas
7	Daelim	South Korea	Natural gas
8	Daewoo Shipbuilding & Marine Engineering	South Korea	Oil tankers
9	Edison	Italy	Oil exploration and production
10	ENI	Italy	Oil exploration and production
11	Gazprom	Russia	Oil exploration and production, pipeline
12	GS	South Korea	Natural gas
13	Haldor Topsoe	Denmark	Refining
14	*Hinduja"* (Ashok Leyland Project Services)	*"United Kingdom"* (India)	Oil exploration and production, natural gas
15	Hyundai Heavy Industries	South Korea	Oil tankers
16	INA	Croatia	Oil exploration and production, natural gas
17	Indian Oil Corporation	India	Natural gas
18	Inpex	Japan	Oil exploration and production
19	JGC Corporation	Japan	Refining
20	Lukoil	Russia	Oil exploration and production
21	LyondelBasell	Netherlands	Petrochemicals
22	Oil India Ltd.	India	Natural gas
23	Oil and Natural Gas Corporation	India	Oil exploration and production, natural gas
24	OMV	Austria	Natural gas
25	ONGC Videsh Ltd.	India	Natural gas
26	Petrobras	Brazil	Oil exploration and production
27	Petrofield	Malaysia	Natural gas
28	Petroleos de Venezuela S.A.	Venezuela	Natural gas
29	Petronet LNG	India	Natural gas
30	PGNiG	Poland	Natural gas
31	PTT Exploration & Production	Thailand	Natural gas
32	Repsol	Spain	Natural gas
33	Royal Dutch Shell	Netherlands	Natural gas
34	Sinopec	China	Oil exploration and production, refining
35	SKS Ventures	Malaysia	Natural gas
36	Snamprogetti	Italy	Pipeline
37	StatoilHydro	Norway	Oil exploration and production, natural gas
38	Tecnimont	Italy	Petrochemicals

	Firm [a]	Country [b]	Sector
39	Total	France	Natural gas
40	Turkish Petroleum Company	Turkey	Natural gas
41	Uhde	Germany	Petrochemicals

Source: GAO analysis of open source information.

[a] Following the March 2010 publication of this table, four firms (Ashok Leyland, Repsol, Statoil, and Tecnimont) informed us that they had not gone forward with the projects cited in the table.

[b] The country listed is the physical location of the firm.

Appendix II. Firms Reported in Open Sources as Having Both Commercial Activity in the Iranian Energy Sector and U.S. Government Contracts

			U.S. Government obligations			
Firm/country [a]	FY 2005	FY 2006	FY 2007	FY 2008	FY 2009	Total
Repsol/Spain	$40 million	$37 million	$110 million	$81 million	$51 million	$319 million
Total/France	$0	$27 million	$0	$154 million	$131 million	$312 million
Daelim Industrial Co./South Korea	$0	$0	$0	$0	$111 million	$111 million
ENI/Italy	$9 million	$88 million	Less than $100,000	$0	$0	$97 million
PTT Exploration and Production/Thailand	$21 million	$4 million	$6 million	$1 million	$3 million	$35 million
Hyundai Heavy Industries/South Korea	$1 million	$2 million	$1 million	$0	$0	$5 million
GS Engineering and Construction/South Korea	Less than $100,000	$0	$0	$0	$0	Less than $100,000
Total	$71 million	$158 million	$117 million	$236 million	$296 million	$879 million

Source: GAO analysis of Federal Procurement Data System-Next Generation records and other government records.

Note: Totals may not add due to rounding.

[a]The country listed is the physical location of the firm as reported in open sources.

End Notes

[1]GAO, Iran Sanctions: Firms Reported to Have Commercial Activity in the Iranian Energy Sector and U.S. Government Contracts, GAO-10-721T (Washington, D.C.: May 12, 2010); Firms Reported to Have Commercial Activity in the Iranian Energy Sector and U.S. Government Contracts, GAO-10-639R (Washington, D.C.: May 4, 2010); Firms Reported in Open Sources as Having Commercial Activity in Iran's Oil, Gas, and Petrochemical Sector, GAO-10-515R (Washington, D.C.: March 23, 2010); Iran Sanctions: Complete and Timely Licensing Data Needed to Strengthen Enforcement of Export Restrictions, GAO-10-375 (Washington, D.C.: March 4, 2010); and Iran Sanctions: Impact in Furthering U.S. Objectives Is Unclear and Should Be Reviewed, GAO-08-58 (Washington, D.C.: December 18, 2007).

[2]See generally, 31 C.F.R. part 560.

[3] 31 C.F.R. § 560.204.

[4] 31 C.F.R. § 560.205.

[5] Pub. L. No. 111-195, § 102(g). This reporting requirement applies only to activities described in section 5(a) of the ISA.

[6] The firm also stated that it, rather than "Hinduja," should have been identified as a firm with commercial activities in Iran's natural gas sector.

In: U.S. Led Sanctions on Iran
Editors: Robert K. Figg and Danielle A. Wilson
ISBN: 978-1-62100-414-1

Chapter 3

IRAN SANCTIONS: FIRMS REPORTED TO HAVE COMMERCIAL ACTIVITY IN THE IRANIAN ENERGY SECTOR AND U.S. GOVERNMENT CONTRACTS*

United States Government Accountability Office

Statement of Joseph A. Christoff, Director
International Affairs and Trade

Mr. Chairman and Members of the Committee:

I am pleased to be here today to discuss our work regarding foreign firms with commercial interests in Iran's energy sector. In March 2010, we issued a report identifying 41 foreign firms that have commercial activity in Iran's energy sector. The report released today identifies which of the 41 foreign firms also have U.S. government contracts.[1]

Iran's energy sector is vital to its economy and government. In recent years, oil export revenues have accounted for 24 percent of Iran's gross domestic product and between 50 and 76 percent of the Iranian government's revenues. However, Iran has not reached peak crude oil production levels since 1978, does not produce sufficient natural gas for domestic use, and lacks the refining capacity to meet domestic demand for gasoline. Accordingly, Iran is seeking the participation of foreign firms in providing financing and technical assistance in numerous energy projects. IHS Global Insight reports that Iran's priorities for the next 5 years are to (1) raise oil production and exports as much as possible, (2) increase natural gas production for domestic use, and (3) expand refining capacity. In November 2008, the Deputy Minister of the National Iranian Oil Company stated that Iran would need about $145 billion in new investment over the next 10 years to build a thriving energy sector.

U.S. law restricts U.S. firms from investing in Iran's energy sector through sanctions to discourage Iran from supporting terrorism and developing nuclear weapons.[2] In addition, the Iran Sanctions Act (ISA) provides for sanctions against persons, including foreign firms, who invest more than $20 million in Iran's energy sector in any 12-month period.[3] The act allows

---

* This is an edited, reformatted and augmented version of the United States Government Accountability Office publication GAO-10-721T, dated May 12, 2010.

the President, who delegated authority under the act to the Secretary of State, to ban such persons from U.S. government procurement, including contracts for goods or services.[4] The Secretary of State is responsible for determining whether a firm's activities meet the legal criteria for an investment, and the firm could therefore be subject to actions under the Iran Sanctions Act. The Secretary of State may waive the sanctions if the Secretary determines it is in the national interests of the United States to do so.[5]

The Secretary has not determined that a firm's activities have met the legal criteria for sanctions under the Iran Sanctions Act since 1998. At that time, the Secretary waived sanctions on three foreign energy firms—Total (France), Gazprom (Russia), and Petronas (Malaysia). We did not attempt to determine whether the activities of the 41 firms we identified meet the legal criteria for an investment under the Iran Sanctions Act. To identify firms reported in open sources as having commercial activity in the Iranian energy sector, we relied only on government reports and information, about 200 energy trade publications, and corporate Web site information and statements. We excluded sources deemed insufficiently reliable, such as newspaper reports, newswires and news releases from the Iranian government. We listed a firm as having commercial activity in Iran's energy sector if three reputable industry publications or the firm's corporate statements reported the firm to have (1) signed an agreement to conduct business; (2) invested capital; or (3) received payment for providing goods or services in connection with a specific Iranian energy project. We provided the firms on our list an opportunity to comment on our findings.

To determine the extent to which the firms we identified also had contracts with the U.S. government, we searched the Federal Procurement Data System-Next Generation (FPDS-NG) for references to the firms.[6] We verified that the firms in FPDS-NG were matches to firms on our list by using the U.S. government central contractor registration to confirm identifying information. We took steps to corroborate key FPDS-NG information by obtaining U.S. government documents and public statements that confirmed the firms' U.S. contracts.

We conducted our work from September 2009 to April 2010 in accordance with all sections of GAO's Quality Assurance Framework that are relevant to our objectives. The framework requires that we plan and perform the engagement to obtain sufficient and appropriate evidence to meet our stated objectives and discuss any limitations in our work.

SUMMARY

Based on our review of open source information, we identified 41 firms that had commercial activity in the Iranian energy sector between 2005 and 2009. Of these firms, seven had contracts with the U.S. government. From fiscal years 2005 through 2009, the U.S. government obligated almost $880 million in contracts to these seven firms.[7] U.S. agencies obligated almost 90 percent of these funds for purchases of fuel and petroleum products overseas. Thirteen of the 41 firms listed in our March 2010 report responded to our inquiries regarding their commercial activities in Iran, including two of the seven firms with U.S. government contracts. Since the report was released, four more firms responded, including one firm that noted it had not made a decision about finalizing its commercial activities in Iran.

BACKGROUND

Iran seeks commercial investments to increase its oil and natural gas production, refining capacity, and pipeline and tanker infrastructure.

Iran has the world's third largest oil reserves, or about 140 billion barrels, and produces about 4.2 million barrels per day. However, Iran's oil production has remained virtually flat in recent years and will likely stagnate in the medium term due to insufficient investment, according to the International Monetary Fund. Iran requires increasingly modern and advanced oil recovery technologies to stop natural declines of oil production, but has found advanced technology difficult to import due to international sanctions and high costs.

According to DOE, Iran does not currently have sufficient refining capacity to meet its domestic demand for gasoline. Iran imported approximately 130,000 barrels of gasoline per day in 2009, as well as other refined products such as diesel fuel. Iran's nine refineries are operated by the National Iranian Oil Refining and Distribution Company. With the potential participation of foreign companies, Iran plans to add capacity at eight refineries to fully meet domestic demand for gasoline by 2013 or 2014, according to DOE officials.

Iran has one of the world's largest natural gas reserves, second only to Russia. Iran's domestic consumption of natural gas has increased rapidly over the past 20 years, and development of natural gas resources would better position Iran to meet domestic demand. According to U.S. officials, between 20 and 25 percent of Iran's natural gas is currently reinjected into mature oil fields to enhance oil recovery. Iran plans to expand its development of liquefied natural gas, but this plan requires significant investment from international partners.[8]

Iranian officials have stated that Iran needs large investments in its natural gas infrastructure, including pipelines. In addition, while Iran has over 40 tankers, Iran purchased additional tankers for shipping crude oil in 2009.

FORTY-ONE FOREIGN FIRMS HAD COMMERCIAL ACTIVITY IN IRAN'S OIL, GAS, OR PETROCHEMICAL SECTORS FROM 2005 TO 2009

Based on our review of open source information, we identified 41 foreign firms that had commercial activity in the development of the Iranian oil, gas, and petrochemical sectors from 2005 to 2009. We define commercial activity as having signed an agreement to conduct business, invested capital, or received payment for the provision of goods or services in Iran's energy sector. We did not review the contracts and documents underlying these transactions and did not independently verify these transactions. These firms are listed in table 1. Open source information stated that these firms supported activities throughout Iran that involved the exploration and development of oil and gas, petroleum refining, or the construction of pipelines and tankers for the transport of oil or gas. The firms provide technical expertise, equipment, or funding that enables Iran to increase the productive capacity and profitability of its oil, gas, and petrochemical sectors.

Table 1. Foreign Firms Publicly Reported to Have Commercial Activity in the Iranian Oil, Gas, or Petrochemical Sectors

Firm	Country[a]	Sector
ABB Lummus	Not applicable	Refining, petrochemicals
Amona	Malaysia	Oil exploration and production
Belneftekhim	Belarus	Oil exploration and production
China National Offshore Oil Corporation	China	Natural gas
China National Petroleum Corporation	China	Oil exploration and production, natural gas
Costain Oil, Gas & Process Ltd.	United Kingdom	Natural gas
Daelim	South Korea	Natural gas
Daewoo Shipbuilding & Marine Engineering	South Korea	Oil tankers
Edison	Italy	Oil exploration and production
ENI	Italy	Oil exploration and production
Gazprom	Russia	Oil exploration and production, pipeline
GS	South Korea	Natural gas
Haldor Topsoe	Denmark	Refining
Hinduja	United Kingdom	Oil exploration and production, natural gas
Hyundai Heavy Industries	South Korea	Oil tankers
INA	Croatia	Oil exploration and production, natural gas
Indian Oil Corporation	India	Natural gas
Inpex	Japan	Oil exploration and production
JGC Corporation	Japan	Refining
Lukoil	Russia	Oil exploration and production
LyondelBasell	Netherlands	Petrochemicals
Oil India Ltd.	India	Natural gas
Oil and Natural Gas Corporation	India	Oil exploration and production, natural gas
OMV	Austria	Natural gas
ONGC Videsh Ltd.	India	Natural gas
Petrobras	Brazil	Oil exploration and production
Petrofield	Malaysia	Natural gas
Petroleos de Venezuela S.A.	Venezuela	Natural gas
Petronet LNG	India	Natural gas
PGNiG	Poland	Natural gas
PTT Exploration & Production	Thailand	Natural gas
Repsol	Spain	Natural gas
Royal Dutch Shell	Netherlands	Natural gas
Sinopec	China	Oil exploration and production, refining
SKS Ventures	Malaysia	Natural gas
Snamprogetti	Italy	Pipeline
StatoilHydro	Norway	Oil exploration and production, natural gas
Tecnimont	Italy	Petrochemicals
Total	France	Natural gas
Turkish Petroleum Company	Turkey	Natural gas
Uhde	Germany	Petrochemicals

Source: GAO analysis of open source information.
[a]The country listed is the physical location of the firm.

The 41 firms listed in table 1 represent a minimum of firms with commercial activity in Iran's energy sectors (see GAO-10-515R for details on our methodology). We provided the 41 firms an opportunity to comment on our findings. Thirteen firms responded before we issued the March 2010 report, and confirmed our findings.[9] Four firms responded after we issued the report. An official from Statoil stated that the information in our March 2010 report was accurate.

Tecnimont noted that the contract we described had never entered into force due to a lack of financing. Repsol stated that it had not yet made a final investment decision on the project that we identified. ENI neither confirmed nor denied the information that we reported.

Seven of the Foreign Firms Also Had Contracts with the U.S. Government

From fiscal years 2005 through 2009, the U.S. government obligated almost $880 million in contracts to seven of these 41 firms. U.S. agencies obligated almost 90 percent of these funds for purchases of fuel and petroleum products overseas. The firms are presented in table 2 in order of magnitude of obligations, as reported in FPDS-NG.

Table 2. Firms Reported in Open Sources as Having Both Commercial Activity in the Iranian Energy Sector and U.S. Government Contracts

	U.S. Government obligations					
Firm/country [a]	FY 2005	FY 2006	FY 2007	FY 2008	FY 2009	Total
Repsol/Spain	$40 million	$37 million	$110 million	$81 million	$51 million	$319 million
Total/France	$0	$27 million	$0	$154 million	$131 million	$312 million
Daelim Industrial Co./South Korea	$0	$0	$0	$0	$111 million	$111 million
ENI/Italy	$9 million	$88 million	Less than $100,000	$0	$0	$97 million
PTT Exploration and Production/Thailand	$21 million	$4 million	$6 million	$1 million	$3 million	$35 million
Hyundai Heavy Industries/South Korea	$1 million	$2 million	$1 million	$0	$0	$5 million
GS Engineering and Construction/ South Korea	Less than $100,000	$0	$0	$0	$0	Less than $100,000
Total	$71 million	$158 million	$117 million	$236 million	$296 million	$879 million

Source: GAO analysis of Federal Procurement Data System-Next Generation records and other government records.

Note: Totals may not add due to rounding.

[a] The country listed is the physical location of the firm as reported in open sources.

According to FPDS-NG, the Department of Defense (DOD) obligated funds to

- Repsol of Spain for the purchase of fuel for naval and aviation purposes;
- Total of France for the purchase of fuel, including jet fuel, gasoline, and diesel;
- Daelim Industrial Co. of South Korea for the construction of family housing at a U.S. Army base in South Korea;'0

- ENI of Italy for the purchase of petroleum products;
- PTT Exploration and Production of Thailand for the purchase of jet fuel and other petroleum products;
- Hyundai Heavy Industries of South Korea for the purchase of power transformers;[11] and
- GS Engineering and Construction of South Korea (then known as LG Engineering and Construction) for the construction of office buildings in South Korea.

According to DOD, these firms are qualified to contract with the U.S. government based on reviews of the Excluded Parties Listing System and the Office of Foreign Assets Control Specially Designated Nationals List, maintained by the Departments of State and Treasury. DOD also stated that these contracts are critical to support mission requirements of worldwide military operations.

Mr. Chairman, this concludes my statement. I would be pleased to answer any questions that you or other members may have at this time.

End Notes

[1] See GAO, Firms Reported to Have Commercial Activity in the Iranian Energy Sector and U.S. Government Contracts, GAO-10-639R (Washington, D.C.: May 3, 2010) and Firms Reported in Open Sources as Having Commercial Activity in the Iran's Oil, Gas and Petrochemical Sectors, GAO-10-515R (Washington, DC.: Mar. 23, 2010)

[2] See e.g. Exec. Order 13,059, 62 Fed. Reg. 44,531 (Aug. 19, 1997).

[3] Iran-Libya Sanctions Act of 1996, Pub. L. No. 104-172, § 5, 110 Stat. 1541, 1543 as amended. The act also allows for sanctions against persons providing goods, technology, or services to Iran knowing that such provision would contribute materially to Iran's ability to acquire or develop chemical, biological, or nuclear weapons or related technologies; or acquire or develop destabilizing numbers and types of advanced conventional weapons

[4] Pub. L. No. 104-172, §§ 5-6; Memorandum: Delegation of Responsibilities Under the Iran and Libya Sanctions Act of 1996, 61 Fed. Reg. 64,249 (Nov. 21, 1996). Other sanctions include a denial of Export-Import Bank assistance, a ban on issuing licenses to export controlled technologies to the sanctioned firm, and other sanctions to restrict imports with respect to the sanctioned person in accordance with the International Emergency Economic Powers Act.

[5] Pub. L. No. 104-172, § 9; 61 Fed. Reg. 64,249.

[6] FPDS-NG is the primary governmentwide contracting database. More than 60 government agencies, departments, and other entities submit contract data to FPDS-NG. FPDS-NG can be accessed at https://www.fpds.gov/fpdsng_cms/. Reporting requirements for FPDS-NG are in Federal Acquisition Regulation (FAR) subpart 4.6. FPDS-NG data are described in FAR 4.602.

[7] An obligation is recorded when a government agency enters into a binding agreement to purchase services or goods.

[8] Iran has three major liquefied natural gas (LNG) projects in various stages of development—Iran LNG, Pars LNG, and Persian LNG—all of which are associated with a phase of the South Pars development. The South Pars natural gas field has a 25 phase development scheme spanning 20 years.

[9] See GAO-10-515R for summaries of these firms' comments.

[10] The U.S. Army Corps of Engineers has announced that it has contracted with Daelim Industrial to construct family housing at a U.S. base in South Korea. See http://www.army.mil/-news/2009/08/09/25673-corps-of-engineers-awards-contract-for-new-family-housing-at-usag-humphreys/.

[11] According to FPDS-NG, DOE also obligated funds to Hyundai Heavy Industries of South Korea for the purchase of power transformers.

In: U.S. Led Sanctions on Iran
Editors: Robert K. Figg and Danielle A. Wilson
ISBN: 978-1-62100-414-1

Chapter 4

FIRMS REPORTED TO HAVE COMMERCIAL ACTIVITY IN THE IRANIAN ENERGY SECTOR AND U.S. GOVERNMENT CONTRACTS*

United States Government Accountability Office

May 4, 2010

The Honorable Joseph I. Lieberman
Chairman

The Honorable Susan Collins
Ranking Member
Committee on Homeland Security and Governmental Affairs
United States Senate

The Honorable Jon Kyl
Ranking Member
Subcommittee on Terrorism and Homeland Security Committee on the Judiciary
United States Senate

On March 23, 2010, we issued a report entitled *Firms Reported in Open Sources as Having Commercial Activity in Iran's Oil, Gas, and Petrochemical Sectors*.[1] Based on open sources, we identified 41 foreign firms as having commercial activity in these vital sectors of Iran's economy from 2005 to 2009.[2] As you requested, this report identifies which of the 41 firms in our March 2010 report had contracts with the United States government from fiscal years 2005 to 2009.

Our March 2010 report and this report are intended to support congressional consideration of U.S. sanctions against Iran, including proposed legislation to expand the Iran Sanctions Act (ISA). We did not use ISA criteria or monetary thresholds when identifying

* This is an edited, reformatted and augmented version of the United States Government Accountability Office publication, dated May 4, 2010.

firms and did not attempt to determine whether firms meet the legal criteria for an investment specified in ISA.[3] Under the existing Iran Sanctions Act, persons, including firms, that invest more than $20 million in Iran's energy sector in any 12-month period may be banned from U.S. government procurement.[4] In 1998, the United States made its first and only determination that a firm's investments constituted activity covered by the Iran Sanctions Act. The sanctions were waived because the Secretary of State determined it was in the national interest to do so. The U.S. Senate and House of Representatives have passed separate bills to expand U.S. sanctions against Iran and are now working to resolve differences.[5]

To identify which of the 41 firms listed in our March 2010 report also had U.S. government contracts, we searched the Federal Procurement Data System-Next Generation (FPDS-NG) for fiscal years 2005 through 2009. We first searched in FPDS-NG for firms with identical names and other identifying information as the firms listed in our March 2010 report, and we found seven firms with identical names. We verified that those seven firms were among the firms listed in our March 2010 report. We then corroborated the information in FPDS-NG on the seven firms by obtaining U.S. contracts and other evidence that confirmed the existence of contracts with these firms. Enclosure I provides our scope and methodology for this report and enclosure II lists the 41 firms from our March 2010 report.

We conducted our work from March to April 2010 in accordance with all sections of GAO's Quality Assurance Framework that are relevant to our objective. The framework requires that we plan and perform the engagement to obtain sufficient and appropriate evidence to meet our stated objective and discuss any limitations in our work. We believe that the information and data obtained, and the analysis conducted, provide a reasonable basis for any findings and conclusions.

Seven Firms with Commercial Activity in the Iranian Energy Sector Also Had Contracts with the U.S. Government

From fiscal years 2005 through 2009, the U.S. government obligated almost $880 million in contracts to seven of the 41 firms identified in our March 2010 report.[6] U.S. agencies obligated almost 90 percent of these funds for purchases of fuel and petroleum products overseas. The firms are presented in table 1 in order of magnitude of obligations, as reported in FPDS-NG.

According to FPDS-NG, the Department of Defense (DOD) obligated funds to

- Repsol of Spain for the purchase of fuel for naval and aviation purposes;
- Total of France for the purchase of fuel, including jet fuel, gasoline, and diesel;
- Daelim Industrial Co. of South Korea for the construction of family housing at a U.S. Army base in South Korea;[7]
- ENI of Italy for the purchase of petroleum products;
- PTT Exploration and Production of Thailand for the purchase of jet fuel and other petroleum products;
- Hyundai Heavy Industries of South Korea for the purchase of power transformers;[8] and

- GS Engineering and Construction of South Korea (then known as LG Engineering and Construction) for the construction of office buildings in South Korea.

Table 1. Firms Reported in Open Sources as Having Commercial Activity in the Iranian Energy Sector and Reported to Have U.S. Government Contracts

Firm/country [a]	U.S. Government obligations [b]					
	FY 2005	FY 2006	FY 2007	FY 2008	FY 2009	Total
Repsol/Spain	$40 million	$37 million	$110 million	$81 million	$51 million	$319 million
Total/France	$0	$27 million	$0	$154 million	$131 million	$312 million
Daelim Industrial Co./South Korea	$0	$0	$0	$0	$111 million	$111 million
ENI/Italy	$9 million	$88 million	Less than $100,000	$0	$0	$97 million
PTT Exploration and Production/Thailand	$21 million	$4 million	$6 million	$1 million	$3 million	$35 million
Hyundai Heavy Industries/South Korea	$1 million	$2 million	$1 million	$0	$0	$5 million
GS Engineering and Construction/South Korea	Less than $100,000	$0	$0	$0	$0	Less than $100,000
Total	$71 million	$158 million	$117 million	$236 million	$296 million	$879 million

Source: GAO analysis of Federal Procurement Data System-Next Generation records and other government records.

Note: Totals may not add due to rounding.

[a] The country listed is the physical location of the firm as reported in open sources.

[b] We confirmed that each of these firms had U.S. government contracts by obtaining official documents and statements that confirmed the existence of contracts with these firms. Of the obligation amounts reported in the table, we tested 8 instances against U.S. government contractual documents and official statements. We determined the amounts were consistent with the information reported in FPDS-NG.

Agency Comments

We provided the Departments of State and Defense a draft of this report for comment. The Department of State provided technical suggestions which we have incorporated as appropriate.

DOD provided oral comments on the draft. DOD stated that it contracts for services, supplies, and construction worldwide in support of military operations. According to DOD, these contracts are critical to meeting mission requirements; however, contracting overseas is compounded by a limited number of contractors who are able to perform where DOD requires support. DOD stated it must meet Federal Acquisition Regulation requirements to evaluate the qualifications of a contractor. A DOD review of current and active records in the Excluded Parties Listing System and the Office of Foreign Assets Control Specialty Designated Nationals List, operated by the Departments of State and Treasury, did not find any contractors listed in this report. According to DOD, the seven firms listed in this report are qualified to contract with the federal government and DOD and are not excluded from such contracts.

As agreed with your offices, unless you publicly announce the contents of this report earlier, we plan no further distribution until 30 days from the report date. At that time, we will send copies of the report to interested committees, the Secretary of State, and the Secretary of Defense. In addition, the report will be available at no charge on the GAO Web site at http://www.gao.gov.

If you or your staffs have any questions about this report, please contact me at 202-512-8979 or christoffj@gao.gov. Major contributors to this report include Tetsuo Miyabara (Assistant Director), JoAnna Berry, Colleen Candrl, Jon Fremont, Julia Kennon, Lauren Membreño, and Pierre Toureille. Technical support was provided by Martin De Alteriis, Grace Lui, Jodi Munson, and Joseph Carney.

Sincerely,
Joseph A. Christoff
Director, International Affairs and Trade

ENCLOSURE I. SCOPE AND METHODOLOGY

To determine the extent to which firms identified in open sources as having commercial activity in Iran's energy sector also have contracts with the U.S. government, we searched the Federal Procurement Data System-Next Generation (FPDS-NG) for references to the 41 firms identified in our March 2010 report. As we described in that report, each of these 41 firms had (1) been cited in at least three standard industry publications as having commercial activity in a specific project, or (2) provided information on its corporate web site about its involvement in a specific project *and* had been cited as having been involved in the same project by at least one standard industry publication.[9] We chose FPDS-NG to determine if any of these 41 firms also had contracts with the U.S. government because FPDS-NG has served as the primary governmentwide contracting database since 1978. Congress, executive branch agencies, and the public rely on FPDS-NG for a broad range of data on agency contracting actions, procurement, and spending.[10] The Office of Management and Budget established FPDS-NG, and the U.S. General Services Administration administers the system.[11] More than 60 government departments, agencies, and other entities submit contract data to FPDS-NG . FPDS-NG contains data on obligations, which are recorded when a government agency enters into a contract to purchase services or goods.

We searched the FPDS-NG archives from fiscal years 2005 through 2009 using search terms that would select any record with the same firm name as identified in our March 2010 report. After matching firms from our March 2010 list with records in FPDS-NG, we obtained the Data Universal Numbering System (DUNS) numbers for the firms determined to be identical matches, and searched FPDS-NG for these DUNS numbers.[12] With certain exceptions, all firms that do business with U.S. agencies are required by the U.S. government to register with the U.S. government central contractor registration (CCR) and obtain a unique DUNS number. We matched all of the data in table 1 to individual firms' DUNS numbers.

We took steps to corroborate key FPDS-NG information by obtaining U.S. government documents and public statements that confirmed that these seven firms have U.S. contracts. To do so, we searched (1) the Department of Defense's Electronic Document Access system[13] to locate copies of relevant contract documents and (2) the U.S. Army Corps of Engineers website for announcements of contracts.

Our searches for U.S. contracts only covered firms that we had identified as being directly involved in commercial activity in the Iranian energy sector. Therefore we included a parent firm or subsidiary only if that firm had also been reported in open sources as having commercial activity in the Iranian energy sector. For example, in our March 2010 report, we included two parent firms and two of their subsidiaries because all were reported in open sources as having commercial activity in the Iranian energy sector.

Enclosure II. Foreign Firms Publicly Reported to Have Commercial Activity in the Iranian Oil, Gas, or Petrochemical Sectors

This table provides information from our March 2010 report. We did not attempt to determine if these firms meet the legal criteria specified in the Iran Sanctions Act.

Table 2. Foreign Firms Publicly Reported to Have Commercial Activity in the Iranian Oil, Gas, or Petrochemical Sectors

Firm	Country[a]	Sector
ABB Lummus	Not applicable	Refining, petrochemicals
Amona	Malaysia	Oil exploration and production
Belneftekhim	Belarus	Oil exploration and production
China National Offshore Oil Corporation	China	Natural gas
China National Petroleum Corporation	China	Oil exploration and production, natural gas
Costain Oil, Gas & Process Ltd.	United Kingdom	Natural gas
Daelim	South Korea	Natural gas
Daewoo Shipbuilding & Marine Engineering	South Korea	Oil tankers
Edison	Italy	Oil exploration and production
ENI	Italy	Oil exploration and production
Gazprom	Russia	Oil exploration and production, pipeline
GS	South Korea	Natural gas
Haldor Topsoe	Denmark	Refining
Hinduja	United Kingdom	Oil exploration and production, natural gas
Hyundai Heavy Industries	South Korea	Oil tankers
INA	Croatia	Oil exploration and production, natural gas
Indian Oil Corporation	India	Natural gas
Inpex	Japan	Oil exploration and production
JGC Corporation	Japan	Refining

Table 2. (Continued)

Firm	Country[a]	Sector
Lukoil	Russia	Oil exploration and production
LyondelBasell	Netherlands	Petrochemicals
Oil India Ltd.	India	Natural gas
Oil and Natural Gas Corporation	India	Oil exploration and production, natural gas
OMV	Austria	Natural gas
ONGC Videsh Ltd.	India	Natural gas
Petrobras	Brazil	Oil exploration and production
Petrofield	Malaysia	Natural gas
Petroleos de Venezuela S.A.	Venezuela	Natural gas
Petronet LNG	India	Natural gas
PGNiG	Poland	Natural gas
PTT Exploration & Production	Thailand	Natural gas
Repsol	Spain	Natural gas
Royal Dutch Shell	Netherlands	Natural gas
Sinopec	China	Oil exploration and production, refining
SKS Ventures	Malaysia	Natural gas
Snamprogetti	Italy	Pipeline
StatoilHydro	Norway	Oil exploration and production, natural gas
Tecnimont	Italy	Petrochemicals
Total	France	Natural gas
Turkish Petroleum Company	Turkey	Natural gas
Uhde	Germany	Petrochemicals

Source: GAO analysis of open source information.

[a] The country listed is the physical location of the firm as reported in open sources.

(320763)

End Notes

[1] GAO, Firms Reported in Open Sources as Having Commercial Activity in Iran's Oil, Gas, and Petrochemical Sectors, GAO-10-515R (Washington, D.C.: Mar 23, 2010).

[2] Iran's energy industry is vital to its economy and government. However, Iran has not reached peak crude oil production levels since 1978, does not produce sufficient natural gas for domestic use, and lacks the refining capacity to meet domestic demand for gasoline, according to the Department of Energy (DOE) and IHS Global Insight. Accordingly, Iran is seeking the participation of foreign firms in providing financing and technical assistance in numerous oil, gas, and petrochemical projects, according to DOE.

[3] The Secretary of State is responsible for making such determinations. Our complete methodology for identifying the 41 firms is described in GAO-10-515R.

[4] Iran-Libya Sanctions Act of 1996, Pub. L. No. 104-172, § 5, 110 Stat. 1541, 1543 as amended. Other sanctions include a denial of Export-Import Bank assistance, a ban on issuing licenses to export controlled technologies to the sanctioned firm, and other sanctions that fall under the powers of the International Emergency Economic Powers Act.

[5] The House of Representatives passed H.R. 2194, the Iran Refined Petroleum Sanctions Act of 2009, on December 15, 2009. On March 11, 2010, the Senate amended and passed H.R. 2194, renaming it the Comprehensive Iran Sanctions, Accountability, and Divestment Act of 2009. The Senate also asked for a conference on the bill on March 11, 2010.

[6] An obligation is recorded when a government agency enters into a binding agreement to purchase services or goods.

[7] The U.S. Army Corps of Engineers has announced that it has contracted with Daelim Industrial to construct family housing at a U.S. base in South Korea. See http://www.army.mil/-news/2009/08/09/25673-corps-of-engineers-awards-contract-for-new-family-housing-at-usag-humphreys/.

[8] According to FPDS-NG, the Department of Energy also obligated funds to Hyundai Heavy Industries of South Korea for the purchase of power transformers.

[9] Our complete methodology for identifying these 41 firms is described in GAO, Firms Reported in Open Sources as Having Commercial Activity in Iran's Oil, Gas, and Petrochemical Sectors, GAO-10-515R (Washington, D.C.: Mar 23, 2010). As noted in GAO-10-515R, we did not attempt to determine whether the listed firms meet the legal criteria for an investment specified in the Iran Sanctions Act. The Secretary of State is responsible for making such determinations.

[10] FPDS-NG can be accessed at https://www.fpds.gov/fpdsng_cms/. Reporting requirements for FPDS-NG are in Federal Acquisition Regulation (FAR) subpart 4.6, FPDS-NG data are described in FAR 4.602.

[11] For more information on FPDS-NG and other federal procurement data systems, see GAO, Federal Contracting: Observations on the Government's Contracting Data Systems, GAO-09-1032T (Washington, D.C.: Sept. 29, 2009).

[12] Data Universal Numbering System (DUNS) numbers are 9-digit identifying numbers obtained by firms through Dun and Bradstreet to uniquely identify a firm. Dun and Bradstreet is a leading source of commercial information, and maintains a commercial database with more than 140 million business records. U.S. vendors must be registered in the U.S. Central Contract Registry prior to the award of a U.S. government contract and a firm must have a DUNS number to register. We also compared the street addresses of the firms listed in our March 2010 report with street addresses listed in the U.S. government central contractor registration (CCR) data system (https://www.bpn.gov/ccr/).

[13] The Electronic Document Access system is a Department of Defense online system designed to provide acquisition-related information.

In: U.S. Led Sanctions on Iran
Editors: Robert K. Figg and Danielle A. Wilson

ISBN: 978-1-62100-414-1

Chapter 5

FIRMS REPORTED IN OPEN SOURCES AS HAVING COMMERCIAL ACTIVITY IN IRAN'S OIL, GAS, AND PETROCHEMICAL SECTORS*

United States Government Accountability Office

The Honorable Joseph I. Lieberman
Chairman
Committee on Homeland Security and Governmental Affairs
United States Senate

The Honorable Jon Kyl
Ranking Member
Subcommittee on Terrorism and Homeland Security
Committee on the Judiciary
United States Senate

Iran's oil and gas industry is vital to its economy and government. Oil export revenues have accounted for more than 24 percent of Iran's gross domestic product and between 50 and 76 percent of the Iranian government's revenues in recent years.[1] Iran has the world's third largest oil reserves and second largest gas reserves, according to the Congressional Research Service (CRS), and is the world's fourth largest producer of crude oil, according to the Central Intelligence Agency (CIA) World Factbook. [2] However, Iran has not reached peak crude oil production levels since 1978, does not produce sufficient natural gas for domestic use, and lacks the refining capacity to meet domestic demand for gasoline, according to the Department of Energy (DOE) and IHS Global Insight.[3] IHS Global Insight reports that Iran's priorities for the next five years are to (1) raise oil production and exports as much as possible, (2) increase natural gas production for domestic use, and (3) expand refining capacity if financially and technically possible. CRS reported that the Deputy Minister of the

---

* This is an edited, reformatted and augmented version of the United States Government Accountability Office publication, dated March 23, 2010.

National Iranian Oil Company said in November 2008 that Iran would need about $145 billion in new investment over the next 10 years to build a thriving energy sector. Accordingly, Iran is seeking the participation of foreign firms in providing financing and technical assistance in numerous oil, gas, and petrochemical projects, according to DOE. Although Iran prohibits non-Iranian firms from obtaining an ownership interest by investing in oil and gas fields, Iran allows them to enter into "buy-back" arrangements in which the foreign firms may receive entitlements to oil or gas for a limited time in exchange for the funds they expend on the project, according to DOE.[4]

U.S. law restricts U.S. firms from investing in Iran's energy sector through a variety of sanctions administered by the Department of the Treasury to discourage Iran from supporting terrorism and developing nuclear weapons.[5] In addition, the Iran Sanctions Act, as amended, provides for sanctions against persons, including foreign firms, who invest more than $20 million in Iran's energy sector in any 12-month period.[6] For example, the Act allows the President, who delegated authority under the Act to the Secretary of State, to restrict loans to sanctioned firms and ban them from U.S. government procurement.[7] The Secretary of State may waive the sanctions if the Secretary determines that it is important to the national interests of the United States to do so.[8] For example, in 1998, the Secretary of State waived sanctions against a consortium of foreign firms due, in part, to the high level of cooperation with the European Union on counterproliferation and counterterrorism efforts involving Iran.[9] See enclosure IV for more on the Iran Sanctions Act.

Our December 2007 report on Iran sanctions included a list of foreign firms potentially investing in Iran's energy sector from 2003 to 2007.[10] In 2009, a majority of members of Congress sponsored the Iran Refined Petroleum Sanctions Act of 2009, which would impose sanctions against firms that export gasoline and other refined petroleum products to Iran.[11] As of March 2010, Congress was considering this proposed legislation. This correspondence (1) provides a list of foreign firms reported in open sources as engaging in commercial activity in Iran's oil, gas, or petrochemical sectors from 2005 to 2009 and (2) provides information about these sectors.[12] We define commercial activity as having signed an agreement to conduct business, invested capital, or received payment for the provision of goods or services in the Iranian oil, gas, or petrochemical sectors. We did not review the contracts and documents underlying these transactions and did not independently verify these transactions. We did not attempt to determine whether the firms in this list meet the legal criteria for an investment specified in the Iran Sanctions Act. The Secretary of State is responsible for making such determinations.

To accomplish our objectives, we reviewed open source information, including industry standard trade publications and corporate statements. We listed a firm as having commercial activity in Iran's oil, gas, or petrochemical sectors if three reputable industry publications or the firm's corporate statements reported the firm to have signed an agreement to conduct business; invested capital; or received payment for providing goods or services in connection with a specific Iranian oil, gas, or petrochemical project. We provided the firms on our list an opportunity to comment on the information in our table. While we obtained information from DOE, the Department of State, and U.S. intelligence agencies, we used only open source data for this report. See enclosure I for a full description of our scope and methodology.

We conducted our work from September 2009 to March 2010 in accordance with all sections of GAO's Quality Assurance Framework that are relevant to our objective. The framework requires that we plan and perform the engagement to obtain sufficient and appropriate evidence to meet our stated objective and discuss any limitations in our work.

FORTY-ONE FOREIGN FIRMS HAD COMMERCIAL ACTIVITY IN IRAN'S OIL, GAS, OR PETROCHEMICAL SECTORS FROM 2005 TO 2009, ACCORDING TO OPEN SOURCE INFORMATION

Based on our review of open source information, we identified 41 foreign firms that had commercial activity in the development of the Iranian oil, gas, and petrochemical sectors from 2005 to 2009. These firms are listed in table 1. Open source information stated that these firms supported activities throughout Iran that involved the exploration and development of oil and gas, petroleum refining, or petrochemicals, including the construction of pipelines and tankers for the transport of oil or gas. (See figure 1 for a map of Iranian oil, gas, and petrochemical activities). According to the open source information, the firms provide technical expertise, equipment, or funding that enables Iran to increase the productive capacity and profitability of its oil, gas, and petrochemical sectors. See enclosure II for a more detailed description of the firms' reported activities in Iran, and see enclosure III for a glossary of terms used in this report.

The following table presents information gathered from reputable industry standard publications and firms' public statements. We did not attempt to determine whether the firms in this list meet the legal criteria specified in the Iran Sanctions Act.

FOREIGN FIRMS ARE REPORTEDLY SUPPORTING MULTIPLE IRANIAN OIL, GAS, OR PETROCHEMICAL SECTOR ACTIVITIES

According to open sources, foreign firms are supporting Iranian activities in oil and gas exploration and production, refining, petrochemicals, and pipelines and tankers. While some firms are reported to be involved in multiple activities, most were involved in a single activity. Using open source information, we identified 14 firms as involved in exploration and production of crude oil resources, 4 firms in expanding refining capacity, 23 firms in the development of natural gas resources, 4 firms in the production of petrochemicals, and 4 firms in oil and gas pipelines and tankers. Open source information reported that 8 firms were involved in multiple activities (such as natural gas and petrochemicals), and these firms are counted in each of the activity descriptions.

Oil Exploration and Production

Using open source information, we identified 14 foreign firms as having commercial activity in Iran's crude oil exploration and production efforts.

Table 1. Foreign Firms' Publicly Reported to Have Commercial Activity in the Iranian Oil, Gas, or Petrochemical Sectors

Firm	Country [a]	Sector
ABB Lummus	Not applicable [b]	Refining, petrochemicals
Amona	Malaysia	Oil exploration and production
Belneftekhim	Belarus	Oil exploration and production
China National Offshore Oil Corporation	China	Natural gas
China National Petroleum Corporation	China	Oil exploration and production, natural gas
Costain Oil, Gas & Process Ltd.	United Kingdom	Natural gas
Daelim	South Korea	Natural gas
Daewoo Shipbuilding & Marine Engineering	South Korea	Oil tankers
Edison	Italy	Oil exploration and production
ENI	Italy	Oil exploration and production
Gazprom	Russia	Oil exploration and production, pipeline
GS	South Korea	Natural gas
Haldor Topsoe	Denmark	Refining
Hinduja	United Kingdom	Oil exploration and production, natural gas
Hyundai Heavy Industries	South Korea	Oil tankers
INA	Croatia	Oil exploration and production, natural gas
Indian Oil Corporation	India	Natural gas
Inpex	Japan	Oil exploration and production
JGC Corporation	Japan	Refining
Lukoil	Russia	Oil exploration and production
LyondelBasell	Netherlands	Petrochemicals
Oil India Ltd.	India	Natural gas
Oil and Natural Gas Corporation	India	Oil exploration and production, natural gas
OMV	Austria	Natural gas
ONGC Videsh Ltd.	India	Natural gas
Petrobras	Brazil	Oil exploration and production
Petrofield	Malaysia	Natural gas
Petroleos de Venezuela S.A.	Venezuela	Natural gas
Petronet LNG	India	Natural gas
PGNiG	Poland	Natural gas
PTT Exploration & Production	Thailand	Natural gas
Repsol	Spain	Natural gas
Royal Dutch Shell	Netherlands	Natural gas
Sinopec	China	Oil exploration and production, refining
SKS Ventures	Malaysia	Natural gas
Snamprogetti	Italy	Pipeline
StatoilHydro	Norway	Oil exploration and production, natural gas
Tecnimont	Italy	Petrochemicals

Firm	Country [a]	Sector
Total	France	Natural gas
Turkish Petroleum Company	Turkey	Natural gas
Uhde	Germany	Petrochemicals

Source: GAO analysis of open source information.

[a] The country listed is the physical location of the firm as reported in open sources.

[b] ABB Lummus no longer exists as a firm. ABB of Switzerland sold the Lummus Group in 2007 to Chicago Bridge and Iron Company (CB&I) of the United States. ABB and CB&I told us they no longer have commercial activity in Iran.

Source: GAO analysis of U.S. Department of Energy data.

Figure 1. Map of Iranian Oil, Gas, and Petrochemical Activities.

For example, the China National Petroleum Corporation is reported to be financing 90 percent of the development of the North Azadegan oil field, in an agreement estimated at more than $2 billion. As of January 2010, Iran faces a funding shortage and is reportedly prioritizing foreign investment in oil exploration and development efforts at the expense of downstream sectors, according to IHS Global Insight. Iran particularly needs technological assistance to increase the level of oil production in fields where oil reserves have declined over time, according to DOE. According to the IMF, Iran's oil production has remained virtually flat in recent years and will likely stagnate in the medium term due to insufficient investment. Iran requires increasingly modern and advanced enhanced oil recovery technologies in order to stop natural declines of oil production, but has found advanced technology difficult to import due to international sanctions and high costs. As a result, Iran depends on older methods to maintain oil recovery from its mature oil fields, such as injecting massive quantities of natural gas into oil reservoirs, according to DOE and IHS Global Insight. Due to the lack of investment, the natural decline in oil reserves, and other factors, Iran has been unable to continue producing oil at its peak level of over 5 million barrels per day since 1978.[13]

Refining Capacity

Using open source information, we identified 4 firms that are involved in expanding and upgrading the refining capacity of Iran. For example, JGC Corporation of Japan is reported to be assisting in the expansion of the Arak refinery, in an agreement estimated at $25 million. According to DOE, Iran does not currently have sufficient refining capacity to meet its domestic demand for gasoline. In 2007 and 2008, Iranian gasoline production averaged less than 300,000 barrels per day, while daily domestic gasoline consumption averaged approximately 400,000 barrels. Although Iran imposed gasoline rationing in 2007, it imported approximately 130,000 barrels of gasoline per day in 2009, as well as other refined products such as diesel fuel. Iran's nine refineries are operated by the National Iranian Oil Refining and Distribution Company (NIORDC), according to DOE. With the potential participation of foreign companies, Iran plans to add capacity at 8 refineries to fully meet domestic demand for gasoline by 2013 or 2014, according to CRS and DOE officials. However, Iran's plans for doing so may fall behind schedule because it has recently placed a higher priority on finding and developing crude oil to address funding shortages, according to IHS Global Insight.

Natural Gas

Using open source information, we identified 23 firms as having commercial activity in the development of Iran's natural gas resources. For example, Hinduja of the United Kingdom and Oil and Natural Gas Corporation of India reportedly signed an agreement in December 2009 for a 40 percent stake in developing phase 12 of Iran's massive South Pars offshore gas field, a project estimated to cost $7.5 billion. Iran's domestic consumption of natural gas has increased rapidly over the past 20 years, and development of natural gas resources would better position Iran to meet domestic demand. According to U.S. officials, between 20 and 25 percent of Iran's natural gas is currently reinjected into mature oil fields to enhance oil recovery. According to IHS Global Insight, Iran has failed to develop its natural gas production quickly enough and is only preventing shortages by importing natural gas from other countries, such as Turkmenistan. Iran also plans to expand its development of liquefied natural gas (LNG), but this plan requires significant investment from international partners and has become less of a priority as Iran has recently focused limited funds on oil exploration and production projects. However, Iran continues to have three major LNG projects in various stages of development—Iran LNG, Pars LNG, and Persian LNG—all of which are associated with a phase of the South Pars development.[14]

Petrochemicals

Using open source information, we identified 4 firms as involved in the production of petrochemicals. For example, LyondelBasell of the Netherlands is reported to be licensing technology for a petrochemical plant that is expected to increase capacity by 300,000 metric tons per year. The main raw materials used in petrochemical production are derived from oil and natural gas, according to

DOE. Natural gas and other products of the refining process are shipped to chemical plants, where they are used to manufacture more complex petrochemicals and plastics. Petrochemical products include ethylene, propylene, benzene, and similar nonfuel products, such as asphalt, road oil, lubricants, solvents, and wax. According to *Oil and Gas Journal*, expanding petrochemical production allows a country with large oil and natural gas resources to use them more profitably.

Pipelines and Tankers

Using open source information, we identified 4 firms as having commercial activity in Iran's oil and gas pipelines and tankers. For example, in 2009, Daewoo Shipbuilding and Marine Engineering of South Korea reportedly delivered crude oil tanker ships to Iran, as part of a contract valued at $384 million. Iranian officials have stated that Iran needs large investments in its natural gas infrastructure, including pipelines. In addition, while Iran has over 40 tankers, Iran recently purchased additional tankers for shipping crude oil. The total capacity of Iran's tankers is 9.56 million deadweight tons (for a total capacity of 70 million barrels, or about 2.4 percent of the world total oil tanker capacity).

Agency Comments

We provided a draft report to the Department of State and Department of Energy for their review. The agencies provided technical comments which were incorporated into the report.

As agreed with your offices, unless you publicly announce the contents of this report earlier, we plan no further distribution until 30 days from the report date. At that time, we will send copies to interested committees, the Secretary of State, and the Secretary of Energy. In addition, the report will be available at no charge on the GAO Web site at http:// www.gao.gov.

If you or your staffs have any questions about this report, please contact me at 202-512-8979 or christoffj@gao.gov. Contact points for our Offices of Congressional Relations and Public Affairs may be found on the last page of this report. Major contributors to this report include Tetsuo Miyabara (Assistant Director), JoAnna Berry, Colleen Candrl, Jon Fremont, Phillip Farah, Lauren Membreño, and Pierre Toureille. Technical support was provided by Martin De Alteriis, Grace Lui, Rebekah Boone, and Patrick Breiding.

Sincerely,

Joseph A. Christoff
Director, International Affairs and Trade

ENCLOSURE I. SCOPE AND METHODOLOGY

To develop this report, we analyzed open source information that was determined to be credible and comprehensive by information specialists and an energy expert within GAO. Open source information data is overt, publicly available information, as opposed to covert or classified sources. Open source information is a key component of traditional intelligence and information-gathering agencies, such as the Central Intelligence Agency. Open source information can provide a very broad range of useful data for analysis, but the validity of an analysis can be put at risk if it relies on open sources that contain inaccurate, imprecise, incomplete, or otherwise faulty information. We took a series of steps to mitigate this risk in developing our analysis.

First, we relied only on government reports and information, energy industry trade publications from around the world, corporate web site information, and professional trade association analysis. We obtained reports and information from the Department of Energy (DOE), the Congressional Research Service (CRS), other U.S. government agencies, the International Monetary Fund, and the Organization of Petroleum Exporting Countries (OPEC). We searched information from approximately 200 industry trade publications from January 2005 to December 2009, including *Oil and Gas Journal, Oil and Gas News, Platt's Publications, Petroleum Economist, Energy Compass,* and *World Refining & Fuels Today*. We excluded sources deemed insufficiently reliable, such as newspaper reports, newswires, and direct news releases from the Iranian government. We searched company web sites for press releases and corporate statements that made their activities in Iran public, or corrected information that had been publicly reported. In addition, we interviewed officials from the Department of Energy, the Department of State, and U.S. intelligence agencies.

Second, we required multiple corroborating sources of information for every entry in our list of firms reported to have commercial activity in Iran's oil, gas, and petrochemical sectors (see tables 1 and 2). We collected and reviewed thousands of articles; extracted relevant information about firms involved in Iran; organized and analyzed the information using data-analysis software designed to aid in processing unstructured data from multiple sources; and developed a final listing based on an evidentiary threshold established through consistently-applied decision rules. We generated a preliminary listing of firms reported to have commercial activity in Iran's oil, gas, or petrochemical sectors. We defined commercial activity as having signed an agreement to conduct business, invested capital, or received payment for the provision of goods or services in the Iranian oil, gas, or petrochemicals sectors. To generate the preliminary listing, we analyzed information in *Oil and Gas Journal's WorldWide Construction Update* reports from 2005 through 2009. This publication conducts a global survey of ongoing and planned oil and gas contractors and firms working in sectors such as pipelines, refining, and engineering, and is greatly trusted and utilized by other U.S. government agencies and those familiar with the international oil industry. We verified the survey methodology with *Oil and Gas Journal*'s Survey Editor and found it was sufficiently reliable for our purposes. We then began to confirm these firms' commercial activity in Iran by conducting searches in approximately 200 industry trade publications between January 2005 and December 2009. The trade publications were compiled by Nexis and include publications where more than 60 percent of the stories pertain to the oil industry.

This generated several thousand additional articles listing firms with potential commercial activity in Iran. To expand the scope of our searches, we searched our sources for specific firms named in U.S. government reports as investors in Iran's oil, gas, or petrochemical sectors. The U.S. government reports were from DOE, CRS, and other government agencies. Finally, we reviewed the source information and extracted details about the firm and their projects in Iran, such as the purpose of the projects, the amount of the firm's commercial activity, and the projects' status. These details were systematically organized and tracked using software designed to synthesize large quantities of textual information.

To determine whether the preliminary listing reflected sufficient evidence that a firm had commercial activity in Iran, a team of analysts reviewed the list and confirmed that one of the following criteria had been met: (1) at least three standard industry publications cited the firm as having commercial activity in a specific project, or (2) the firm provided information on its corporate web site about its involvement in a specific project *and* the firm's involvement in the specific project was also cited by at least one standard industry publication. If not all analysts were completely satisfied that these criteria were met, the firm was not included in our listing. Like all GAO products, our evidence also had to convince independent GAO fact-checkers—who confirmed that the appropriate criteria had been met for all firms—before it could be included in our final listing. Our list, therefore, represents a minimum of firms with commercial activity in Iran's oil, gas, or petrochemical sectors.

After confirming that a firm had commercial activity in a specific project in Iran, we obtained additional information presented in the table—including the firm's commercial activity and the project's status—from the industry standard publications. When reports varied about certain details of a firm's project, we presented the information reported in the most recent source available. Where information was not available on the value of a specific firm's commercial activity, we reviewed the relevant sources to determine the total value of the project in which the firm was involved. In some cases, specific information was not reported and is reflected as such in the tables.

Finally, analysts fluent in the appropriate language contacted the firms directly by telephone in order to introduce GAO, explain our project, and obtain an appropriate point of contact within the firm to officially comment on the reported information. Beginning January 14, 2010, we e-mailed the firms a letter containing information from enclosure II concerning the firms' reported activities, giving each firm an opportunity to comment. As of March 22, 2010, 13 of the firms responded and we have incorporated these responses into enclosure II.

Enclosure II. Publicly Reported Commercial Activity of Foreign Firms in the Iranian Oil, Gas, or Petrochemical Sectors

The following table presents information gathered and organized from reputable industry standard publications and firms' public statements. The details and terminology presented in the table are as reported in the original sources. See enclosure III for a glossary of terms presented in this table. We provided all firms with an opportunity to comment on the information found in open sources. We did not attempt to determine whether the firms in this list meet the legal criteria specified in the Iran Sanctions Act.

Table 2. Foreign Firms Publicly Reported Commercial Activity in Iran and Firms' Comments Regarding Their Activity

Firm/country[a]	Firm activity	Status	Commercial activity	Firm comment
ABB Lummus / Not applicable[b]	Catalytic cracker in a refining expansion in	Expected completion 2009-2010.	Total project to expand refinery	ABB and Chicago Bridge and Iron Company (CB&I)
Amona/ Malaysia	Rehabilitation of the Resalat oil field in the Lavan area.Drilling 30 wells and building a processing plant, to increase output to 47,000 bbl/d.	Expected completion September 2011.	Project valued at $1.53 billion.	Contacted on February 17, 2010; no response as of March 22, 2010.
Belneftekhim/ Belarus	Oil production in Jofeir field, increasing production by 40,000 bbl/d.	Talks under way to produce oil as of June 2009.	Two-year contract signed in 2007 valued at $450 million.	Contacted on February 18, 2010; no response as of March 22, 2010.
China National Offshore Oil Corporation (CNOOC)/ China	Development of natural gas field and construction of liquefied natural gas (LNG) plant.	Initial agreement reached 2006- 2007; final agreement signed 2009; expected completion in 2015.	Project valued at $16 billion. CNOOC to receive 50% share of LNG product.	Contacted on February 19, 2010; no response as of March 22, 2010.
China National Petroleum Corporation (CNPC)/ China	Oil exploration and development in Masjed-i-Suleiman oil field. Development of the North Azadegan oil field. LNG project in South Pars phase 11.	Agreement approved and drilling started in 2007. Contract signed in January 2009. Contract signed June 2009.	CNPC has a 75% holding in project. Providing 90% of the financing for Azadegan under a buy-back contract, a more than $2 billion investment. 12.5% share of project valued at more than $13 billion.	Contacted on February 19, 2010; no response as of March 22, 2010.
Costain Oil, Gas & Process Ltd./ United Kingdom	Gas refinery/processing plant at Bid Boland II.	Expected completion 2009.	Part of consortium whose contract is valued at $1.7 billion.	Contacted on January 14, 2010; no response as of March 22, 2010.
Daelim/ South Korea	Construction of liquid storage tanks for Iran LNG project that will be fed by phase 12 of South Pars gas field.	Expected completion by January 2011.	Total cost of Iran LNG project is $5 billion, which includes other components.	Confirmed role in project is an engineering and procurement contractor, and the value of their work is $162 million.
Daewoo Shipbuilding and Marine Engineering/ South Korea	Construction of crude oil tanker ships.	Delivery was scheduled for 2009, as of 2005.	Contract for $384 million. Total cost of Iranian tanker building program estimated at $2.4 billion.	Confirmed delivery of tanker ships in August 2009, at an estimated contract cost of $384 million. No other sales planned.
Edison/ Italy	Oil exploration in offshore Dayyer block in the Persian Gulf.	In 2009, signed contract for four- year exploration period.	Four-year contract valued at around $44 million.	Noted the exploration contract was signed on January 8, 2008 and not in 2009.
ENI/Italy	Development and operation of first and	Signed 5.5 year buy-back contract in 2001;	2001 contract worth $1 billion and 60%	Contacted on February 19, 2010; no response as of March

Firm/country[a]	Firm activity	Status	Commercial activity	Firm comment
Gazprom/ Russia	Construction of new gas pipeline from Iran to Armenia. Exploration and development of Azar oil fields of Anaran block; field expected to produce up to 65,000 bbl/d when fully developed. Possible exploration and development of Azadegan oil field.	Pipeline inaugurated May 2009. Memorandum of Understanding signed in November 2009. General cooperation agreement between Iran and Gazprom signed in July 2008. Talks continuing as of July 2009.	Project valued at $120 million, with Gazprom's share at 45%. Not reported. Not reported.	Contacted on February 11, 2010; no response as of March 22, 2010.
GS/South Korea	Gas sweetening facility in Phases 6-8 of the South Pars gas field. Development of South Pars phases 9 and 10, which is expected to produce 50 million cubic meters per day of natural gas.	Agreement signed October 2009. Expected completion in March 2009.	Value of contract is $1.24 billion. $1.6 billion development contract with GS to lead consortium; project valued at $4 billion.	Contacted on February 11 and 19, 2010; no response as of March 22, 2010.
Haldor Topsoe/ Denmark	Licensor of a hydrotreater for refinery in Esfahan.	Completed in 2009.	Not reported.	Confirmed activity. Noted expected completion of activity is 2013 to 2014.
Hinduja/ United Kingdom	Development of natural gas field in South Pars phase 12. Project to convert natural gas into LNG for export. Development of the Azadegan oil field.	Agreement signed in December 2009. Agreement signed in December 2009. Company involvement reported in 2008 and 2009.	Along with India's ONGC, 40% stake in project, estimated to cost $7.5 billion to develop. Along with India's ONGC and Petronet LNG, 20% stake in project, estimated cost of plant is $4.35 billion. Along with India's Oil and Natural Gas Corporation (ONGC), 45% stake in the project. Cost of development estimated at $2.5 to $3 billion.	GAO letter was sent on February 18, 2010, to the only Hinduja entity in the United Kingdom listed on Hinduja's web site. The entity responded on March 5, 2010, that it was not the firm cited in our sources. A representative did not address our repeated requests for contact information for Hinduja (United Kingdom).
Hyundai Heavy Industries/South Korea	Construction of crude oil tanker ships.	Delivery was scheduled for 2009, as of 2005.	Total cost of Iranian tanker building program estimated at $2.4 billion.	Contacted on February 19, 2010; no response as of March 22, 2010.
INA/ Croatia	Exploration of Moghan 2 oil and gas block project in Ardebil province.	Contract signed April 2008.	Contract worth at least $140 million.	Confirmed activity. Noted contract value is $40 million.

Table 2. (Continued)

Firm/country[a]	Firm activity	Status	Commercial activity	Firm comment
Indian Oil Corporation/ India	Development of Farzad-B natural gas field in the Farsi block.	Part of consortium that is exploring the Farsi block and that submitted a 2009 plan to develop the gas field over a 7-to 8-year period.	40% stake in the project, with an estimated total investment of $5 billion.	Contacted on February 19, 2010; no response as of March 22, 2010.
Inpex/Japan	Development of Azadegan oil field.	Initial agreement in 2004, revised in 2006. Iran proceeding with initial development using local companies.	75% share was reduced to 10% in 2006.	Confirmed share was reduced to 10% in October 2006, and the role of operator was transferred to an Iranian company.
JGC Corporation/ Japan	Expansion of Arak refinery to produce 250,000 bbl/d.	Completion was estimated for 2009.	Arak refinery expansion project worth $25 million.	Confirmed activity. Noted involvement was in the initial project design, and their activity was completed nearly 5 years ago.
Lukoil/Russia	Oil exploration and development of the Anaran block in Zagros Mountains, including Azar, Changuleh West, Dehloran, and Musian.	Activities reported halted in 2007 due to threat of U.S. sanctions.	Lukoil had 25% stake in project; project cost is more than $1billion.	Contacted on February 18, 2010; no response as of March 22, 2010.
LyondelBasell/ The Netherlands	Supplying technology for new HDPE petrochemical plant in Kermanshah, increasing capacity by 300,000 metric tons per year. Supplying technology for LDPE plant in Sanandaj.	Expected completion 2009 to 2010. Startup was scheduled for 2008.	Not reported. Not reported.	Confirmed activities. Noted that profits from the two projects are small compared to its European operations.
Oil India Ltd. (OIL)/ India	Development of Farzad-B natural gas field in the Farsi block.	Part of a consortium that is exploring the Farsi block and that submitted a 2009 plan to develop the gas field over a 7-to 8-year period.	20% stake in the project, with an estimated total investment of $5 billion.	Contacted on February 18, 2010; no response as of March 22, 2010.

Firm/country[a]	Firm activity	Status	Commercial activity	Firm comment
Oil and Natural Gas Corporation (ONGC)/ India	Development of natural gas field in South Pars phase 12. Project to convert natural gas from South Pars into LNG for export. Development of the Azadegan oil field.	Agreement signed in December 2009. Agreement signed in December 2009. Company involvement reported in 2008.	Along with United Kingdoms's Hinduja, 40% stake in project, estimated to cost $7.5 billion to develop. Along with Hinduja and India's Petronet LNG, 20% stake in project. Estimated cost of plant is $4.35 billion Along with Hinduja, 45% stake in the project. Cost of development estimated at $2.5 to $3	Contacted on February 18, 2010; no response as of March 22, 2010.
OMV/ Austria	Development of South Pars natural gas fields and share of Iran LNG.	Signed preliminary agreement in 2007.	Total project value is potentially $30 billion.	Confirmed that agreement was signed with the National Iranian Oil Company in 2007 to develop South Pars phase 12 and Iran LNG. Since 2007, further nonbinding negotiations. Also noted a 2001 exploration contract for Mehr block that ended in 2009 due to technical and economical constraints.
ONGC Videsh Ltd. (OVL)/India	Development of Farzad-B natural gas field in the Farsi block.	Part of consortium that is exploring the Farsi block and which submitted a 2009 plan to develop the gas field over a 7-to 8-year period.	40% stake in the project (along with India Oil Corporation and Oil India Ltd.), with an estimated total investment of $5 billion.	Contacted on February 19, 2010; no response as of March 22, 2010.
Petrobras/ Brazil	Completed exploratory activities in the Tusan block.	Returned its concession in 2009.	Spent $178 million before returning its concession.	In 2004, a subsidiary of Petrobras signed service contract to explore Tusan; contract expired in July 2008. Confirmed project costs of $178 million. Currently no activities or plans in Iran.
Petrofield[c]/ Malaysia	Developing an LNG plant on Iran's gulf coast to process natural gas from the Golshan and Ferdos fields in southern Iran.	Agreement made in 2008.	Will finance 100% of the LNG plant. Investment will be repaid in 7 years through the sale of gas and related products.	Contacted on February 10, 2010; no response as of March 22, 2010.
Petroleos de Venezuela S.A. (PDVSA)/ Venezuela	Development of natural gas field in South Pars phase 12.	Project initiated in 2009.	10% stake in project, valued at $760 \million.	Contacted on February 18, 2010; no response as of March 22, 2010.
Petronet LNG/ India	Project to convert natural gas from South Pars into LNG for export.	Memorandum of Agreement signed December 2009.	Part of a consortium with India's ONGC and UK's Hinduja to take a 20% stake in the project.	Contacted on February 18, 2010; no response as of March 22, 2010.

Table 2. (Continued)

Firm/country[a]	Firm activity	Status	Commercial activity	Firm comment
PGNiG/ Poland	Development of natural gas fields. Development of offshore natural gas field at Lavan.	Memorandum of Intent signed February 2008. Project under negotiation in 2008.	Not reported. Buy-back agreement with Iranian Offshore Oil Company valued at $2 billion.	Contacted on February 11, 2010; no response as of March 22, 2010.
PTT Exploration and Production/ Thailand	Exploration and development of the Saveh block natural gas field.	Signed a 25-year contract in 2005.	Has a 100% stake in the Saveh block.	Contacted on February 19, 2010; no response as of March 22, 2010.
Repsol/ Spain	Development of South Pars natural gas fields (also known as Persian LNG).	Signed a framework agreement.	25% stake in project, with an estimated total cost of $10 billion.	Contacted on February 9, 2010; no response as of March 22, 2010.
Royal Dutch Shell/ The Netherlands	Development of South Pars natural gas fields (also known as Persian LNG).	Signed a framework agreement.	25% stake in project, with an estimated total cost of $10 billion.	Confirmed signing a framework agreement. Stated that the agreement would give it a 50% share in development of South Pars phases and 25% share of liquefaction company. Stated that it has not yet decided whether to proceed.
Sinopec/ China	Development of Yadavaran oil field. Expansion and upgrade of the Arak refinery.	Contract signed in 2007. As of 2008, estimated completion was 2011.	Contract valued at $2 billion. Contract valued at $2.8 billion.	Contacted on February 19, 2010; no response as of March 22, 2010.
SKS Ventures/ Malaysia	Development of two offshore natural gas fields Golshan and Ferdos in southern Iran.	Signed a contract in 2008; development expected to take over 5 years.	Buy-back contract is valued at $5 to $6 billion.	Contacted on February 19, 2010; no response as of March 22, 2010.
Snamprogetti [d]/ Italy	Feasibility study of underwater route for Iran-India pipeline from South Pars.	Study being conducted in 2005.	Not reported.	Contacted on February 18, 2010; no response as of March 22, 2010.
StatoilHydro/ Norway	Development of South Pars natural gas fields. Oil exploration and development of the Anaran block in Zagros Mountains, including Azar, Changuleh West, Dehloran, and Musian.	Froze new investments in Iran in 2008. Activities reported halted in 2007 due to threat U.S. sanctions.	Acquired 37% share in 2002. StatoilHydro had 75% stake in the project; project cost is more than $1 billion	Contacted on February 18, 2010; no response as of March 22, 2010.
Tecnimont/ Italy	Engineering, procurement, and construction contractor for a LDPE plant in Sanandaj that will produce 300,000 metric tons per year.	Startup was scheduled for 2008.	Not reported.	Contacted on February 18, 2010; no response as of March 22, 2010.

Firm/country[a]	Firm activity	Status	Commercial activity	Firm comment
Total/ France	Development of South Pars natural gas fields.	No final agreement or investment as of December 31, 2009.	Possible 30% share of a $4 billion project	Confirmed that Total has been a significant investor in the Iranian energy sector for the past 20 years. Confirmed discussions with Iranian authorities regarding development of South Pars phase 11 and the Pars LNG project. Does not anticipate new investments in the near future.
Turkish Petroleum Company (TPAO)/ Turkey	Development of natural gas field in South Pars phases 22-24. Total production is projected to be 35 billion cubic meters per year.	Preliminary agreement to be finalized by February 2010.	Memorandum of Understanding agreement signed in 2007.	Contacted on February 9, 2010; no response as of March 22, 2010.
Uhde/ Germany	Building new petrochemical plant in Kermanshah, increasing capacity by 300,000 metric tons per year.	Expected completion 2009 to 2010.	Not reported.	Contacted on February 18, 2010; no response as of March 22, 2010.

Source: GAO analysis of open source information.

[a] T he country listed is the physical location of the firm as reported in open sources.

[b] ABB Lummus no longer exists as a company. ABB of Switzerland sold the Lummus Group in 2007 to Chicago Bridge and Iron Company (CB&I) of the United States. Both ABB and CB&I commented that they no longer have any commercial activity in Iran.

[c] Petrofield is a subsidiary of SKS Ventures.

[d] Snamprogetti is a subsidiary of ENI.

ENCLOSURE III. GLOSSARY OF TERMS AND ABBREVIATIONS[15]

Barrel- A unit of volume equal to 42 U.S. gallons.

bbl- The abbreviation for barrel(s).

bbl/d- The abbreviation for barrel(s) per day.

Butane- A normally gaseous hydrocarbon extracted from natural gas or refinery gas streams.

Butylene- A hydrocarbon recovered from refinery processes.

Buy-back contract:- Under "buy-back" arrangements, foreign firms may receive entitlements to oil or gas for a limited time in exchange for the funds they invest.

Buy-back oil- Crude oil acquired from a host government whereby a portion of the government's ownership interest in the crude oil produced in that country may or should be purchased by the producing firm.

Catalytic cracking- The refining process of breaking down the larger, heavier, and more complex hydrocarbon molecules into simpler and lighter molecules. Catalytic cracking is accomplished by the use of a catalytic agent and is an effective process for increasing the yield of gasoline from crude oil.

Catalytic hydrocracking- A refining process that uses hydrogen and catalysts with relatively low temperatures and high pressures for converting middle boiling or residual material to high octane gasoline, reformer charge stock, jet fuel, or high-grade fuel oil.

Catalytic hydrotreating- A refining process for treating petroleum fractions from atmospheric or vacuum distillation units (e.g., naphthas, middle distillates, reformer feeds, residual fuel oil, and heavy gas oil) and other petroleum (e.g., cat cracked naphtha, coker naphtha, gas oil, etc.) in the presence of catalysts and substantial quantities of hydrogen.

Commercial activity- We define commercial activity as having signed an agreement to conduct business, invested capital, or received payment for the provision of goods or services in the Iranian oil, gas, or petrochemicals sectors.

Consortium- Group of companies formed to promote a common objective or engagement in a project of benefit to all members. The relationship normally entails cooperation and a sharing of resources, sometimes even common ownership.

Construction- An energy-consuming subsector of the industrial sector that consists of all facilities and equipment used to perform land preparation and construct, renovate, alter, install, maintain, or repair major infrastructure or individual systems therein. Infrastructure includes buildings; industrial plants; and other major structures, such as tanks, towers, monuments, roadways, tunnels, bridges, dams, pipelines, and transmission lines.

Crude oil- A mixture of hydrocarbons that exists in liquid phase in natural underground reservoirs and remains liquid at atmospheric pressure after passing through surface separating facilities. Liquids produced at natural gas processing plants are excluded. Crude oil is refined to produce a wide array of petroleum products, including heating oils; gasoline, diesel, and jet fuels; lubricants; asphalt; ethane, propane, and butane; and many other products used for their energy or chemical content.

Deadweight tons- The lifting capacity of a ship expressed in long tons (2,240 pounds), including cargo, commodities, and crew.

Development- The preparation of a specific mineral deposit for commercial production; this preparation includes construction of access to the deposit and of facilities to extract the minerals. The development process is sometimes further distinguished between a preproduction stage and a current stage, with the distinction being made on the basis of whether the development work is performed before or after production from the mineral deposit has commenced on a commercial scale.

Diesel fuel- A fuel composed of distillates obtained in a petroleum refining operation or blends of such distillates with residual oil used in motor vehicles. The boiling point and specific gravity are higher for diesel fuels than for gasoline.

Downstream- When referring to the oil and gas industry, this term indicates the refining and marketing sectors of the industry. More generically, the term can be used to refer to any step further along in the process.

Ethane- A normally gaseous hydrocarbon extracted from natural gas and refinery gas streams.

Ethanol- A clear, colorless, flammable oxygenated hydrocarbon. Ethanol is typically produced chemically from ethylene, or produced biologically from fermentation of various sugars from carbohydrates found in agricultural crops and cellulosic residues from crops or wood.

Ethylene- A hydrocarbon recovered from refinery processes or petrochemical processes. Ethylene is used as a petrochemical feedstock for numerous chemical applications and the production of consumer goods.

Exploration, drilling- Drilling done in search of new mineral deposits, on extensions of known ore deposits, or at the location of a discovery up to the time when the company decides that sufficient ore reserves are present to justify commercial exploration. Assessment drilling is reported as exploration drilling.

Exploratory well- A hole drilled: (a) to find and produce oil or gas in an area previously considered to be an unproductive area; (b) to find a new reservoir in a known field (i.e. one previously producing oil and gas from another reservoir); or (c) to extend the limit of a known oil or gas reservoir.

Field- An area consisting of a single reservoir or multiple reservoirs all grouped on, or related to, the same individual geological structural feature or stratigraphic condition. There may be two or more reservoirs in a field that are separated vertically by intervening impervious strata or laterally by local geologic barriers, or by both.

Firm- An association, company, corporation, estate, individual, joint venture, partnership, or sole proprietorship, or any other entity, however organized, including (a) charitable or educational institutions; (b) the federal government, including corporations, departments, federal agencies, and other instrumentalities, and state and local governments. A firm may consist of (1) a parent entity, including the consolidated and unconsolidated entities (if any) that it directly or indirectly controls; (2) a parent and its consolidated entities only; (3) an unconsolidated entity; or (4) any part or combination of the above.

Gas- A nonsolid, nonliquid combustible energy source that includes natural gas, coke-oven gas, blast-furnace gas, and refinery gas.

Gas plant operator- Any firm, including a gas plant owner, which operates a gas plant and keeps the gas plant records. A gas plant is a facility in which natural gas liquids are separated from natural gas or in which natural gas liquids are fractionated or otherwise separated into natural gas liquid products or both.

Gas processing unit- A facility designed to recover natural gas liquids from a stream of natural gas that may or may not have passed through lease separators or field separation facilities. Another function of natural gas processing plants is to control the quality of the processed natural gas stream. Cycling plants are considered natural gas processing plants.

Gas sweetening- conditioning for the removal of acid gases, which can cause corrosion to gas flowlines (pipelines) and can also be harmful to consumers.

Gas to liquids (GTL)- A process that combines the carbon and hydrogen elements in natural gas molecules to make synthetic liquid petroleum products, such as diesel fuel.

HDPE- High-density polyethylene, a petrochemical derivative.

Hydrocarbon- An organic chemical compound of hydrogen and carbon in the gaseous, liquid, or solid phase. The molecular structure of hydrocarbon compounds varies from the simplest (methane, a constituent of natural gas) to the very heavy and very complex.

Hydrotreater- See *catalytic hydrotreating.*

LDPE- Low-density polyethylene, a petrochemical derivative.

LNG- Liquefied natural gas.

Liquefied natural gas (LNG)- Natural gas (primarily methane) that has been liquefied by reducing its temperature to -260 degrees Fahrenheit at atmospheric pressure.

Mcf- One thousand cubic feet.

Methane- A colorless, flammable, odorless hydrocarbon gas (CH_4), which is the major component of natural gas. It is also an important source of hydrogen in various industrial processes.

Metric ton- A unit of weight equal to 2,204.6 pounds, used to measure products such as LDPE and HDPE.

MMbbl/d- One million barrels of oil per day.

Natural gas- A gaseous mixture of hydrocarbon compounds, the primary one being methane.

Natural gas liquids (NGL)- Those hydrocarbons in natural gas that are separated from the gas as liquids through the process of absorption, condensation, adsorption, or other methods in gas processing or cycling plants. Generally, such liquids consist of propane and heavier hydrocarbons and are commonly referred to as lease condensate, natural gasoline, and liquefied petroleum gases. Natural gas liquids include natural gas plant liquids (primarily ethane, propane, butane, and isobutane) and lease condensate (primarily pentanes produced from natural gas at lease separators and field facilities).

Natural gas liquids production: The volume of natural gas liquids removed from natural gas in lease separators, field facilities, gas processing plants, or cycling plants during the report year.

Natural gas processing plant- Facilities designed to recover natural gas liquids from a stream of natural gas that may or may not have passed through lease separators or field separation facilities. These facilities control the quality of the natural gas to be marketed.

Offshore- That geographic area that lies seaward of the coastline. In general, the coastline is the line of ordinary low water along with that portion of the coast that is in direct contact with the open sea or the line marking the seaward limit of inland water.

Offshore reserves and production- Unless otherwise dedicated, reserves and production that are in either state or federal domains, located seaward of the coastline.

Oil- A mixture of hydrocarbons usually existing in the liquid state in natural underground pools or reservoirs. Gas is often found in association with oil. Also see *petroleum*.

OPEC (Organization of the Petroleum Exporting Countries)- An intergovernmental organization created in 1960 whose stated objective is to "coordinate and unify the petroleum policies of member countries." Current members include Algeria, Angola, Ecuador, Iran, Iraq, Kuwait, Libya, Nigeria, Qatar, Saudi Arabia, United Arab Emirates, and Venezuela.

Operated- Exercised management responsibility for the day-to-day operations of natural gas production, gathering, treating, processing, transportation, storage, or distribution facilities or a synthetic natural gas plant.

Petrochemical feedstocks- Chemical feedstocks derived from petroleum principally for the manufacture of chemicals, synthetic rubber, and a variety of plastics.

Petrochemicals- Organic and inorganic compounds and mixtures that include but are not limited to organic chemicals, cyclic intermediates, plastics and resins, synthetic fibers, elastomers, organic dyes, organic pigments, detergents, surface active agents, carbon black, and ammonia.

Petroleum- A broadly defined class of liquid hydrocarbon mixtures. Included are crude oil, lease condensate, unfinished oils, refined products obtained from the processing of crude oil, and natural gas plant liquids.

Petroleum products- Petroleum products are obtained from the processing of crude oil (including lease condensate), natural gas, and other hydrocarbon compounds. Petroleum products include unfinished oils, liquefied petroleum gases, pentanes plus, aviation gasoline, motor gasoline, naphtha-type jet fuel, kerosene-type jet fuel, kerosene, distillate fuel oil, residual fuel oil, petrochemical feedstocks, special naphthas, lubricants, waxes, petroleum coke, asphalt, road oil, still gas, and miscellaneous products.

Petroleum refinery- An installation that manufactures finished petroleum products from crude oil, unfinished oils, natural gas liquids, other hydrocarbons, and alcohol.

Processing plant- A surface installation designed to separate and recover natural gas liquids from a stream of produced natural gas through the processes of condensation, absorption, adsorption, refrigeration, or other methods and to control the quality of natural gas marketed or returned to oil or gas reservoirs for pressure maintenance, repressuring, or cycling.

Production, crude oil: The volumes of crude oil that are extracted from oil reservoirs. These volumes are determined through measurement of the volumes delivered from lease storage tanks or at the point of custody transfer.

Production, natural gas- The volume of natural gas withdrawn from reservoirs less (1) the volume returned to such reservoirs in cycling, repressuring of oil reservoirs, and conservation operations; less (2) shrinkage resulting from the removal of lease condensate; and less (3) nonhydrocarbon gases where they occur in sufficient quantity to render the gas unmarketable. Volumes of gas withdrawn from gas storage reservoirs and native gas, which has been transferred to the storage category, are not considered production. Flared and vented gas is also considered production.

Production, oil and gas- The lifting of oil and gas to the surface and gathering, treating, field processing (as in the case of processing gas to extract liquid hydrocarbons), and field storage. The production function shall normally be regarded as terminating at the outlet valve on the lease or field production storage tank. If unusual physical or operational circumstances exist, it may be more appropriate to regard the production function as terminating at the first point at which oil, gas, or gas liquids are delivered to a main pipeline, a common carrier, a refinery, or a marine terminal.

Propylene- Propylene is intended for use in nonfuel applications such as petrochemical manufacturing. Nonfuel propylene includes chemical-grade propylene, polymer-grade propylene, and trace amounts of propane. Nonfuel propylene also includes the propylene component of propane/propylene mixes where the propylene will be separated from the mix in a propane/propylene splitting process. Nonfuel propylene excludes the propylene component of propane/propylene mixes where the propylene component of the mix is intended for use as fuel.

Refined petroleum products- Refined petroleum products include but are not limited to gasolines, kerosene, distillates, liquefied petroleum gas, asphalt, lubricating oils, diesel fuels, and residual fuels.

Refiner- A firm or the part of a firm that refines products or blends and substantially changes products, refines liquid hydrocarbons from oil and gas field gases, or recovers liquefied petroleum gases incident to petroleum refining and sells those products to resellers, retailers, reseller/retailers, or ultimate consumers. "Refiner" includes any owner of products that contracts to have those products refined and then sells the refined products to resellers, retailers, or ultimate consumers.

Refinery- An installation that manufactures finished petroleum products from crude oil, unfinished oils, natural gas liquids, other hydrocarbons, and oxygenates.

Reinjected- The forcing of gas under pressure into an oil reservoir in an attempt to increase recovery.

Reserve- That portion of the demonstrated reserve base that is estimated to be recoverable at the time of determination. The reserve is derived by applying a recovery factor to that component of the identified coal resource designated as the demonstrated reserve base.

Upstream- The exploration and production portions of the oil and gas industry.

ENCLOSURE IV. IRAN SANCTIONS ACT

Under the Iran Sanctions Act, a person can be sanctioned for an investment, made on or after August 5, 1996, of $20 million or more (or any combination of investments of at least $5 million each, which in the aggregate equals or exceeds $20 million in any 12 month period).[16] However, this investment must be made with actual knowledge and it must be an investment that directly and significantly contributed to the enhancement of Iran's ability to develop the petroleum resources of Iran.[17]

The act requires the President, delegated to the Secretary of State, to impose at least two of the following sanctions:

- denying Export-Import Bank assistance for exporting to the foreign person;
- banning licenses to export controlled technologies to the sanctioned person;
- banning U.S. financial institutions from loaning the sanctioned person more than $10 million in a 1-year period unless such person is engaged in activities to relieve human suffering and the loans or credits are provided for such activities;
- if the sanctioned person is a financial institution, prohibiting the designation of that institution as a primary dealer in U.S. government debt instruments or serving as an agent for the U.S. government or as repository for U.S. government funds; and
- banning U.S. government procurement from the sanctioned person, and
- as well as other sanctions that fall under the powers of the International Emergency Economic Powers Act (IEEPA), including IEEPA-derived executive orders, to restrict imports with respect to the sanctioned person.[18]

The President may waive these sanctions if the President determines that doing so is important to the national interest of the United States.[19]

(320727)

End Notes

[1] Based on International Monetary Fund (IMF) data from 2005 to 2008, and data from the Economist Intelligence Unit (*The Economist*), Iran Country Report (Dec. 8, 2009).

[2] Central Intelligence Agency, World Factbook, https://www.cia.gov/library/publications/the-world-factbook/ rankorder /2173rank.html?cou, accessed on February 18, 2010.

[3] IHS Global Insight provides economic and financial information for the energy industry on a contract basis, including analysis and forecasting for the Iranian oil, gas, and petrochemical sectors discussed in this report.

[4] Foreign firms typically hand over operations to the National Iranian Oil Company after the development phase, according to DOE.

[5] *See e.g.* Exec. Order 13,059, 62 Fed. Reg. 44,531 (Aug. 19, 1997).

[6] Iran-Libya Sanctions Act of 1996, Pub. L. No. 104-172, § 5, 110 Stat. 1541, 1543 as amended. The act also allows for sanctions against persons providing goods, technology, or services to Iran knowing that such provision would contribute materially to Iran's ability to acquire or develop chemical, biological, or nuclear weapons or related technologies; or acquire or develop destabilizing numbers and types of advanced conventional weapons.

[7] Pub. L. No. 104-172, § 6; Memorandum: Delegation of Responsibilities Under the Iran and Libya Sanctions Act of 1996, 61 Fed. Reg. 64,249 (Nov. 21, 1996). Other sanctions include a denial of Export-Import Bank assistance, a ban on issuing licenses to export controlled technologies to the sanctioned firm, and other sanctions that fall under the powers of the International Emergency Economic Powers Act (IEEPA).

[8] Pub. L. No. 104-172, § 9; 61 Fed. Reg. 64,249.

[9] This instance was the first and only time that the United States has publicly made a determination that a firm's investment violated the Iran Sanctions Act.

[10] GAO, *Iran Sanctions: Impact in Furthering U.S. Objectives Is Unclear and Should Be Reviewed*, GAO-08-58 (Washington, D.C.: Dec. 18, 2007).

[11] Iran Refined Petroleum Sanctions Act of 2009, H.R. 2194, 111th Cong. (2009). We will issue an additional report on firms that export refined petroleum products to Iran.

[12] We present the activities from what are considered "upstream" sectors, such as drilling for oil, to "downstream" sectors, such as exporting refined products in tankers.

[13] According to the 2009 Economist Intelligence Unit (The Economist) Iran Country Report, oil production was at 3.8 million barrels per day in 2008.

[14] According to DOE, South Pars natural gas field has a 25 phase development scheme spanning 20 years.

[15] The U.S. Energy Information Administration, an independent agency within the U.S. Department of Energy, was the primary source for definitions contained in this glossary.

[16] Pub. L. No. 104-172, § 5, as amended.

[17] *Id.*

[18] Pub. L. No. 104-172, § 6, as amended.

[19] Pub. L. No. 104-172, § 9, as amended.

In: U.S. Led Sanctions on Iran
Editors: Robert K. Figg and Danielle A. Wilson
ISBN: 978-1-62100-414-1

Chapter 6

IRAN SANCTIONS: COMPLETE AND TIMELY LICENSING DATA NEEDED TO STRENGTHEN ENFORCEMENT OF EXPORT RESTRICTIONS*

United States Government Accountability Office

WHY GAO DID THIS STUDY

In 1995, the United States banned exports to Iran of most U.S. goods without a Treasury Department license. In 2008, the U.S. media, citing U.S. government statistics, reported that U.S. firms were exporting numerous goods to Iran. The statistics are maintained by the Census Bureau and are based on data filed by exporters or their agents. The United States has also generally banned unlicensed transshipments of U.S. goods to Iran via other nations. In this report, GAO assesses the extent to which (1) U.S. trade statistics accurately depict exports to Iran, (2) Treasury licenses exports to Iran in accordance with the trade restrictions and provides licensing data to enforcement agencies and Congress, and (3) Iran obtains U.S. military and dual-use goods through transshipment. GAO analyzed Census export data, a randomly selected sample of Treasury export licenses, Treasury licensing information systems, and U.S. government transshipment data. It also interviewed relevant U.S. government officials.

WHAT GAO RECOMMENDS

GAO recommends that Treasury develop the capability to provide complete and timely information on all licenses for the export of goods to Iran. Treasury commented that it was upgrading its licensing system for agricultural and medical exports, but it did not specify when it would upgrade its licensing system for dual-use items with potential military uses.

* This is an edited, reformatted and augmented version of the United States Government Accountability Office publication GAO-10-375, dated March 2010.

What GAO Found

U.S. trade statistics for exports to Iran erroneously include goods that were not exported to Iran. While the statistics indicate that U.S. firms exported 278 types of goods to Iran from 2004 to 2008, 97 of these types of goods were instead exported to Ireland, Iraq, and other countries. The misidentification of Iran as the recipient resulted from errors in export data filings that Census did not detect or correct. As a result of our review, Census officials stated, Census has begun manually checking all new filings of exports to Iran and posting corrections to a Census Web page.

While Treasury is licensing exports to Iran in accordance with export restrictions, it cannot provide complete and timely information about the licenses it has issued. Its paper-based licensing information systems cannot be searched to quickly identify licenses for exports of goods to Iran. For example, Treasury was unable to address a 2009 request from U.S. Customs and Border Protection (CBP) officials for complete and timely licensing data to support CBP inspectors at U.S. ports. Treasury's information systems weaken the ability of the government to assess compliance with Iran sanctions. Treasury plans to upgrade its licensing information system for agricultural and medical exports to Iran. However, the upgrade would not address its inability to readily identify licenses for other goods, including civilian items with potential military uses.

A wide range of U.S. military and dual-use goods are illegally transshipped to Iran through the United Arab Emirates (UAE), Malaysia, Singapore, and other countries, according to U.S. officials. The Justice Department has prosecuted several individuals for efforts to transship military aircraft parts to Iran.

Abbreviations

AECA	Arms Export Control Act
AES	Automated Export System
CBP	Customs and Border Protection
Census	U.S. Census Bureau
CENTCOM	Defense Department Central Command
IEEPA	International Emergency Economic Powers Act
MTCR	Missile Technology Control Regime
OFAC	Office of Foreign Assets Control
TSRA	Trade Sanctions Reform and Export Enhancement Act of 2000
WMD	weapons of mass destruction

March 4, 2010

The Honorable Howard Berman
Chairman
Committee on Foreign Affairs House of Representatives

The Honorable David M. Scott
House of Representatives

Iran's actions to enrich uranium, conceal its nuclear program, and sponsor international terrorism present significant challenges to U.S. national interests. In response, the United States has banned the export of most U.S. goods to Iran without an export license from the Department of the Treasury. According to Treasury officials, Treasury's general policy is to deny most license applications for Iran with the exception of agricultural and medical goods specified in a 2000 law.[1] Treasury is responsible for maintaining records of its export licensing decisions. In 2008, the U.S. media, citing U.S. government official trade statistics, reported that U.S. firms had exported a wide range of restricted goods to Iran, including military rifles. At that time, Treasury officials questioned the statistics' accuracy and stated that Treasury had licensed exports to Iran in compliance with U.S. law and policy. The statistics, which are maintained by the U.S. Census Bureau (Census), are based on data that exporters or their agents file.[2] In addition to restricting direct exports, the United States has also generally prohibited U.S. firms from knowingly shipping goods to Iran through other nations without a Treasury license.[3] This prohibition includes dual-use goods (civilian goods with potential military applications) that the Department of Commerce has licensed for export to other countries. The Departments of Commerce, Defense, Justice, and Homeland Security are responsible for detecting and prosecuting illegal transshipment of U.S. goods to Iran.

In this report, we assess the extent to which (1) U.S. trade statistics accurately depict U.S. exports to Iran, (2) Treasury licenses U.S. exports to Iran in accordance with the trade restrictions and provides complete and timely licensing data to enforcement agencies and Congress, and (3) Iran obtains U.S. military and dual-use items through illegal transshipments. We also present information in appendix II regarding U.S. legal tools for sanctioning foreign firms that export sensitive non-U.S. technologies to Iran.

To assess the extent to which U.S. statistics accurately depict U.S. exports to Iran, we asked Census to review the export statistics for Iran and identify the addresses of the recipients of the exports. We also met with Census officials to determine their methods and policies for assuring the accuracy of the statistics. To assess Treasury's licensing activities, we selected a random sample of Treasury export licenses for agricultural and medical goods and determined if the goods and recipients cited in the licenses were consistent with U.S. law. We also reviewed Treasury documents concerning the systems Treasury uses to record its licensing activities, interviewed Treasury and other executive branch officials, and requested detailed licensing data from Treasury. To review the extent to which U.S. goods are illegally transshipped to Iran, we obtained and analyzed lists of relevant criminal prosecutions from the Department of Justice. We also discussed transshipment issues with officials of the Departments of Commerce, Defense, Homeland Security (including U.S. Customs and Border Protection and U.S. Immigration and Customs Enforcement), Justice, and the Treasury; the Federal Bureau of Investigation; and other government agencies. The Department of Commerce (Commerce) provided us with transshipment-related information that it controls as being "for official use only." We have not included that information in this report but have instead incorporated it into a "For Official Use Only" report that is not publicly available.

We conducted this performance audit from May 2009 to March 2010 in accordance with generally accepted government auditing standards. Those standards require that we plan and perform the audit to obtain sufficient, appropriate evidence to provide a reasonable basis for our findings and conclusions based on our audit objectives. We believe that the evidence obtained provides a reasonable basis for our findings and conclusions based on our audit objectives. Our scope and methodology are described in greater detail in appendix I.

RESULTS IN BRIEF

The U.S. government's official statistics for U.S. exports to Iran erroneously include goods that were exported to countries other than Iran. These statistics indicate that U.S. exporters shipped a total of 278 different types of goods to Iran from 2004 to 2008. However, we found that 97 of these types of goods, including military rifles, were shipped not to Iran but to a variety of other nations, including Ireland, Israel, and Iraq. The remaining 181 types of goods consisted primarily of agricultural, medical, humanitarian, and informational items. The misidentification of Iran as the recipient country in the statistics resulted from export data filing errors that Census did not detect or correct because of the low dollar value of the export transactions. Although their dollar value is small relative to the value of all U.S. exports, the accuracy of the Iran export statistics is important because the United States has severely restricted trade with Iran as a state sponsor of terrorism. Census officials stated that, as a result of our review, they have initiated a manual check of new filings of exports to Iran, required filers of export data to select recipient countries from a list instead of allowing them to enter a two-letter international standard country code, and begun posting newly-detected corrections to Iran export data on a Census Web page. According to Census officials, it is too soon to determine whether these actions will improve the accuracy of future U.S. trade statistics for Iran.

Treasury is issuing export licenses for Iran in accordance with export regulations but cannot routinely provide complete and timely information about those licenses. We reviewed a random sample of 58 licenses drawn from 1,833 agricultural and medical export licenses issued from late 2006 to mid-2009 and found that the sampled licenses were consistent with U.S. export regulations related to agricultural and medical items. We also determined that Treasury had complied with legal restrictions applicable to licensing the export of dual-use technology to insure the safety of civil aviation and safe operation of U.S.-origin commercial aircraft. However, we identified weaknesses in Treasury's ability to retrieve and provide complete information about its licensing decisions. Treasury uses two paper-based information systems to record data on all Iran-related licensing decisions. The systems are not integrated with one another, and neither can be searched to specifically identify licenses for the export of goods to Iran. As a result, Treasury has been unable to consistently provide timely responses to requests for complete information on such licenses. For example, Treasury was unable to respond to a 2009 request from U.S. Customs and Border Protection (CBP) officials for complete and timely Iran licensing data. CBP officials stated that they sought the information to help CBP inspectors verify that goods at U.S. ports had been properly licensed for export to Iran. Because Treasury administers the U.S. sanctions program on Iran, its inability to provide complete and timely information on export licenses undermines the U.S. government's ability to assess compliance with the sanctions. Treasury is planning to upgrade its system for tracking licenses for agricultural and medical exports to Iran, which are permitted by U.S. law. However, the upgrade would not include the small number of export licenses for other types of goods, such as civilian aircraft safety equipment with potential military uses.

Iran is obtaining U.S. military and dual-use goods that are illegally transshipped through intermediaries in third-party nations, according to U.S. officials. Goods involved in cases of actual or attempted transshipment include parts for Iran's U.S.-built fighter aircraft, military helicopters, and air defense systems; night vision equipment; submachine guns; computers; laboratory equipment; specialized steel; pumps with nuclear applications; and electronic components for missiles. Criminal cases handled by the Justice Department indicate that U.S. goods are often transshipped to Iran through the United Arab Emirates, Malaysia, or Singapore. To address the problem, U.S. agencies have conducted investigations to uncover Iranian procurement networks and prosecuted at least 30 firms and individuals during 2007 through September 2009.

To help ensure that U.S. agencies have timely access to reliable data concerning licensed U.S. exports to Iran, we are recommending that the Secretary of the Treasury ensure that Treasury develop the capability to provide other agencies and Congress with complete and timely information concerning all licenses issued for the export of goods to Iran.

In commenting on a draft of this report, Treasury stated that it was upgrading the licensing system that tracks agricultural and medical exports to Iran. However, it did not specify when similar upgrades would occur for a licensing system that tracks other exports, including dual-use items that have potential military applications. We therefore have not changed our recommendation. Treasury also stated that the title of our draft report implied that its information systems weakened implementation of sanctions on Iran. We therefore modified the title to clarify our message and reinforce our recommendation. Treasury's comments are reproduced in appendix III.

The Department of Commerce provided technical comments in writing, which we have incorporated as appropriate and reproduced in appendix IV. The other agencies cited in this report did not provide formal comments. CBP, U.S. Immigration and Customs Enforcement, and Treasury provided technical comments, which we incorporated as appropriate.

BACKGROUND

The U.S. government's official trade statistics are maintained by the U.S. Census Bureau for use as economic indicators and measures of the U.S. balance of trade with other countries. The statistics are based primarily on data filed by exporters and their agents[4] into the electronic Automated Export System (AES) database.[5] Census maintains the AES data on a mainframe computer operated by the Department of Homeland Security's U.S. Customs and Border Protection. While most filers enter data through the Census Bureau's AESDirect or a related Census system, others have developed their own software for this purpose. The data filed into AES includes the recipient country. Until recently, filers of export data designated the recipient country by choosing a two-letter international standard country code. Data filers also designate the type of good being exported from a list of more than 8,000 internationally harmonized commodity codes. According to these statistics, the United States exported worldwide nearly $1.3 trillion during 2008.

U.S. exports to Iran are severely restricted by U.S. laws and regulations. Before 1979, the United States enjoyed good relations with the Iranian government and exported military equipment to Iran. However, U.S.- Iranian relations deteriorated sharply following the 1979 Iranian revolution and the consequent seizure of U.S. embassy personnel. Iran's subsequent efforts to enrich uranium and support international terrorism prompted the United States to impose numerous sanctions on Iran, including a 1995 ban on almost all U.S. exports to that country.[6] The current ban is administered by the Office of Foreign Assets Control of the U.S. Department of the Treasury, which is also responsible for licensing financial transactions with Iran and imports from Iran.[7] Under the ban, in general, a U.S. person must obtain a Treasury license before exporting or selling goods to Iran.[8] Congress had already restricted exports to Iran by prohibiting the export of dual-use goods (civilian goods with potential military applications) to Iran.[9] This prohibition can be waived by the President if the President determines that doing so is essential to the national interests of the United States.[10]

According to Treasury officials, Treasury policy is to generally deny license applications for the export of U.S. goods to Iran, with the exception of goods covered by the Trade Sanctions Reform and Export Enhancement Act of 2000 (TSRA). TSRA requires the President to terminate any unilateral agricultural or medical sanctions against a foreign country or foreign entity.[11] TSRA also states that the export of agricultural commodities, medicine, or medical devices to a designated state sponsor of terrorism, such as Iran,[12] shall only be made pursuant to 1-year licenses.[13] As a result, Treasury licenses the export of agricultural goods, medicines, and medical goods to Iran and other sanctioned countries.[14] Treasury has issued a growing number of licenses for agricultural and medical exports to Iran following passage of TSRA, as shown in figure 1. TSRA licenses may not be granted for exports to entities linked to international terrorism, the proliferation of weapons of mass destruction, or narcotics trafficking.

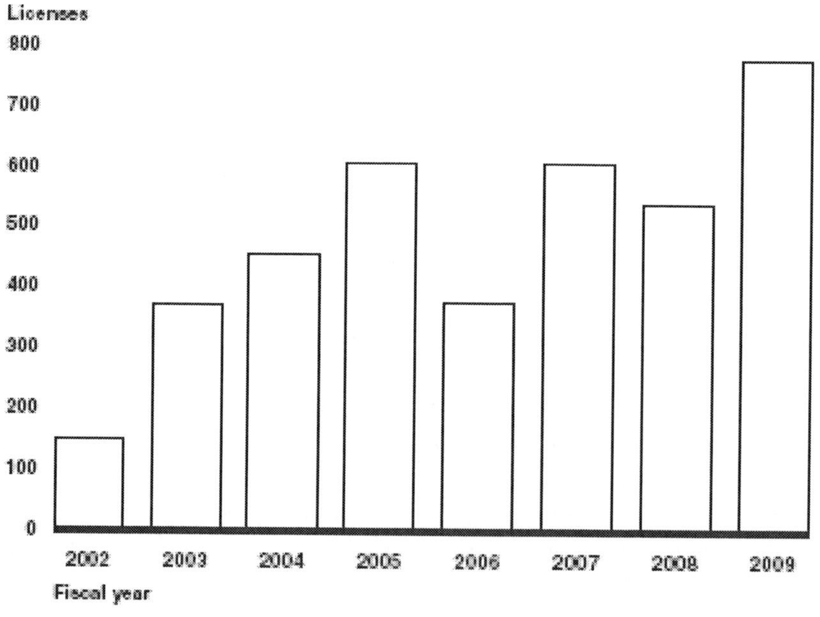

Source: GAO analysis of Treasury data.

Figure 1. TSRA Licenses Issued by Treasury for Exports to Iran, 2002-2009.

The trade ban also generally prohibits exports of U.S. goods (including dual-use items) to countries other than Iran without a Treasury license if the exporter has reason to know the goods are specifically intended for transshipment to Iran.[15] Foreign firms are generally prohibited from knowingly reexporting goods on Commerce's list of controlled dual use goods to Iran even if those goods were originally legally exported from the United States to a third country under a Commerce license.[16] For example, dual-use U.S. goods exported to countries other than Iran under a Commerce license may not be subsequently transshipped to Iran without a Treasury license if the exporter knew or had reason to know that such goods were intended for Iran. The Departments of Commerce, Defense, Homeland Security, Justice, and the Treasury investigate allegations of illegal transshipment of U.S. goods to Iran. Exporters who knowingly ship U.S. goods to Iran via other countries without a Treasury license are subject to prosecution by the Department of Justice. Congress is considering new sanctions that would restrict Iran's ability to import goods from other countries.[17]

U.S. Export Statistics for Iran Erroneously Include Goods Not Exported to Iran

The U.S. government's official statistics for U.S. exports to Iran erroneously include many types of goods that U.S. firms did not export to Iran. The misidentification of Iran as the recipient country in the statistics is the result of export data filing errors that Census did not detect or correct. Census officials stated that, as a result of our review, Census has begun manually checking new export filings reporting exports to Iran. While Census policy is not to correct errors in the statistics that are older than 1 year, it has begun posting Iran-related corrections on a separate Web page.

U.S. Export Statistics Contain Numerous Erroneous Entries for Iran

U.S. export statistics erroneously indicate that U.S. exporters shipped 278 types of goods to Iran from 2004 to 2008. At our request, Census reviewed its records and determined that more than a third (97) of these types of goods had not been exported to Iran. As shown in table 1, the types of goods erroneously included in the Iran export statistics include military rifles exported to Iraq and aircraft parts exported to Ireland, Israel, and Iraq.[18] The remaining types of goods in the export statistics for Iran are primarily agricultural, medical, humanitarian, or informational.

Table 1. Selected Goods Erroneously Included in Export Statistics for Iran

Type of Good	Total value shipped (2004-2008)	Actual countries ofdestination
Civilian aircraft, engines, and parts	$640,235	Ireland, Israel, Iraq
Military rifles	106,635	Iraq
Military rifle parts	8,760	Iraq
Military equipment	33,197	Iraq, Kyrgyzstan
Specially designed vehicles	21,000	Iraq
Work trucks	60,713	Israel
Cinema cameras	3,000	Iraq
Perfumes and toilet waters	8,938	Israel
String musical instruments	8,123	Ireland

Source: GAO analysis of Census data.

The misidentification of Iran as the recipient country for these and other exports was the result of errors made by filers of export data into the Automated Export System. In checking its records at our request, Census determined the addresses of the recipients to which the shipment were to be delivered. It found many cases of "improbable" addresses, such as "Dublin, Iran." In these cases, exporters apparently mistook the two-letter country code for Iran ("IR") for the code for the actual recipient country. For example, exporters shipping goods to Ireland might enter "IR" instead of the correct code for Ireland ("IE"). Table 2 depicts the code for Iran and the codes for several other recipient countries.

Table 2. Selected Countries and Country Codes

Country	Standardized country code
Iran	IR
Ireland	IE
Israel	IL
Iraq	IQ
Italy	IT

Source: U.S. Census Bureau.

Census Did Not Detect or Correct Errors in Export Data for Iran

Census officials stated that they did not detect or correct all of the Iran-related errors in new exporter filings or in the export statistics for previous years. The officials focused on detecting errors involving high-dollar value transactions because of the statistics' use in determining the U.S. balance of trade rather than the sensitivity of the reported recipient country. The officials stated that they did not focus on detecting errors in the data for exports to Iran because the value of such exports was relatively small. In 2008, the reported value of U.S. exports to Iran was $683 million, while the total value of all U.S. exports worldwide was nearly $1.3 trillion.19 Moreover, the officials stated, the policy of the Census Bureau is not to make changes in trade statistics that are more than a year old. For example, Census officials have not corrected an erroneous entry in the statistics concerning the alleged export of rifles to Iran in 2004, although they learned of the error in 2008. Census officials also stated that Census is not involved in enforcing U.S. export controls on Iran.

Although the dollar value of U.S. exports to Iran is small relative to the value of all U.S. exports, the accuracy of the Census Bureau's Iran export statistics is important. The nature and composition of the U.S. exports to Iran is sensitive because the United States has severely restricted trade with Iran as a state sponsor of terrorism. Also, other U.S. government agencies use these statistics in connection with the trade with Iran. For example, Commerce and Homeland Security enforcement officials use the statistics as part of their enforcement targeting efforts. In addition, officials from the Department of State stated that they employ these statistics in defending U.S. trade policy with Iran in discussion with other governments.

Census Has Taken Action in Response to Our Review

In response to our review, Census officials have taken action to improve the accuracy of statistics concerning current U.S. exports to Iran.

- Beginning in August 2009, Census officials began routine accuracy checks of new filings of exports to Iran and other heavily sanctioned countries (Cuba, North Korea, and Sudan), regardless of the dollar value of the exports. Census officials stated that they are now checking recipient addresses to verify that they match the reported country of destination and are calling filers of export data to verify questionable entries. Although they have not formalized the process, Census officials have stated that they intend to continue these accuracy checks.
- Census also clarified the country selection process in AESDirect, the filing system used by most exporters to enter information into the Automated Export System. Because exporters often apparently assumed that "IR" was the code for other countries, Census has changed the data entry process to include a pull-down menu that lists all the countries of the world by their complete names.
- In June 2009, Census began posting an online list of corrections to Iran export data.[20] However, Census officials stated that they will continue their policy of not correcting errors in the trade statistics older than 1 year.[21]
- Census officials stated that it is too early to determine the extent to which these recent efforts may improve the accuracy of U.S. statistics concerning exports to Iran.

TREASURY IS LICENSING EXPORTS TO IRAN IN ACCORDANCE WITH TRADE BAN BUT CANNOT PROVIDE COMPLETE AND TIMELY INFORM ATION ON ITS LICENSING DECISIONS

Treasury is licensing exports to Iran in accordance with the trade ban but cannot provide other agencies or Congress with complete and timely licensing information. It is hindered by paper-based information systems that cannot be searched to identify licenses for the export of goods to Iran. As a result, Treasury has been unable to quickly respond to requests for complete information on such licenses. Treasury is planning to upgrade its system for tracking licenses for agricultural and medical exports to Iran, which are permitted by TSRA. However, the upgrade would not include the small number of export licenses for other types of goods, such as dual- use civilian aviation equipment with potential military uses.

Treasury Licenses for Exports to Iran Are in Accordance with the Trade Ban

Our review of a sample of TSRA licenses found no evidence that Treasury has issued TSRA licenses for the export of goods other than those covered by TSRA. We also found no evidence that TSRA licenses involved recipients engaged in forbidden activities. We selected a random sample of 58 licenses from 1,833 TSRA export licenses issued by Treasury between October 2006 and August 2009. The licenses selected authorized the export of more than 275 types of goods. None of the licenses in our sample authorized the export of nonagricultural or nonmedical items. Also, none of the end users listed on the licenses in our sample appeared on Treasury's Specially Designated Nationals and Blocked Persons List, which contains individuals known to be linked to international terrorism, the proliferation of weapons of mass destruction, and narcotics trafficking.

We also reviewed 34 non-TSRA licenses that Treasury issued between January 2008 and July 2009. As shown in table 3, we found that all but one of the licenses involved the return of human remains to Iran; official U.S. government and law enforcement matters; educational, research, and exchange programs; and media-related enterprises for broadcasting or Internet connectivity. The remaining license involved the export of dual-use equipment to help ensure the safety of Iran's U.S.-built civilian airliners. U.S. law prohibits the export of any dual-use item to Iran and states that the President may waive the prohibition if doing so is essential to the interests of the United States.[22] The President has delegated the authority to issue such waivers to the Secretary of State.[23] We obtained a list of waivers from the Department of State and confirmed that a waiver had been issued for this dual-use export.

Table 3. Non-TSRA Licenses Issued 2008 to August 2009

Purpose of licenses	Number of licenses
Transport of human remains to Iran	13
U.S. Government/Law Enforcement	9
Educational/Research/Exchange Programs	8

Media/Broadcasting/Internet Connectivity	3
Aircraft Safety (dual-use)	1
Total	34

Source: GAO analysis of Treasury data.

Treasury Information Systems Cannot Provide Complete and Timely Licensing Data to other Agencies and Congress

Treasury cannot provide other agencies or Congress with complete and timely information concerning the licenses it has issued. It cannot do so because it relies on paper-based information systems that cannot be searched to identify licenses for the export of goods to Iran. Treasury's primary licensing information system for export licenses is based on correspondence tracking software. According to a Treasury official familiar with the system, it contains nonstandardized data for license applications entered before 2007, relies on manual data entry, and requires time-consuming case-by-case review by licensing officials to ensure its reliability and suitability for release. Treasury's secondary information system was created by TSRA licensing personnel to support the licensing of exports of TSRA goods. In January 2009, an internal Treasury budget request characterized the TSRA information system as a "largely paper-based" system that hinders "the speed, efficacy, reliability, and security of [Treasury's] licensing, enforcement and compliance activities." Treasury officials must manually review all TSRA licensing data for Iran to identify licenses that authorize the export of goods. Because the TSRA system is not integrated with Treasury's primary licensing information system, TSRA licensing officials must manually enter the same data into both systems.

Treasury has been unable to consistently provide timely and complete licensing information for Iran to other agencies and Congress. For example, a Treasury official informed U.S. Customs and Border Protection (CBP) officials in 2009 that Treasury's information systems could not provide CBP with complete and timely information on licenses issued for the export of goods to Iran. CBP officials stated that they had sought the information to help CBP officers at U.S. ports quickly determine whether goods slated for export to Iran had been properly licensed by Treasury. CBP officers currently use a more time-consuming process to access limited Treasury data through a third agency. Treasury officials stated in January 2010 that their licensing information systems focus on the exceptions that Treasury grants to the Iran trade embargo, rather than on controls over the export of specific goods.

Similarly, as of March 1, 2010, Treasury had yet to provide Congress with a required biennial report on TSRA licenses issued to Iran from October 1, 2006 to September 30, 2008.[24] Treasury officials noted that Treasury has published quarterly reports that contain the number of TSRA licenses issued during this period. However, the data in the quarterly reports were not consistent with data that Treasury provided us during our review. A TSRA official stated that Treasury could not resolve the inconsistencies in a timely manner because of information system limitations. In addition, Treasury required more than 2 months to provide GAO with adequate data concerning its TSRA licenses.

Treasury has begun work to upgrade its system for managing TSRA licensing information. During our review, Treasury hired a contractor in September 2009 to begin designing a system to better manage TSRA licensing information. The stated goal of the project is to provide Treasury with an integrated, largely paperless TSRA database that would allow it to better collect and manage information, conduct analysis, improve efficiency, provide U.S. law enforcement agencies with better information, and improve the timeliness of reports to Congress. Treasury intends to complete the upgrade by September 2010. Treasury officials informed us that they gave priority to upgrading the TSRA database because of the volume of licensing requests.

However, the new TSRA system would not include licenses that Treasury has issued for the export of goods that are not agricultural or medical in nature, including dual-use civilian goods with potential military applications. Congress has prohibited the export of any dual-use item to Iran and has stated that the President may waive the prohibition if doing so is essential to the interests of the United States.[25] Treasury has had difficulty in identifying licenses for dual-use items. For example, Treasury officials informed a Defense Department Central Command (CENTCOM) official in 2009 that they could not provide CENTCOM with a list of Treasury licenses for the export of U.S. dual-use civilian aircraft parts to Iran. According to the CENTCOM official's report, Treasury officials stated they could not do so because of information system limitations.[26] Similarly, Treasury took more than 4 months to provide GAO with adequate data concerning a dual-use export license and 33 other non-TSRA licenses issued during the preceding 18 months (January 1, 2008-July 2009). Treasury officials stated in December 2009 that Treasury had yet to determine when it might upgrade its licensing information system for nonTSRA export licenses.

In 2007, we identified the lack of data concerning U.S. trade sanctions as a governmentwide problem affecting the U.S. government's ability to assess the impact of the sanctions on Iran.[27] Given Treasury's central role in licensing exports to Iran, its inability to provide complete and timely licensing information weakens government efforts to determine whether dual-use and other goods exported to Iran have been properly licensed and to assess compliance with the trade ban.

Iran Is Obtaining Illegal Transshipments of U.S. Military and Dual-Use Goods through Other Countries

According to U.S. officials, Iran is obtaining U.S. military and dual-use goods that are being illegally transshipped by firms and individuals through locations in numerous countries, including the United Arab Emirates, Malaysia, and Singapore. The goods include components for U.S.-built fighter aircraft, electronics, and specialized metals. To address the problem, U.S. agencies have conducted undercover investigations to detect Iranian procurement networks, prosecuted criminal cases against at least 30 firms and individuals for transshipping or attempting to transship goods to Iran, and provided export control training and support to the United Arab Emirates and other countries.

Wide Range of Military and Dual-Use Goods Involved in Iran Transshipment Cases

Firms and individuals have transshipped or attempted to transship a wide range of U.S. military and dual-use goods to Iran, according to U.S. officials. The Department of Justice reported in September 2009 that individuals and firms were seeking to transship military components to Iran. For example, the department listed nine major criminal prosecutions between 2007 and September 2009 that involved transshipment of components for Iran's U.S.-built fighter aircraft. These aircraft include the F-14 fighter, a highly capable aircraft used by the U.S. Navy until 2006 (see fig. 2); the F-4 fighter-bomber; and the F-5 fighter. The department also reported efforts to transship parts for Iran's U.S.-built military helicopters, military-grade night vision equipment, submachine guns, computers, and specialized laboratory equipment. Immigration and Customs Enforcement officials expressed concern regarding Iranian efforts to acquire through transshipment electronic components for missiles, parts for Iran's U.S.- built Hawk anti-aircraft missiles, specialized steel, and pumps with nuclear applications.

Sources (left to right): U.S. Navy (F-14) and U.S. Air Force (F-4).

Figure 2. F-14 and F-4 Aircraft.

Goods Are Transshipped through Several Nations

Firms and individuals have transshipped or attempted to transship goods though intermediaries in several countries. A 2009 report by the Justice Department cited 30 cases that involved the use of intermediaries in the United Arab Emirates (UAE), Malaysia, Singapore, Thailand, Australia, Canada, Colombia, Brazil, Austria, France, Germany, Luxembourg, The Netherlands, and the United Kingdom. As shown in figure 3, the cases involved efforts to ship the goods to Iran through the use of intermediaries in these countries. More than 50 percent of the cases listed involved use of intermediaries in the UAE for transshipment. About 20 percent involved the use of Malaysia and Singapore.28 U.S. goods involved in these cases included U.S. military aircraft components, laboratory equipment, specialty alloy pipes, night vision goggles, and sensitive technologies sent to Iranian missile and nuclear entities.

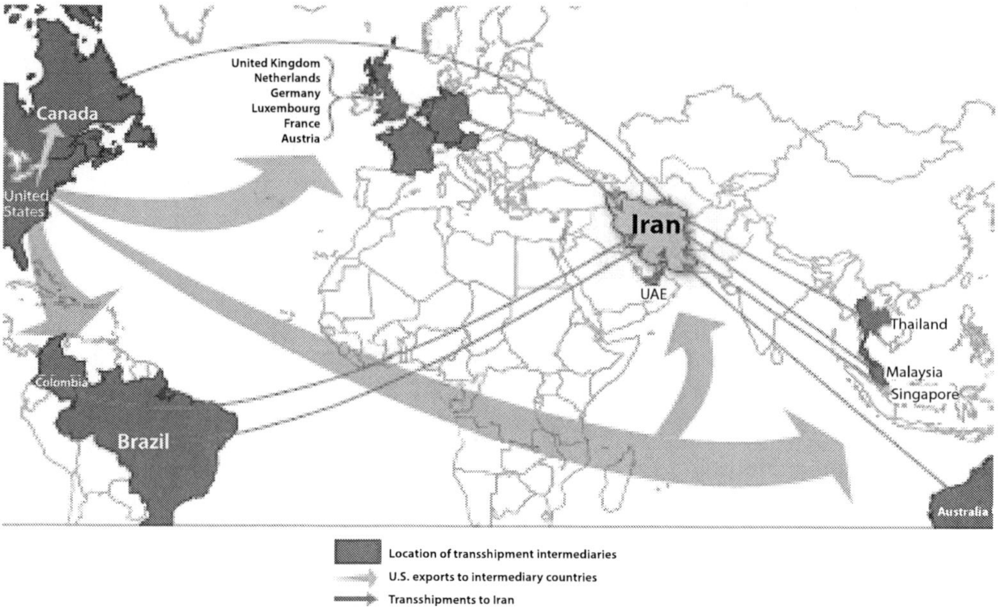

Source: GAO analysis of Justice Department data; Map Resources (map).

Figure 3. Illegal Transshipment Routes Cited in Cases Prosecuted 2007-2009.

U.S. officials stated that the UAE has taken steps to address the use of its territory for transshipment. They noted that the UAE has increased cooperation with U.S. enforcement entities and enacted new export control legislation in 2007. According to the UAE government, the new law addresses goods subject to import and export control procedures, bans the export or re-export of strategic goods (including arms and military hardware, chemical and biological materials, and dual-use items) without a special license, and specifies penalties of imprisonment of up to a year and fines totaling over $270,000. U.S. officials met with UAE officials in June 2009 to discuss the implementation of the new law. Commerce officials stated that the law contains the basic elements of an export control regime to combat transshipment. However, some U.S. officials also stated that individuals involved in illegal transshipment may shift their operations to other nations, such as Malaysia and Singapore.

Actions Are Being Taken by U.S. Agencies to Combat Transshipment

U.S. enforcement officials stated that they pursue allegations of transshipment. For example, Defense Criminal Investigative Services and U.S. Immigration and Customs Enforcement officials stated they conduct undercover investigations to detect efforts by Iranian procurement agents to obtain U.S. goods in response to requests from Iran's military-industrial establishment. To do so, procurement agents may seek to build long-term relationships with suppliers by initially buying small quantities of relatively-innocuous items before seeking more sensitive items. Defense Criminal Investigative Services and U.S. Immigration and Customs Enforcement officials stated that, in one case, a procurement agent with ties to the Iranian military attempted to procure about 700 goods, including aircraft parts and radar components. Most of the goods would have required U.S. government licenses to be exported to their alleged destination in the United Arab Emirates. The individual seeking the parts typically identified himself as a United Arab Emirates businessman in approaching U.S. firms, according to U.S. enforcement officials. The individual provided false documents and attempted to convince the U.S. firms that they did not need to obtain export licenses.

U.S. law provides criminal penalties for the illegal transshipment of goods to Iran.[29] For example, violators of Treasury's Iranian Transactions Regulations may receive sentences of up to 20 years imprisonment and fines of up to $1 million. The Justice Department has reported that from January 2007 to September 2009 it handled at least 30 criminal prosecutions involving actual or attempted transshipments to Iran. Five individuals convicted in connection with these cases received sentences of imprisonment that ranged from 6 months to more than 5 years.

The Commerce Department is responsible for licensing U.S. exports of dual-use items to the UAE, as well as countries other than Iran. To help detect illegal transshipments of U.S. dual-use goods, Commerce enforcement personnel select a sample of previously shipped goods and attempt to verify they are located and being used in accordance with licensing conditions.[30]

U.S. agencies have provided export control assistance to countries that have been used by intermediaries to transshipment goods to Iran. For example, the UAE has received assistance provided by U.S. agencies, including the Department of Homeland Security and the Department of Energy. The Departments of Commerce and Justice have also worked with the UAE in improving its controls over exports.

CONCLUSIONS

While the United States government has severely restricted U.S. exports to Iran, it cannot readily determine the extent to which it has issued licenses for such exports or the extent to which goods marked for Iran are leaving U.S. ports. U.S. agencies should have complete, reliable, and timely information concerning these matters to ensure the U.S. government is implementing the ban on exports to Iran. While covert transshipments of U.S. goods through third-party countries are inherently difficult to detect, erroneous reports of overt shipments of U.S. goods to Iran have prompted concerns that the United States is not abiding by its own export ban. The Census Bureau has taken some steps to detect and correct errors in its latest statistics, but the Treasury Department has yet to take action to ensure that it can retrieve complete and timely data on which exports to Iran it has licensed and which it has not.

RECOMMENDATION FOR EXECUTIVE ACTION

To help ensure that U.S. agencies have timely access to reliable data concerning licensed U.S. exports to Iran, we recommend that the Secretary of the Treasury ensure that the Department of the Treasury develop the capability to provide other agencies and Congress with complete and timely information concerning all licenses issued for the export of goods to Iran.

Agency Comments and Our Evaluation

Treasury provided written comments regarding a draft of our report, which are reprinted in appendix III. With regard to our recommendation, Treasury stated that it is already able to access, review, and share information relating to TSRA licenses and that it "hopes" to enhance its abilities to process non-TSRA licensing information. It also indicated that it plans to share licensing data with CBP in the future through the Automated Commercial Environment (ACE) system. Treasury acknowledged that its ability to search some parts of its current licensing databases is limited and that its data systems could be improved. Treasury also acknowledged that it "has work to do" before it can provide CBP with the specific data CBP needs to validate licensed exports. While Treasury is able to access and share licensing information, it cannot do so in a complete and timely manner. As noted in our draft report, Treasury required more than 2 months to provide us with complete licensing data for agricultural and medical exports and more than 4 months to access and share 34 recent export licenses for other types of goods, including a dual-use good with potential military applications. The ACE system is still in development and is not ready to receive Treasury's export data. We therefore have not changed our recommendation that Treasury develop the ability to provide complete and timely information regarding all export licenses for Iran.

Treasury also stated that, contrary to the notion that the administration of the sanctions program had been weakened, nothing in our draft report indicated that enforcement actions regarding exports to Iran, or the implementation of the sanctions, had been impaired by incomplete and untimely licensing data. Treasury's assertion is in contrast with a 2009 internal Treasury budget request, in which Treasury officials stated that

1) Treasury's information processes were hampering "the speed, efficacy, reliability and security" of its enforcement and compliance activities and
2) Treasury would be able to provide better information to law enforcement agencies if it upgraded its TSRA information system. Also, as noted in our report, limitations in Treasury's information systems prevented it from responding to a request from U.S. Customs and Border Protection officials for more complete and timely licensing information to aid CBP agents at U.S. ports.

Treasury also stated that it appreciated the report's finding that Treasury is licensing the export of goods to Iran in accordance with the laws and regulations imposing sanctions on Iran. However, it expressed concern that our draft report title conveyed an impression that Treasury's information systems were weakening the implementation of economic sanctions against Iran. We therefore modified the title of our report to clarify our message and reinforce our recommendation.

The Department of Commerce provided formal written comments concerning the Census Bureau's maintenance of U.S. export statistics. Commerce's comments were technical in nature and did not address our findings or recommendation. We have incorporated Commerce's comments in our text as appropriate and reproduced them in appendix IV. The other agencies cited in this report did not provide formal comments. CBP, U.S. Immigration and Customs Enforcement, and Treasury provided technical comments, which we incorporated as appropriate.

We are sending copies of this report to the Departments of Commerce, Defense, Energy, Homeland Security, Justice, State, and the Treasury, as well as interested congressional committees. In addition, the report will be available at no charge on the GAO Web site at http://www.gao.gov.

If you or your staffs have any questions about this report, please contact me at (202) 512-8979 or christoffj@gao.gov. Contact points for our Offices of Congressional Relations and Public Affairs may be found on the last page of this report. Key contributors are listed in appendix V.

Joseph A. Christoff
Director,
International Affairs and Trade

Appendix I. Objectives, Scope, and Methodology

To assess the extent to which U.S. statistics accurately depict U.S. exports to Iran, we analyzed the results of a Census Bureau review of records regarding all types of goods reportedly shipped to Iran from 2004 through 2008 to determine the specific destinations of those goods. In reviewing its records, Census checked the shipping address of the ultimate recipient for each good. Based on the results of its review, Census provided us with the actual country of destination and the total dollar value of each type of good that was sent to a country other than Iran. We used that information to adjust the data found in the U.S. export statistics. We also reviewed a Census Web page listing corrections to U.S. export data concerning Iran to corroborate the posted corrections with those that Census had provided to us. We also met with Census officials to determine their methods and policies for assuring the accuracy of the statistics.

To assess the Treasury Department's licensing activities, we first reviewed U.S. laws and regulations that established sanctions on U.S. exports to Iran, including Treasury's Iranian Transaction Regulations. We then reviewed a random sample of 58 licenses that were issued by Treasury to exporters from October 2006 to August 2009. With this probability sample, each member of the study population had a nonzero probability of being included, and that probability could be computed for any member. The random sample was taken from a list of 1,833 licenses provided to us by Treasury. On the basis of the sample, we estimate no more than 5 percent of the population contained errors, at a 95 percent confidence level,[1] which we judged to be sufficiently reliable for our review. In the digital PDF copies of licenses we obtained, we verified that all licenses were for agricultural goods, medicines, and medical devices allowed under TSRA and the Iranian Transactions Regulations. We also looked at the intended end users in the license to verify that none were sponsors of international terrorism. The names of end users in the licenses were compared with a search of Treasury's Specially Designated Nationals and Blocked Persons list, which is maintained and updated daily on Treasury's Web site.[2] For non-TSRA goods, we reviewed all non-TSRA licenses provided by

Treasury for January 2008 to June 2009. For dual-use items, we verified that a waiver had been obtained for the export of goods to Iran before a license was granted. We also interviewed officials from the Departments of the Treasury and State on their collaboration and joint decision-making for licenses granted for export to Iran that required a presidential waiver. To assess Treasury's ability to provide complete and timely licensing data to other agencies and Congress, we obtained documents concerning Treasury information systems, including contracting and budget documents for a planned upgrade. We obtained a Treasury presentation on the TSRA Database and Foreign Assets Control Database systems used to store records of its licensing activities. We also obtained and reviewed all of the mandated biennial and quarterly reports for TSRA on Treasury's Web site.[3] We compiled these reports into a comprehensive total of licenses issued by Treasury and then compared it with the list Treasury provided to us for the overlapping time periods. We also interviewed relevant Treasury licensing, information technology, and enforcement officials. We interviewed officials from the Departments of Commerce and Homeland Security and other entities who use Treasury licensing information. In addition, we requested detailed licensing data from Treasury and monitored its ability to comply with our request.

To review the extent to which U.S. goods are being illegally transshipped to Iran, we obtained and analyzed lists of relevant criminal prosecutions from the Department of Justice. We also discussed transshipment issues with officials of the Departments of Commerce, Defense, Homeland Security, Justice, and the Treasury; the Federal Bureau of Investigation; and other government agencies. We relied on secondary sources for descriptions of foreign laws.

APPENDIX II. U.S. LEGAL TOOLS FOR SANCTIONING FOREIGN COMPANIES THAT TRANSFER SENSITIVE TECHNOLOGY

The U.S. government has a number of legal tools to exert pressure on foreign entities that transfer foreign sensitive technologies to Iran.[1] These tools allow the United States to penalize foreign entities by freezing their U.S. properties, limiting their ability to trade with the United States, prohibiting them from obtaining U.S. government procurement contracts, or otherwise impairing their ability to work with U.S. entities. Some of these tools are specifically focused on the transfer of technologies to Iran, while others can be applied to a wider range of actions. The laws presented below are discussed only in the context of non-U.S. entities transferring sensitive non-U.S. technologies to Iran from outside the United States. Please refer to the original text of the laws for the full content.

Executive Orders 13382, 12938, and 13094

These executive orders establish criteria for the application of sanctions on foreign firms that provide sensitive technologies to Iran. The orders draw their authority from the International Emergency Economic Powers Act (IEEPA) and several other acts of Congress.

- Executive Order 13382 allows the Secretary of State or the Secretary of the Treasury, in consultation with each other and other relevant agencies, to freeze the assets of persons designated as being engaged in the proliferation of weapons of mass destruction (WMD), as well as members of their support networks.2 The order also states that frozen assets may not be transferred, paid, exported, withdrawn or otherwise dealt in and prohibits any transactions by a U.S. person or within the United States taken to evade or avoid such prohibitions.3 Foreign persons can be designated under the order if they have engaged, or attempted to engage, in activities or transactions that have materially contributed to the proliferation of (or pose a risk of doing so) WMD or WMD delivery systems (such as missiles capable of delivering WMD). Such activities include efforts by any person or country of proliferation concern to manufacture, acquire, possess, develop, transport, transfer, or use WMD or WMD delivery systems.
- Executive Order 12938 allows the Secretary of State to impose sanctions against foreign persons if the Secretary has made a determination that such persons have, on or after November 16, 1990, knowingly and materially contributed to the efforts of any foreign country, project, or entity to use, develop, produce, stockpile, or otherwise acquire chemical or biological weapons.[4] The United States government is prohibited from procuring goods or services from a designated person or importing products produced by a designated person, unless exempted from these sanctions by the Secretaries of State and the Treasury for certain reasons, such as U.S. military requirements or defense production needs.
- Executive Order 13094 expanded Executive Order 12938 to impose sanctions when the Secretary of State determines that a foreign person on or after November 16, 1990, has materially contributed or attempted to contribute materially to the efforts of any foreign country, project, or entity of proliferation concern to use, acquire, design, develop, produce, or stockpile weapons of mass destruction or missiles capable of delivering such weapons.[5] The penalties that could be imposed under Executive Order 12938 remained the same.

Iran, North Korea, and Syria Nonproliferation Act

This act allows the President to sanction foreign persons with respect to whom there is credible evidence indicating that such persons transferred sensitive goods, services, or technology to Iran after a certain date.[6] Under the act, the President is required to report to the Senate Foreign Relations Committee and the House Foreign Affairs Committee every 6 months identifying foreign persons with respect to whom there is credible evidence that such persons have, on or after January 1, 1999, transferred goods, services, or technology listed in specified multilateral export control lists to Iran.[7] The act allows the President to impose a number of measures to a foreign person appearing in the report, such as a ban of U.S. government procurement from the designated person, a ban of U.S. government arms sales to the foreign person,[8] or the denial or suspension of licenses to export dual-use items to the foreign person.[9]

Iran-Iraq Arms Nonproliferation Act of 1992

This act requires the President[10] to sanction persons who, by transferring or retransferring goods or technology, "knowingly and materially" contribute to Iran's efforts to acquire chemical, biological, or nuclear weapons, or destabilizing numbers and types of advanced conventional weapons.[11] Mandatory sanctions under the act include (1) a ban on U.S. government procurement from sanctioned persons and (2) a ban on licenses for export to or by the foreign person.[12] The sanctions are to be imposed and last for 2 years, unless the President issues a waiver on the basis that it is essential to U.S. national interests.[13] The President is required to report to the Senate Armed Services, Senate Foreign Relations, House Armed Services, and House Foreign Affairs committees if the President determines that a person has made a transfer subject to sanction under the act.[14] In the report, the President must identify the person, provide details of the transfer, and describe the actions taken or to be taken under the act.[15]

Iran Sanctions Act

This act allows the President to sanction persons who provide Iran with goods, technology, or services if they know that doing so would contribute materially to Iran's ability to acquire or develop (1) chemical, biological, or nuclear weapons or related technologies or (2) destabilizing numbers and types of advanced conventional weapons.[16] The act requires the President to impose at least two of the following sanctions:

- denying Export-Import Bank assistance for exporting to the foreign person;
- banning licenses to export sensitive technologies to the sanctioned person;
- banning U.S. financial institutions from loaning the sanctioned person more than $10 million in a 1-year period;
- if the sanctioned person is a financial institution, banning that institution from dealing in U.S. debt instruments or serving as repositories for U.S. government funds; and
- banning U.S. Government procurement, as well as other sanctions that fall under the powers of the International Emergency Economic Powers Act, including IEEPA-derived executive orders.[17]

The President may waive these sanctions if the President determines that doing so is important to the national interest of the United States.[18]

Nuclear Proliferation Prevention Act of 1994

This act directs the President, with exceptions, to sanction persons if the President determines in writing that such persons have "materially and with requisite knowledge" contributed, through the transfer of certain specified goods or technology,[19] to the efforts of any individual, group, or non-nuclear-weapon state to (1) acquire unsafeguarded special nuclear material or (2) to use, develop, produce, stockpile, or otherwise acquire any nuclear explosive device.[20] The penalty is a ban on United States government procurement from the sanctioned person lasting at least 1 year. The President may waive the penalty after the sanction has been imposed for a year if the President determines, and certifies in writing to Congress, that continuation would have a serious adverse effect on vital United States interests. The act further requires the President to sanction persons if the President determines in writing that a United States person or a foreign person has (by providing financing) knowingly, materially, and directly contributed or attempted to contribute to an individual, group, or non-nuclear weapon state's (1) acquisition of unsafeguarded special nuclear material or (2) the use, development, production, stockpiling, or other acquisition of any nuclear explosive device.[21] For at least 1 year, sanctioned persons may not be primary dealers in U.S. government debt instruments, serve as depositories of U.S. government funds, directly or indirectly commence any line of business in the United States, or directly or indirectly conduct new business from a new location in the United States. The President may waive these sanctions after a year if the President determines in writing, and certifies to Congress, that their continuation would have a serious adverse effect on the on the safety and soundness of the domestic or international financial system or on domestic or international payments systems.

Arms Export Control Act

Portions of the Arms Export Control Act (AECA) require the President to sanction foreign persons that the President has determined to have (1) provided to certain countries missile equipment or technology or (2) contributed to certain countries' acquisition of chemical or biological weapons.

- Section 73 (22 U.S.C. § 2797b): Under this section, subject to exceptions, the President shall impose sanctions when the president determines that a foreign persons have knowingly exported, transferred, or otherwise engaged in the trade of missile equipment or technology controlled under the Missile Technology Control Regime (MTCR)[22] that contributes to the acquisition, design, development, or production of missiles in a country that is not an MTCR adherent. The President shall also apply sanctions when he has made a determination with respect to a foreign person under section 2410b(b)(1) of Title 50, Appendix (discussed later). Depending on the nature of the equipment and technology involved, sanctions could include (1) denying the foreign persons U.S. government contracts related to missile equipment or technology, (2) denying the foreign persons any U.S. government contracts, (3) denying licenses for transfers of missile equipment or technology controlled under the Arms Export Control Act to the sanctioned persons, (4) denying licenses for the transfer of all items on the United States Munitions List to the sanctioned persons, or (5) prohibiting the importation of products produced by the sanctioned persons into the United States. The President may waive these sanctions in certain cases specified in the act. The President may also decide to apply a waiver with respect to a product or service if the President certifies to Congress that (1) the product or service is essential to the national security of the United States and (2) such person is a sole source supplier of the product or service, and an alternative is not available and cannot be made available in a timely manner.

- Section 81 (22 U.S.C. § 2798): Under this section, the President is required to sanction, subject to certain exceptions, foreign persons the President determines to have knowingly and materially contributed, through the export of certain goods or technology or any other transaction not already subject to sanctions under the Export Administration Act, to the efforts of certain foreign countries to use, develop, produce, stockpile, or otherwise acquire chemical or biological weapons. The sanctions are a ban on U.S. government procurement from the foreign person and a ban on imports into the United States from the foreign person for at least 12 months. After a year of imposing the sanctions, the President may waive the sanctions by certifying to Congress that doing so is important to the national security interests of the United States.

Export Administration Act

Portions of this act require the President to sanction foreign persons that are determined to have (1) provided to certain countries missile equipment or technology or (2) contributed to certain countries' acquisition of chemical or biological weapons.

- Section 11B (50 app. U.S.C. § 2410b): Subject to certain exceptions, the President shall impose sanctions when the President determines that a foreign person has knowingly exported, transferred, or otherwise engaged in the trade of any MTCR equipment or technology that contributes to the design, development, or production of missiles in a non-MTCR country.[23] The section also calls for sanctions on persons who have conspired or attempted to engage in or facilitated such export, transfer, or trade. The President shall also impose sanctions under this act if the President makes a determination with respect to a foreign person under section 73(a) of the Arms Export Control Act (22 U.S.C. § 2797b(a)) (discussed above). Depending on circumstances specified in this section, sanctions could include a 2-year denial of specified licenses for the transfer to the sanctioned person of AECA-controlled missile equipment or technology and a 2-year ban on imports into the United States of products produced by the foreign person. The President may waive these sanctions in certain specified cases.
- Section 11C (50 app. U.S.C. § 2410c): This section requires the President to impose sanctions, subject to certain exceptions, on foreign persons determined to have "knowingly and materially" contributed to the efforts of state sponsors of terrorism24 and certain other countries25 to use, develop, or acquire chemical or biological weapons through certain exports from a foreign country. The exported goods or technology must be items that the United States would control under the Export Administration Act if the items were of U.S. origin. Foreign persons are subject to bans of at least 1 year on U.S. government procurement and on imports into the United States from the foreign person. The President may issue a waiver after 12

months by certifying to Congress that doing so is important to the national security interests of the United States.

Appendix III. Comments from the Department of the Treasury

Note: GAO comments supplementing those in the report text appear at the end of this appendix.

DEPARTMENT OF THE TREASURY
WASHINGTON, D.C. 20220

Joseph Christoff
Director
International Affairs and Trade
U.S. Government Accountability Office
44 G Street, N.W.
Washington, D.C. 20548

Dear Mr. Christoff:

This responds to your electronic transmission of January 19, 2010, to the U.S. Department of the Treasury (Treasury) attaching a copy of the draft entitled "Incomplete and Untimely Licensing Data Weaken Ability of the United States to Assess and Enforce its Export Restrictions" (GAO-10-375) and its "For Official Use Only" version (GAO-10-339SU). We have reviewed the portions of the report pertaining to matters administered by the Office of Foreign Assets Control ("OFAC"). We are providing the following comments regarding the recommendations and assertions contained in the report produced by the Government Accountability Office.

See comment 1.

We appreciate the report's findings that OFAC is licensing the export of goods to Iran in accordance with the laws and regulations imposing sanctions on Iran. We also acknowledge and welcome the observation that Treasury can improve its data systems, which has been a longstanding OFAC objective. However, it is troubling that the title of this report does not accurately reflect its contents. Despite an explicit, positive finding that Treasury has issued licenses for exports to Iran in accordance with laws and regulations imposing sanctions on Iran, the title of your report would lead the reader into believing that certain limitations in Treasury's ability to process licensing data have actually resulted in problems with the enforcement of export restrictions on Iran. However, contrary to the notion that the administration of the sanctions program has been weakened, nothing in the report indicates that any enforcement action regarding exports to Iran, or the implementation of sanctions with respect to Iran, have been impaired by "incomplete and untimely" licensing data. We thus urge you to change the title to one that fairly represents your report.

While Treasury acknowledges certain limitations with respect to its ability to search some parts of OFAC's current licensing databases, a complete understanding of OFAC's work in administering the more than 20 sanctions programs mandated by the President and Congress, including those related to terrorism, nonproliferation of weapons of mass destruction, narcotics trafficking, and sanctions relating to Iran, Sudan, Cuba and Burma, would lead to refinement of the recommendations. The dedicated professionals of OFAC work tirelessly to enforce these many programs, particularly our sanctions with respect to Iran. It should be emphasized that OFAC licenses for export to Iran only a tiny spectrum of goods, mostly agricultural and medical products under the Trade Sanctions Reform and Export Enhancement Act of 2000 ("TSRA"). Military and dual-use items are ineligible for licenses other than in exceptional circumstances such as for the safety of civil aviation. We wish to reiterate that the completeness or timeliness of licensing data has no bearing on the illegal diversion of military and dual-use items to Iran, and no effect on enforcement efforts to combat illegal diversion.

See comment 2.

As for the report's recommendation that Treasury "develop the capability to provide other agencies and Congress with complete and timely information concerning all licenses issued for the export of goods to Iran," it is important to understand that OFAC is actually already able to access, review, and share information relating to TSRA licenses for the export of agricultural commodities, medicine, and medical devices to Iran. Moreover, as noted in the report, OFAC is currently upgrading and improving its TSRA licensing systems to be able to more efficiently capture information on these licenses. These upgrades were in progress before GAO conducted its review. OFAC hopes to build on this technology to enhance processing capabilities for non-TSRA licensing information. In assessing OFAC's programs, it is critical to recognize that OFAC receives many license requests well beyond requests for the export of goods to Iran. Because the Iranian Transactions Regulations reflect a comprehensive set of trade and financial regulations, these requests are often complex and may involve imports and exports of services, investment transactions, funds transfers, or third country transactions involving the Iranian government or Iranian entities.

In response to the report's specific criticisms about the sharing of licensing data, the report states that systemic limitations have prevented Treasury from sharing licensing data with other agencies, primarily U.S. Customs and Border Protection ("CBP"). Treasury began to address this issue in the 1990s, when it established the International Trade Data System initiative, the purpose of which was to consolidate in one system all import and export data, including export licenses, in part to better support CBP's enforcement at the border. This initiative has become part of CBP's information modernization under the Automated Commercial Environment ("ACE"). Partially in response to the terrorist attacks of September 11, 2001, the project has prioritized the security of our ports and homeland and has thus placed the processing of imports ahead of exports in its development schedule. OFAC fully participates in ACE development, and it plans to include licensing information in the data shared with CBP. The ACE system is not currently ready to incorporate licenses involving exported goods, although OFAC acknowledges that it also has work to do in order to provide the specific data needed by CBP for validating licensed exports.

See comment 3.

We welcome and agree with the report's finding that OFAC is licensing the export of goods to Iran in accordance with laws and regulations imposing sanctions. We also have been working, and will continue to work, towards improving our data systems. It is disappointing and distracting, however, that the title of this report gives the erroneous impression that the ability to search OFAC's data systems somehow weakens the implementation of economic sanctions against Iran.

See comment 4.

Thank you for the opportunity to comment on this report.

Sincerely,

Adam J. Szubin

GAO COMMENTS

The following are GAO's comments on the Department of the Treasury's letter.

1. Treasury's statement is in contrast with statements contained in a 2009 Treasury internal budget request. As cited in our draft report, the request stated that OFAC's information processes were hampering "the speed, efficacy, reliability and security" of OFAC's "enforcement and compliance activities." Our draft report also noted that a Treasury official had informed U.S. Customs and Border Protection officials that Treasury's licensing information systems could not provide CBP with more complete and timely Treasury licensing information. CBP officials stated that they had asked

for the information to help CBP agents at U.S. ports validate licenses for exports to Iran. However, for the sake of clarity, we have modified the title of our report.

2. While Treasury is able to access and share information on licenses for medical and agricultural exports to Iran to some degree, it cannot do so in a timely and complete manner. For example, Treasury required more than 2 months to provide us with requested data on medical and agricultural export licenses. It required more than 4 months to provide us with 34 licenses for the export of other types of goods issued over the preceding 18 months. These licenses included a license for the export of aircraft equipment with potential military applications.
3. ACE is a trade processing system that has been in development by CPB since 2001. Intended to automate border processing, ACE is being deployed in phases. As Treasury notes in its comments, ACE is not ready to accept export data that would be of use to enforcement agencies.
4. As noted above, we have modified the title of our report for the sake of clarity.

APPENDIX IV. COMMENTS FROM THE DEPARTMENT OF COMMERCE

THE SECRETARY OF COMMERCE
Washington, D.C. 20230

February 24, 2010

Mr. Joseph Christoff
Director, International Affairs and Trade
Government Accountability Office
Washington, DC 20548

Dear Mr. Christoff:

The Department of Commerce (Department) appreciates the opportunity to comment on the Government Accountability Office's draft report, "Incomplete and Untimely Licensing Data Weaken Ability of the United States to Assess and Enforce its Export Restrictions" (GAO-10-10-375).

The Department's comments on this report are enclosed.

Sincerely,

Gary Locke

Enclosure

U.S. Department of Commerce
Comments on the
United States Government Accountability Office
Draft Report Entitled *Incomplete and Untimely Licensing Data Weaken Ability of the United States to Assess and Enforce its Export Restrictions*
(GAO-10-10-375)

Highlights page
First paragraph
- **sixth line:** Reads: "did not detect or correct." Should read: "did not detect."
- **seventh line**: Reads: "begun checking all new filings of exports to Iran and posting corrections to a". Should read: "begun manually checking all new filings of exports to Iran, regardless of the dollar value, and have posted corrections to a Census Bureau Web page."

Page 3
First paragraph
- **seventh line:** Reads: "or correct because of the low dollar value of the exports." Should read: "because of the low dollar value of the export transactions."
- **beginning on the tenth line**
  Reads: "terrorism. As a result of our review, Census officials initiated a routine check of new filings of exports to Iran, allowed filers of export data to select recipient countries from a list instead of requiring them to enter a two-letter country code, and began posting corrections to Iran export data on a Census Web page. According to Census officials, it is too soon to determine whether these actions will improve the accuracy of future U.S. trade statistics for Iran."

  Should read: "terrorism. As a result of our review, Census Bureau officials initiated a in-depth manual review of all new filings identifying Iran as the country of destination, implemented a new country selection routine for export filings requiring export filers to select the recipient country from a list containing the full country name instead of allowing them to enter a two-letter International Standards Organization (ISO) country code, and posting corrections to Iran export data, not previously detected, on a Census Web page. According to Census Bureau officials, it is too soon to determine whether these actions will improve the accuracy of future U.S. trade statistics for Iran."

Page 5
First paragraph
- **fourth line:** Reads: "Customs and Border Protection" Should read: Customs and Border Protection (CBP)
- **sixth line:** Reads: "Census-approved" Should read: CBP-approved

Page 5

First paragraph, (continued)

- **eighth line:** Reads: "by choosing a two-lettered standardized code." Should read: by choosing a two-lettered ISO code.

Footnote 4

Reads: "While most data is submitted electronically by exporters and their agents (63 percent), statistics are also compiled using Shipper's Export Declaration documents filed with Customs and Border Protection and sent to the U.S. Census Bureau (3 percent), as well as special computer tapes from Canada for U.S. exports to Canada (34 percent)."

Should read: In general, beginning in July 2008 all export transactions, with the country of destination other than Canada, are submitted electronically by exporters or their agents using the Automated Export System. This accounts for approximately 67 percent of export transactions. The remaining export data are compiled using transactions obtained electronically through the United States/Canada data exchange, accounting for approximately 33 percent of all export transactions."

Page 8

First paragraph

- **second sentence**

Reads: "The misidentification of Iran as the recipient country in the statistics is the result from export data filing errors that Census did not detect or correct. As a result of our review, Census officials have begun routinely checking new export filings reporting exports to Iran. While Census policy is not to correct errors in the statistics that are older than 1 year, it has begun posting Iran related corrections on a separate Web page."

Should read: "The misidentification of 97 records with Iran as the recipient country is the result from export filing errors that the Census Bureau did not detect. As a result of our review, Census Bureau officials have initiated an in-depth manual review of all new export filings reporting Iran as the country of destination. While the Census Bureau's revision policy for international trade data is not to correct errors in the data products that are older than 1 year, it does issue special announcements as warranted with the discovery of large value revisions and has posted corrections older than 1 year on a separate *Special Notices and Corrections* Web page since 2004.

Page 9

- **second line:** Reads: "results of errors made by filers of export data into the Automated Export System. Should read: "results of errors made by filers of export transactions submitted into the AES.

- **sixth line:** Reads: "letter country code" Should read: "letter ISO country code"

<u>Page 10</u>

- **first paragraph**

Reads: "Census officials stated that they did not detect or correct Iran-related errors in new exporter filings or in the export statistics for previous years. The officials focused on detecting errors involving high-dollar values because of the statistics' use in determining the U.S. balance of trade rather than the sensitivity of the reported recipient country. The officials stated that they did not focus on detecting errors in the data for exports to Iran because the value of such exports was relatively small. In 2008, the reported value of U.S. exports to Iran was $683 million, or about one-half of 1 percent of the total value of all U.S. exports. Moreover, the officials stated, the policy of the Census Bureau is not to make changes in trade statistics that are more than a year old. For example, Census officials have not corrected an erroneous entry in the statistics concerning the alleged export of rifles to Iran in 2004, although they learned of the error in 2008. Census officials also stated that Census is not involved in enforcing U.S. export controls on Iran.

Should read: "Census Bureau officials stated that they did not detect all of the Iran-related errors in exporter filings or in the export data products for previous time periods. The officials stated the primary focus is placed on detecting errors involving high-dollar value transactions because of the statistics' use in determining the U.S. balance of trade, one of the principal economic indicators. Census Bureau officials identified all of the Iran related errors and discovered more than 85% of the transactions were valued less than $50 thousand and the highest valued transaction was $1.0 million. In 2008, the reported value of U.S. exports to Iran was $683 million, or about five-hundredths of the total value of all U.S. exports of goods ($1.3 trillion). Moreover, the officials stated that while the Census Bureau's revision policy for international trade data is not to correct errors in the data products that are older than 1 year, it does issue special announcements as warranted with the discovery of large value revisions. The 2004 statistics concerning the alleged export of rifles to Iran will not be corrected in the trade data products since the error was identified in 2008, well past the one-year data product revision period. Beginning in 2004, corrections older than 1 year are posted on a separate "*Special Notices and Corrections*" Web page to supplement the data products. All the corrections for Iran have been posted to this Web site.

- **second paragraph:** the following should be included:

It should be noted that the Census Bureau is not responsible for enforcing export control and enforcement of U.S. regulations and laws regarding U.S. exports to Iran. Those responsibilities fall under the Office of Foreign Asset Control (OFAC) in the Department of Treasury and CBP in the Department of Homeland Security. Additionally, CBP has been delegated the responsibility of enforcing the Census Bureau's Foreign Trade Regulations. Shipments stating the final destination as Iran are available, in real time through the AES, to CBP for monitoring and targeting purposes. The Census Bureau is not responsible for validating the accuracy or need for licensing requirements and has approached OFAC to include licensing requirements in the AES as editing and shipment acceptance criteria. At this point no action has been taken.

Page 11

- **last bullet:**

  Reads: "In June 2009, Census began posting an online list of corrections to Iran export data. However, Census officials stated that they will continue their policy of not correcting errors in the trade statistics older than 1 year."

  Should read: The Census Bureau began posting an on-line list of corrections to Iran under the "Statistical Notices and Corrections" section of their Web site in June 2009. Census officials stated that they will continue their policy of not correcting errors in the trade data products older than 1 year, however they are developing new processing systems that will allow corrections to be applied over several years.

Bureau of Industry and Security Comments

See comment.

Page 6, last paragraph of the Census Comments:

Currently reads "It should be noted that the Census Bureau is not responsible for enforcing U.S. regulations and laws regarding U.S. exports to Iran. Those responsibilities fall under the Office of foreign Asset Control (OFAC) in the Department of Treasury and CBP in the Department of Homeland Security."

Should read "It should be noted that the Census Bureau is not responsible for enforcing export control and enforcement of U.S. regulations and laws regarding U.S. exports to Iran. Those responsibilities fall under the Office of foreign Asset Control (OFAC) in the Department of Treasury, **the Bureau of Industry and Security's Office of Export Enforcement,** and CBP **and ICE** in the Department of Homeland Security."

Page 10, first paragraph

Census states that Iran trade is "five-hundredths of the total value of all U.S. exports of goods"; it appears that such trade is actually five-hundredths of one percent, rather than five-hundredths (which would technically be 5%).

Page 19, last paragraph of the GAO report:

Currently reads "The Commerce Department is responsible for licensing U.S. exports of dual-use items to
the UAE, as well as countries other than Iran."

Should read "The Commerce Department is responsible for licensing **and enforcing** U.S. exports of dual-use items to the UAE, as well as countries other than Iran."

Other assorted, minor issues in these comments:

(a) it appears that Census may consider "export transactions" to be data on export transactions, such that Census frequently makes statements such as "export transactions . . . are submitted electronically . . . " when they seemingly should be saying that "information [or data] on export transactions . . . is [are] submitted electronically . . . . " (see, e.g., comment on footnote 4, Page 5; this issue also appears elsewhere).

(b) Page three, tenth line comment: "and posting corrections to Iran export data" should likely be "and posted corrections to Iran export data" or "and began posting corrections to Iran export data."

(c) Page 8, second sentence correction: "records with Iran as the recipient country is the result from export filing errors" should be "records with Iran as the recipient country is the result of export filing errors"

(d) Page 9, second line: "results" should be "result"

(e) Page 10, replacement first paragraph: "Beginning in 2004, corrections older than 1 year are posted . . . " seemingly should be "Beginning in 2004, corrections older than one year have been posted"

GAO Comment

The following is GAO's comment on the Department of Commerce's letter dated February 24, 2010.

The Bureau of Industry and Security's comments on pages 39 and 40 are not directed at our draft report, but are instead directed at the preceding comments, which were submitted by the Bureau of the Census. The Bureau of Industry and Security and the Bureau of the Census are separate bureaus within the Department of Commerce.

Acknowledgments

Tet Miyabara (Assistant Director), Patrick Breiding, Joseph Clifton, Lynn Cothern, Etana Finkler, Grace Lui, Lauren Membreno, and Pierre Toureille made key contributions to this report. Martin De Alteriis and Justin Fisher provided technical assistance.

End Notes

[1] Trade Sanctions Reform and Export Enhancement Act of 2000, Pub. L. No. 106-387, Title IX, 114 Stat. 1549, 1549A-67 – 1549A-72 (codified as amended at 22 U.S.C. §§ 7201-7211).

[2] The official U.S. trade statistics can be accessed at http://www.usatradeonline.gov/.

[3] 31 C.F.R. § 560.204.

[4] Most data (67 percent) are submitted electronically by exporters and their agents using the Automated Export System, according to Census. The remainder is compiled using data obtained electronically through a U.S. data exchange with Canada.

[5] Section 1404(b) of the Foreign Relations Authorization Act, Fiscal Year 2003 requires the issuance of regulations to require all persons required to file export data to do so through AES. Pub. L. No. 107-228, § 1404(b), 116 Stat. 1350, 1454 (2002).

[6] Exec. Order No. 12,959, 60 Fed. Reg. 24,757 (May 6, 1995). Items exempted from the ban include donations of clothing, food, and medicine to relieve human suffering; and informational materials such as films, posters, and publications.

[7] Iranian Transaction Regulations, 31 C.F.R. part 560.

[8] In this context, a U.S. person is "any United States citizen, permanent resident alien, entity organized under the laws of the United States (including foreign branches), or any person in the United States." 31 C.F.R. § 560.314.

[9] The Iran-Iraq Arms Nonproliferation Act applies to Iran specific sanctions established in section 586G of the Iraq Sanctions Act of 1990, as contained in the Foreign Operations, Export Financing, and Related Programs Appropriations Act, 1991(Pub. L. No. 101-513, §§ 586-586J, 104 Stat. 1979, 2047-55 (1990)). Pub. L. No. 102-484, § 1603, 106 Stat. 2315, 2571 (codified as amended at 50 U.S.C. § 1701 note). These sanctions prohibit exports of dual-use items. See 50 App. U.S.C. §§ 2401-2420; 15 C.F.R. Pt. 774, Supp. 1.

[10] Pub. L. No. 102-484, § 1606. Commerce is generally responsible for licensing dual-use exports but has deferred to Treasury on licensing the export of such items to Iran. 15 C.F.R. § 746.7.

[11] 22 U.S.C. § 7204.

[12] In 1984, the Secretary of State designated Iran as a state sponsor of terrorism. Determination Pursuant to Section 6(i) of the Export Administration Act of 1979 – Iran, 49 Fed. Reg. 2,836 (Jan. 23, 1984).

[13] 22 U.S.C. § 7205.

[14] 31 C.F.R. §§ 560.530, 560.532, 560.533.

[15] 31 C.F.R. §§ 560.204

[16] 31 C.F.R. §§ 560.205

[17] The U.S. export ban (31 C.F.R. part 560) does not apply to foreign firms that export non-U.S. goods to Iran from abroad. U.S. legal tools for sanctioning foreign firms that export sensitive goods to Iran are described in Appendix II. Some of the bills currently under consideration in Congress include the Comprehensive Iran Sanctions, Accountability and Divestment Act of 2009, S. 2799, 111th Cong. (2009); Iran Sanctions Enabling Act of 2009, S. 1065, 111th Cong. (2009); Iran Refined Petroleum Sanctions Act, S. 908, 111th Cong. (2009); Iran Refined Petroleum Sanctions Act of 2009, H.R. 2194, 111th Cong. (2009); and Iran Sanctions Enabling Act of 2009, H.R. 1327, 111th Cong. (2009).

[18] Similarly, U.S. export statistics for 2002 include aircraft launching gear among the items exported to Iran. At our request, Census reviewed its records and determined that this item had been exported to Italy and not to Iran.

[19] According to Census officials, more than 85 percent of the transactions involved in the Iran-related errors were valued at less than $50,000 and the highest-valued transaction was valued at $1 million.

[20] The Census corrections are at http://www.census.gov/foreign-trade/statistics/corrections/iran/. As of December 2009, Census had listed 270 corrections to the Iran export data.

[21] In commenting on a draft of this report in late February 2010, Census officials stated they are "developing new processing systems that will allow corrections to be applied over several years."

[22] Iran-Iraq Arms Non-Proliferation Act of 1992, §§ 1603 and 1606.

[23] Memorandum of the President of the United States, 59 Fed. Reg. 50,685 (Sept. 27, 1994).

[24] 22 U.S.C. § 7205.

[25] Iran-Iraq Arms Non-Proliferation Act of 1992, §§ 1603 and 1606.

[26] Treasury officials stated in January 2010 that they had been unable to develop the list within four hours as requested and that Treasury could have provided the data within a "reasonable" period of time if it had received a written request.

[27] GAO, *Iran Sanctions: Impact in Furthering U.S. Objectives Is Unclear and Should Be Reviewed*, GAO-08-58 (Washington, D.C.: Dec. 18, 2007)

[28] The information made public by Justice does not necessarily include all recent prosecutions of efforts to illegally transship U.S. goods to Iran.

[29] 31 C.F.R. § 560.701.

[30] Additional information regarding Commerce's verification efforts concerning Iran is included in a For Official Use Only version of this report.

End Notes for Appendix I

[1] Because we followed a probability procedure based on random selections, our sample is only one of a large number of samples that we might have drawn. Since each sample could have provided different estimates, we express our confidence in the precision of our particular sample's results as a 95 percent confidence interval (e.g., from zero to 5 percent). This is the interval that would contain the actual population value for 95 percent of the samples we could have drawn.

[2] http://www.ustreas.gov/offices/enforcement/ofac/sdn/t11sdn.pdf.

[3] http://www.ustreas.gov/offices/enforcement/ofac/licensing/agmed/index.shtml.

End Notes for Appendix II

[1] For the purposes of this appendix, sensitive technology includes technology relevant to nuclear and other weapons of mass destruction and advanced conventional weapons (including missiles), as well as any dual-use

technologies (civilian technologies that have security applications). Three United Nations Security Council resolutions call on all United Nations member states to prevent transfer of sensitive technology to Iran. UNSCR 1737 declares that member states should prevent dealings that further Iran's nuclear and missile development and includes a list of entities involved in this development. UNSCR 1747 and UNSCR 1803 add to this list. See S.C. Res. 1737, U.N.Doc. S/RES/1737 (Dec. 27, 2006), S.C. Res. 1747, U.N. Doc. S/RES/1747 (Mar. 24, 2007), and S.C. Res. 1803, U.N. Doc. S/RES/1803 (Mar. 3, 2008).

[2] Exec. Order No. 13,382, 70 Fed. Reg. 38,567 (June 28, 2005).

[3] *Id.*

[4] Exec. Order No. 12,938, 59 Fed. Reg. 58,099 (Nov. 14, 1994).

[5] Exec. Order No. 13,094, 63 Fed. Reg. 40,803 (July 28, 1998).

[6] This law was enacted as the Iran Nonproliferation Act of 2000; Restriction on Extraordinary Payments in Connection with the International Space Station, Pub. L. No. 106-178, 114 Stat. 38 (Mar. 14, 2000); Syria was added to the act by the Iran Nonproliferation Amendments Act of 2005, Pub. L. No. 109-112, §4, 119 Stat. 2366, 2369 (Nov. 22, 2005); and North Korea was added by the North Korea Nonproliferation Act of 2006, Pub. L. No. 109-2353, 120 Stat. 2015 (Oct. 13, 2006).

[7] An example of such a list would be the Missile Technology Control Regime Equipment and Technology Annex of June 11, 1996, as revised. Pub. L. No. 106-178, as amended.

[8] This is a prohibition on United States Government sales of any item on the United States Munitions List as in effect on August 8, 1995, and a termination of sales of any defense articles, defense services, or design and construction services under the Arms Export Control Act, Pub. L. No. 90-269, as amended.

[9] Pub. L. No. 106-178, as amended.

[10] All functions vested in the President under the act were delegated to the Secretary of State, in consultation with heads of other departments and agencies. *See* Memorandum of the President of the United States, 59 *Fed. Reg.* 50,685 (Sept. 27, 1994).

[11] Enacted by the National Defense Authorization Act for fiscal year 1993, Pub. L. No. 102-484, Title XVI, 106 Stat. 2315, 2571-75 (1992).

[12] Pub. L. No. 102-484, § 1604, as amended.

[13] Pub. L. No. 102-484, §§ 1604 and 1606, as amended.

[14] Pub. L. No. 102-484, § 1607, as amended.

[15] *Id.*

[16] This act was originally enacted as the Iran-Libya Sanctions Act of 1996, Pub. L. No. 104-172, 110 Stat. 1541; Libya was removed from the law in 2006 by the Iran Freedom Support Act, Pub. L. No. 109-293, 120 Stat. 1344. Proliferation-related sanctionable activities were added to the law in 2006.

[17] Pub. L. No. 104-172, § 5, as amended.

[18] Pub. L. No. 104-172, § 9, as amended.

[19] The act defines "goods or technology" as (1) nuclear materials and equipment and sensitive nuclear technology as such terms are defined in 22 U.S.C. § 3203, all export items that could be of significance for nuclear explosive purposes and designated by the President as under the control of the Department of Commerce pursuant to section 2139a(c) of Title 42, and all technical assistance requiring authorization under section 2077(b) of Title 42, and (2) in the case of exports from a country other than the United States, any goods or technology that, if exported from the United States, would be goods or technology described in (1).

[20] Nuclear Proliferation Prevention Act, Pub. L. No. 103-236, Title VIII, §§ 801-851, 108 Stat. 382, 507-525 (1994), codified as amended at 22 U.S.C. §§ 6301-6305.

[21] 22 U.S.C. § 6303.

[22] The equipment and technology must be types that would be subject to U.S. jurisdiction under the Arms Export Control Act if it were U.S.-origin equipment or technology.

[23] The equipment and technology must be types that would be subject to U.S. jurisdiction under the Arms Export Control Act if it were U.S.-origin equipment or technology.

[24] As designated under section 6(j) of the Export Administration Act.

[25] The designated countries are any that (1) the President determines has, after January 1, 1980, used chemical or biological weapons in violation of international law, used lethal chemical or biological weapons against its own nationals, or made substantial preparations to engage in such activities, (2) has been designated a state sponsor of terrorism under section 6(j) of the Export Administration Act; or (3) any other foreign country, project, or entity designated by the President for purposes of the act.

INDEX

D

E

F

J

K

L

M

N

O

P

Q

R

S

T

U

V

W

Y